Dynamics of Virtual Work

Series Editors
Ursula Huws
Analytica Social and Economic Research
London, UK

Rosalind Gill
Department of Sociology
City, University of London
London, UK

Technological change has transformed where people work, when and how. Digitisation of information has altered labour processes out of all recognition whilst telecommunications have enabled jobs to be relocated globally. ICTs have also enabled the creation of entirely new types of 'digital' or 'virtual' labour, both paid and unpaid, shifting the borderline between 'play' and 'work' and creating new types of unpaid labour connected with the consumption and co-creation of goods and services. This affects private life as well as transforming the nature of work and people experience the impacts differently depending on their gender, their age, where they live and what work they do. Aspects of these changes have been studied separately by many different academic experts however up till now a cohesive overarching analytical framework has been lacking. Drawing on a major, high-profile COST Action (European Cooperation in Science and Technology) Dynamics of Virtual Work, this series will bring together leading international experts from a wide range of disciplines including political economy, labour sociology, economic geography, communications studies, technology, gender studies, social psychology, organisation studies, industrial relations and development studies to explore the transformation of work and labour in the Internet Age. The series will allow researchers to speak across disciplinary boundaries, national borders, theoretical and political vocabularies, and different languages to understand and make sense of contemporary transformations in work and social life more broadly. The book series will build on and extend this, offering a new, important and intellectually exciting intervention into debates about work and labour, social theory, digital culture, gender, class, globalisation and economic, social and political change.

Suddhabrata Deb Roy

The Rise of the Information Technology Society in India

Capitalism and the Construction of a Vulnerable Workforce

palgrave
macmillan

Suddhabrata Deb Roy
Sociology, Gender Studies and Criminology
University of Otago
Dunedin, New Zealand

ISSN 2947-9290 ISSN 2947-9304 (electronic)
Dynamics of Virtual Work
ISBN 978-3-031-58127-4 ISBN 978-3-031-58128-1 (eBook)
https://doi.org/10.1007/978-3-031-58128-1

© The Editor(s) (if applicable) and The Author(s), under exclusive license to Springer Nature Switzerland AG 2024
This work is subject to copyright. All rights are solely and exclusively licensed by the Publisher, whether the whole or part of the material is concerned, specifically the rights of translation, reprinting, reuse of illustrations, recitation, broadcasting, reproduction on microfilms or in any other physical way, and transmission or information storage and retrieval, electronic adaptation, computer software, or by similar or dissimilar methodology now known or hereafter developed.
The use of general descriptive names, registered names, trademarks, service marks, etc. in this publication does not imply, even in the absence of a specific statement, that such names are exempt from the relevant protective laws and regulations and therefore free for general use. The publisher, the authors and the editors are safe to assume that the advice and information in this book are believed to be true and accurate at the date of publication. Neither the publisher nor the authors or the editors give a warranty, expressed or implied, with respect to the material contained herein or for any errors or omissions that may have been made. The publisher remains neutral with regard to jurisdictional claims in published maps and institutional affiliations.

This Palgrave Macmillan imprint is published by the registered company Springer Nature Switzerland AG.
The registered company address is: Gewerbestrasse 11, 6330 Cham, Switzerland

Paper in this product is recyclable.

To all my cousins, friends, and comrades who work as IT professionals in India and across the world. Without your support and your indulgence, I would not have been able to write the book.

Preface and Acknowledgements

Many who know me on a personal level do not know that I am trained as an electrical engineer and was one of the many millions who had applied for a software/IT job in India back in 2016—eight years ago. It was as if an automated muscle response for me, and many others like me who in their final days of their engineering studies begin to ponder over future possibilities. Fortunately, or unfortunately, I did not get through. In 2012, when I was doing my engineering, a couple of people came to my room and started talking about *big terms* like 'imperialism', 'neoliberalism', and 'nationalism'. Meanwhile, my entire focus was on telling them how glamorous an IT life was—a perception that I had developed over the years. And, then finally one of them asked me, 'Do you think what is happening with the workers at these IT Hubs is a good thing?' That question subsequently had stuck with me and continues to do so till date—the result of which is this book.

Like all my other works, this book would not have been possible without the help of a significant number of people.

Thanks to Ursula Huws, one of the series editors and the person whom I had sent the very first proposal about a project of this kind that I had written some five years ago. She was gracious and kind enough to advise me that without some sort of a fellowship or funding, it would be nearly impossible to do anything regarding the project and since I was unable to get one, I had to drop the plans then. That project under Ursula did not take off, but the kind of support that she offered despite me not working with or under her formally has been exemplary. It exhibits the kind of generous individual that she is. Half a decade later, when we met in

viii   PREFACE AND ACKNOWLEDGEMENTS

London, I spoke to her about this book I had been working on, and she was instantly excited. Thanks for the help, the support, and, of course, the coffee!

Thanks to Marcelle Dawson, the first person with whom I had shared the news when this book got contracted by Palgrave Macmillan. She has been an excellent supervisor and one of the most generous human beings I have met in my life. Without her support, I would not have been able to do half of the things that I have ended up doing in the past five years. Thank you, Marcelle!

Thanks to Annabel Cooper and Simon Barber, the coolest supervisory team that one can have in one's doctoral research. Without them, it would have been a very difficult journey.

Many thanks to Kevin Anderson, Peter Hudis, and Sandra Rein—three people who have contributed immensely to my intellectual development, often at the expense of their sleep and peace of mind. They have often checked draft after draft of whatever I write till we can come at a peaceful co-existence.

Thanks to Debasreeta Deb, the first reader of all my drafts and whose comments help tremendously in shaping anything that I write.

My cousins and friends who work in the IT sector—to whom the book is dedicated to. I will not take their names because of their own security, but I thank them profusely for allowing me into their lives, discussing issues with me and providing me with an intimate view of IT lives.

Thanks to comrades in various IT unions in the country without whose help the book would not have been possible, especially to friends and comrades at the AIITEU. Thanks to Rikta, Cheenangshuk, Suman, and Manas, who have been very helpful to me and my research.

Many thanks to my friends who have been sources of constant support over the many years: Ayush, Nelson, Amitabh, Mrinmoy, Saurav, Brandon, Jonas, Grace, Kieran, Suraj, Sepoy, Chinmay, Ratul, Arif, Himangshu, and Rwituraj.

Thanks to the University of Otago, my alma mater. The university's generous funding and excellent infrastructure made the research possible.

Vote of thanks are also due to the University of Hyderabad and Jorhat Engineering College.

Thanks to the team at Palgrave Macmillan: Sharla Plant and Karthika Devi for their help. They have been extremely helpful and generous.

Dunedin, New Zealand   Suddhabrata Deb Roy

CONTENTS

1 The IT Society in India, Its Inhabitants, and Their Lives of Desperation   1

2 The Exploitative Nature of the IT Spaces   21

3 Social Reproduction and the IT Women   49

4 The Social Construction of Managerial Solutions to Political Problems   77

5 The Invisible Information Technology Workers   105

6 The Arrival of the 'Metro' Middle Class   133

7 Techie Unionisation in the IT Society   161

8 Workers, Middle-Class Employees, Professionals? No, just *the Working Poor*!   191

Index   209

ABOUT THE AUTHOR

Suddhabrata Deb Roy is a research associate-postdoctoral fellow at the Centre for Culture-Centred Approach to Research and Evaluation (CARE), Massey University, New Zealand, where he is working on analysing the causes and impacts of Islamophobia in India. Committed to bridging the epistemological gap between theory and praxis, he mainly works on Marxist theory and believes in doing intensive fieldwork-based research. His works have appeared in journals such as *Capital and Class*, *TripleC*, *Journal of Graphic Novels and Comics*, *Critique*, and so forth. He has written for reputed online platforms including *The Sociological Review Magazine* and *Notes from Below*. He is the author of four books: *Social Media and Capitalism: People, Communities, and Commodities* (2021); *Mass Struggles and Leninism: Reflections on Contemporary Struggles in India* (2022); *Singing to Liberation: Songs of Freedom and Nights of Resistance in Indian Campuses* (2023); and *Pandemic Fissures: COVID-19, Dehumanisation and the Obsolescence of Human Freedom* (Routledge, 2024). This is his fifth book. He can be contacted via email at suddhabratadebroy@gmail.com.

CHAPTER 1

The IT Society in India, Its Inhabitants, and Their Lives of Desperation

INTRODUCTION

India evokes different feelings among different people. If one is a tourist, one might get enamoured by its diverse culture; if one is a sports fan, one might get enamoured by the love that Indians show for cricket. However, the definition of India that attracts much of the Global Financial Capital is its reputation of being a global software and Information Technology hub, which produces around 1.5 million engineers every year (Shah, 2023). The Indian Information Technology (IT) sector

> established a new model for businesses in India, one that was professionally run and meritocracy-based, which was systems—and data-driven, and followed world-class quality and corporate governance standards. They changed the world's perception of India as a land of snake charmers to one of technology-savvy professionals. (Gopalakrishnan et al., 2022, pp. 16–17)

The Indian IT sector has played a critical role in the generation of a global identity for India as a nation. The IT industry in India has become one of the flagship industries that has come to not only define the country but also alter it socio-economically, culturally, and politically. Though computing and software have been a part of the Indian industrial set-up since the 1960s (Gopalakrishnan et al., 2022), the transformation of the

© The Author(s), under exclusive license to Springer Nature
Switzerland AG 2024
S. Deb Roy, *The Rise of the Information Technology Society in India*,
Dynamics of Virtual Work,
https://doi.org/10.1007/978-3-031-58128-1_1

1

Indian IT industry began when in 1991, as Harish Mehta (2022) writes, the Government of India (GOI) commissioned the World Bank to do a survey studying the potential of India as a software hub, of which the National Association of Software and Service Companies (NASSCOM), the premier trade association established in 1988 for serving the Indian IT Sector, was also a part. The results of the survey however were very heart wrenching for those of the ruling class with even Ireland scoring much better than India in certain domains of the survey—a country which is much smaller in size and population than India (Mehta, 2022). From there on India's rising software giants initiated a struggle against the various restrictions put in place by the Nehruvian welfare state, which restricted the monopolisation of capital into the hands of private capitalists. Its main weapon was the large pool of engineers in India who were ready to do quality work for low wages thus providing a significant cost advantage to global corporations (Mehta, 2022; Gopalakrishnan et al., 2022). At the same time, the Indian IT sector's embracement of hyper-productivity as an operating principle made it a lucrative option difficult to be overlooked (Murthy, 2010; Reddy, 2022).

The neoliberal reforms of 1991 altered the Indian society at a structural level initiating a string of changes within the ideological and material contours of the society. Neoliberal reforms had been initiated in India with the intention of establishing a neoliberal bourgeois democracy transforming the private corporate sector—accounting for merely 10 per cent of the economy in the early 1990s—into the leading component of the Indian economy (Vanaik, 2001). The neoliberal reforms of 1991 were a major moment in the history of India because it represented the transformation of India from a semi-feudal welfare state to a neoliberal capitalist economy. Achin Vanaik notes:

> From the fifties to the seventies, India had followed its own distinctive version of the import-substitution industrialisation model, more inward-oriented and state-regulated than elsewhere. The class character of the state was likewise sui generis—a dominant coalition comprising all sections of industrial capital, substantial land-owners, and senior bureaucrats, in which state functionaries operated as overall coordinators. In the eighties, a maturing bourgeoisie, more confident of handling external competition, and a burgeoning 'middle class'—actually an elite of mass proportions—hankering after higher levels of consumption, pushed for a cautious integration into global markets. (Vanaik, 2001, p. 44)

Contemporary India has adopted a highly favourable attitude towards the private sector. The private sector plays an influential role in the way in which the contemporary Indian society manifests itself, both globally and to its own citizens. It controls a significant share of the India's economy and has been often recognised as the chief force behind the recent economic growth in India (World Economic Forum, 2019). Among the service sectors, it is the IT industry that has come to be recognised as the major driver of the growth that India has witnessed in the service sector. The growth of India's economy since the 1980s has often been equated with the growth of the software industry in India because of the number of people that it employs and the revenue that it generates. The Indian IT sector employs close to 5.1 million people directly as of 2022 and is expected to be valued at around US $245 billion during FY2023 according to NASSCOM—growing faster than the Indian economy itself (Ministry of Electronics and IT, 2022; Phadnis, 2023). The estimate is that the IT industry will employ close to 9.5 Million workers by 2026 (Ministry of Electronics and IT, 2022).

Numerous factors have enabled the growth of the IT sector in India, including the extremely cheap rates of data in the country, the tremendous growth of technical education, and the usage of laws related to special economic zones (SEZs) that granted certain special powers to businesses in specific areas (Gopalakrishnan et al., 2022; Mehta, 2022). The middle-class professional service workers played an important role in the neoliberal transformation and were the primary vehicles of India's supposed economic ascension after 1991 (Fernandes, 2006; Chadchan & Shankar, 2012). The new middle class which was employed in various private companies and had formal and secured jobs and earned enough monetary and financial returns was critical to the development of the gentrified spaces deemed to be essential for the socio-economic development in India (Smith, 1979; Fernandes, 2006). A critical role in this transformation was played by the service sector, which commanded an important position in the neoliberal transformation of India. India's service sector contributed around 53 per cent to India's gross value added (GVA) at current prices during the financial year 2021–2022. Service sectors such as Information Technology (IT), business processing outsourcing (BPOs), and other allied services such as education, banking, healthcare, education, communication, and insurance—combined together—contribute around 66 per cent share in India's GDP and generate about 28 per cent of the total employment in India.[1] The growing share of the services within the GDP is a major shift from the predominantly agrarian economy that used to characterise India (Bhalla, 1987). The IT sector in India has played a crucial role in this regard, being the largest employer within the private service sector (Didimishe, 2023).

The changes in the sectoral employment were taking place concurrently with the development of a neoliberal state in India, which restricts itself merely to the creation of newer markets wherever markets are present transforming itself into a substitutive state (Harvey, 2007; Berry, 2022). The Indian state was slowly transforming itself into a state that promotes an economic structure dominated by monopolistic transnational capitalism that goes against the Keynesian welfare models that had dominated the conceptions surrounding welfarism in the twentieth century (Huws, 2017). Under a welfare state, it is the public sector that ensures that the management of the state runs in accordance with democratic principles (Desai, 1984). The structuring of the public sector has been such that it has allowed the middle classes to take greater amount of control over the same. And since the public sector had been the most visible part of the workers' movement in India (Crouch, 1979), the middle class also constructed an important progenitor of left-wing vanguardist politics in India. It was only natural that after the 1991 neoliberal economic reforms, the most eligible section of the population came to be the ones who were entrusted with the responsibility of managing it—the middle class. However, the middle class is also the section which gets aligned with the ideals of capitalist globalisation and neoliberalism easily because it already remained attached to ideas such as personal responsibility, achievement, and so forth (Weiss, 2019). And one of the prime ideas behind the rise of neoliberalism has been the constant erosion of the idea of social responsibility in favour of more personal responsibility (Giroux, 2014).

While under a welfare state that often mainly functions through the public sector enterprises (PSEs), human beings are analysed as citizens, and under neoliberalism, they are analysed as customers because of the neoliberal focus on profits rather than on social well-being (Harvey, 2005). Such changes within the society cannot be brought forward without a compliant middle class because of the hegemonical role that the middle class plays in the society in favour of the status quo either ideologically or politically (Katz, 1993; Harvey, 2005; Weiss, 2019). The growth of the

---

[1] Details are available at the website of the India Brand Equity Foundation: https://www.ibef.org/industry/services [Accessed 05.04.2023].

middle class was antithetical to the binary class structure that was often espoused by orthodox trade unionism in India. The generation of individual subjectivities causes a major divergence within the orthodox Marxist movement that fails to consider the non-economic factors in a social movement. Class belongingness does not emerge only out of the economic conditions but also from other factors such as control and coercive domination (Ehrenreich & Ehrenreich, 1979) that change in the ways in which working individuals construct their social selves. Marginalised individuals remain particularly vulnerable to such changes because the evolving norms of public conduct often do not consider the casteist, majoritarian, and gendered nature of the social spaces within which these individuals have to conduct themselves.

Such tendencies have been constantly validated and often encouraged by the numerous Special Economic Zones (SEZs) and software technology parks of India (STPIs) which have been established with the belief that they would ease the business procedures associated with the IT sector within the IT hubs. Bengaluru was one of the first IT hubs developed in India back in the 1990s. Even today, a significant section of engineers (including engineering students) and others who desire to make a career in IT will often mention Bengaluru to be their first choice when it comes to choosing their employment sites. As a senior trade unionist, Amanullah Khan, stated in an interview to the author:

> Bangalore[2] because of its unique climatic situation[3] was an instant hit with many of the international companies. They set-up offices here, and most of them got a ready-made workforce because there were a lot of software-based PSEs already in the city. Some of the recently retired staff who had settled down in the city served as their initial employees, and then subsequently new people came in, who also settled in. Then their children grew up, and they needed education, so all these engineering colleges were set up.[4] And, now when the second generation has had children, you are seeing

[2] The old name of Bengaluru.

[3] Bengaluru's climate is often ascribed to be the best in the country. More details are available at: https://www.bengaluruonline.in/city-guide/amazing-weather-of-bangalore. For more details on migration to Bengaluru, see https://www.deccanherald.com/india/karnataka/bengaluru/what-brings-so-many-migrants-to-bengaluru-928532.html [Accessed 05.04.2023].

[4] Bengaluru has one of the highest numbers of engineering college density in the country with more than 200 engineering colleges located in and around the city. More details are available at: https://ceo.karnataka.gov.in/uploads/8395 1696398287.pdf [Accessed 05.04.2023].

the boom of universities. It has been a process in itself, but sadly, the only companies who have suffered have been the PSEs.

The growth of the IT sector in the country has resulted in certain changes within the urban spaces in which it was allowed to flourish, Bengaluru in particular. The development of Bengaluru has taken place in a highly gentrified manner whereby significant changes have been implemented into the fabric of the city which have created grounds for privatisation to thrive in the city (Nair, 2007). Bengaluru has become one of the most sought-after models of urban development for any region that desires to develop an IT hub of its own. With time, numerous other IT hubs have been formed in the country: Hyderabad, Gurgaon (now Gurugram), Noida, Kochi, Pune, Chennai, and others. Similar structural changes have been institutionalised in cities such as Gurgaon (Oldenburg, 2018) and Noida (Vasudevan, 2013), widely recognised as one the fastest-growing cities in India. Most of these urban spaces have come to be defined by signs of affluence that the IT industry has come to render mainstream in the society modifying the relationships that its inhabitants have with the marginalised populace that *also* inhabit the space. Most of these hubs have come to be defined by a steady migration of engineers, software professionals, and other such professional workers from the middle classes. At the same time, there has also been large-scale internal migration of low-paid workers into these cities serving the IT industry as support or service workers (Chakraborty, 2021). These workers are key parts of the transformation that is brought forward within the social reality that capitalism produces that tries to achieve a domination over the entire society. They remain one of the worst effected from the exploitation that the IT sector produces receiving low wages and living through extremely precariat states of existence (Chandrasekhar, 2003). As Mario Tronti had argued:

> [T]he relation between capitalist production and bourgeois society, between factory and society, between society and State achieves, to an ever-greater degree a more organic relation. At the highest level of capitalist development, the social relation is transformed into a moment of the relation of production, the whole of society is turned into an articulation of production, that is, the whole of society lives as a function of the factory and the factory extends its exclusive domination to the whole of society. (Tronti, 1962, Para 17)

The IT sector in India has left an indelible mark on the socio-economic structure of the country. SEZs and STPIs, which have been formed to further the sector (Mehta, 2022), have been one of the major hallmarks of the exploitation that is meted out to the IT workers. SEZs and STPIs have rendered mainstream the frequent violation of labour laws and policies (Paul, 2014). The social factory that develops around the IT industry is also nurtured by the constant rise in the number of technology-based institutions which have ensured a constant supply of engineers and other allied professional service workers for the sector to employ (Gopalakrishnan et al., 2022). At the same time, the growth has also been concurrent with a corresponding growth of uneven development and precarity in many of India's non-urban and semi-urban regions, which has created an internal migrant workforce[5] of more than 100 million people according to the 2017 Economic Survey (Tumbe, 2018). The failure of the welfare state in India can be related to capitalism's relationship with the process of uneven development (Desai, 1975). Capitalist development is often highly uneven in nature designed to favour those who possess the requisite socio-economic and cultural resources to utilise the effects of the developmental trajectory to their own benefits (Harvey, 2005; Wainwright, 2013). Uneven development is a result of the ways in which capitalism constantly impoverishes certain regions for achieving development in some select regions for some select individuals leading to the large-scale commodification of labour power in the latter regions (Harvey, 2006). The neoliberal reforms have ensured that India continues to suffer from uneven development, a characteristic feature of the development of capitalism in the 1990s globally. And, one of the most explicit examples of the same is the social composition that one can find in the IT hubs.

The uneven development that characterises India embeds within itself potentially politically explosive factors in certain contexts because '[most] of India's economic development in the past four decades has come from the southern and western states … which have become hubs for manufacturing and high-tech industries [while] the heartland states … have shown little sign of catching up' (The Economist, 2022, Para 5). The distinctiveness of certain regions has always played a key role in the uneven development that many regions in India face, both economically and socially (Prasad, 1988). Even within the various metropolitan areas, cities such as

---

[5] The term here refers to individuals who migrate for economic reasons, mainly to find work.

New Delhi, Hyderabad, and Bengaluru have been characterised by socio-economic growth at a faster rate than other areas such as Kolkata, Chennai, or Guwahati (Telangana Today, 2024). Most of the IT Hubs have been formed by a constant wave of migrations to these urban spaces which have been an important part of the developmental trajectory of the IT hubs in the country. Although no proper survey has been conducted with regards to migrant formal IT workers in the IT Hubs, it can be assumed, as an IT union activist stated, that half of the IT workers in any of the IT hubs are migrants:

> More than three lakh [300,000] people entered Bengaluru in 2022, and that is after Covid. Now, undoubtedly, most of them are precariat migrant workers, but at the same time, we can assume that at least thirty to forty percent of them work in the IT sector if we analyse the recruitment patterns of the IT companies. The government will not conduct a survey because it will reveal the growing stress on the city and expose the sub-regional fault lines.

Such a massive influx of migrants has changed the nature of the spatial process in cities such as Bengaluru, as well as other IT hubs such as Gurugram, Hyderabad,[6] and Noida, altering the dynamics of class structure and consciousness therein. The changing patterns of class identification have a dialectical relationship with the choices that individuals make with regard to their employment. The changing nature of the state and the society also play a critical role in this regard. The delicate balance existing between the drive for financial profits and well-being of the citizens gives rise to conditions where marginalised individuals face an increasing amount of repression and exploitation. For example, a section of eligible Dalits has continued to be funded by private corporations for their education but very few private corporations actually institutionalise affirmative action within their organisations (Khan, 2019). Muslims, continue to be underrepresented in the various formal sectors that provide social security and are mostly employed as self-employed labour that contributes to their marginality (Mansoor, 2021). Women, on the other hand, continue to be viewed as individuals for whom their sexuality or their association with a particular family is an asset that can be used for garnering better

---

[6]Although Hyderabad is the name used, most of the IT offices are located in Cyberabad, a planned part of the city developed specifically for the purpose of IT firms.

advantages within their employment arrangements. The continued relevance of such perceptions has caused certain disparities to arise within the various bodies formed to address these concerns, which go far beyond the economistic arguments given by mainstream trade unions and management strategists, and their normalised organisational philosophy and operational strategies.

The changes that the IT industry has brought within the Indian workers' movement have been diverse, so much so that the conditions of work in the IT sector have also forced many of the public sector enterprises (PSEs) to change their organisational strategies. One senior trade unionist in the public sector banking services stated:

> With the growth of the IT sector, the workers' expectations from their own companies have been changing. In the past, we used to organise *workers*. Now, we organise the middle class—a distinct shift can be seen here. The terms have become enmeshed with each other now. We have even begun to analyse ourselves as being a middle-class union. There is a rise of corporate culture in the offices. That does not change anything organisationally, but it does point out that we are now organising a workforce which hates the term 'workforce', much like how our brothers and sisters in the IT sector hate to be called workers.

The primary problem faced by the workers' movement in this regard has been to rescue or redefine the working-class identity and a sense of social solidarity from the forces of alienation that run amok under neoliberal global capitalism producing segregations between different kinds of workers, often based on skills (Huws, 2017). Most of these tendencies have been aided by a growing authoritarian politics, austerity measures, growth of centralised models of development, and the consistent weakening of structures and networks of solidarity, which have caused a rift to occur between the local structures of solidarity that continue to exist in countries such as India and the kind of structure that neoliberalism desires to create. These changes have been accompanied by a gradual process of de-politicisation which has made it difficult for individual subjectivities to be expressed and catered to (Hardt & Negri, 2000). Conditions such as these bring forward a bio-political mode of control that often makes it difficult for discourses focused on social justice to be propagated among the non-capitalist classes. The generation of an egalitarian discourse focused on workers' welfare and progressive social restructuring is a

10   S. DEB ROY

political process in itself. Historically, the Central Trade Unions (CTUs)[7] have played a critical role in this regard and were instrumental voices against impoverishment. But these organisations have suffered tremendously under neoliberalism which have had their effects on the IT sector as well, especially in the domain of unionisation. While previously, the trade unions only worked with the formal and the informal workforce of a particular workplace, privatisation rendered this two-fold division of workers in the workplace relatively redundant and instead produced a multiplicity of different class positions—sometimes within the same workplace with different class positions often been found among individuals doing the same kind of work.

More than 90 per cent of India's workforce works in the unorganised sectors (Sengupta, 2007). Within the organised sector, the most important role was once played by the various PSEs, which currently employ only around 2.2 per cent of the total employment generated in India, a significant decrease from the 12.2 per cent that it used to employ in 1994 (Chandrashekhar & Ghosh, 2019; Gera, 2022). Such a change has caused numerous alterations to occur in the economic and social lives of individuals. The prominence of the private sector as intrinsic component of economic and human development has converted a section of the middle class into working poor living under deplorable conditions. It has also produced a new middle class that is armed with newer methods of fulfilling their subjective desires. The sense of dependence is a critical part of the neoliberal construction of the middle class (Goldthorpe, 1982). The service sector, which provides working individuals with a fixed salary, a certain amount of job security, and an avenue to gain an improved lifestyle, plays a crucial role in these processes. The proliferation of salaried service workers among a certain section of the population enables structures of control to further capitalist domination by acting as compliant enablers of the philosophy of their employers, who provide them with their salaries (Marcuse, 1964)—more so in the case of India because the salaried service workers control the narrative discourse about socio-political and cultural changes in the country.

---

[7] Three major CTUs of India are the All India Trade Union Congress (AITUC), the Centre of Indian Trade Unions (CITU), and the All India Council of Central Trade Unions (AICCTU) informally affiliated respectively with the Communist Party of India, the Communist Party of India (Marxist), and the Communist Party of India (Marxist-Leninist) Liberation.

When such sectoral shifts—such as the one that India has been witnessing from being a largely agrarian economy to a service oriented one (Gordon & Gupta, 2003)—occur with more workers engaging in either flexible, casual, or (relatively) low-paid work, it can often result in the creation of the working poor in countries of the Global South, because such nations do not have much social security schemes in place (Majid, 2001). Workers coming from the marginalised sections are more at risk of becoming the working poor because they are not only subservient to the established power relations, but also the secondary effects that those power relations have on everyday urban reality (Gilbert, 1998). Conditions contributing to their deplorable living standards are further enhanced by the hostility that the IT sector possesses towards trade unions because the workers are restricted from accessing organisational set-ups that can enable a radical transformation of their workplaces and social lives. They often portray unions to be bodies composed of irresponsible individuals whose sole purpose is to disrupt the social stability. They correspondingly use all the financial and legal powers at their disposal to counter and dismantle any organisational structure within their organisations. The uniqueness of contemporary capitalism is that while in the past, the capitalists used force to ensure compliance from the workers in this regard, the contemporary capitalists have used their financial and disciplinary prowess to develop a sense of consensual submission (Hardt & Negri, 2000; Dekker, 2022). An active embracement of disciplinary methods can be seen in the writings of many of the early progenitors of the Indian IT industry such as Murthy (2010) and Reddy (2022).

Contemporary capitalism aims to achieve a structure of domination that is camouflaged as empowerment despite being more exploitative than most other historical forms of domination. It desires a stable social order in order to further its own accumulation and remains averse to any kind of conflict that can potentially disrupt the everyday functioning of the market. The hegemonical control that is inflicted on the workers is navigated through the institutions of the office, the community, and the family—encompassing the totality of the workers' social existence. Capitalist control over the IT workers benefits from creating a sense of alienation within the workers constructing for the workers—a social reality that converts them into highly compliant subjects. Organisations working among these workers have had to take these factors into account when devising their strategies. The middle class in developing countries is a constructed category which capitalism invents to further oppress the working-class creating avenues for the deeper penetration of neoliberal governmentality among the poorest of the poor while at the same time excluding them from the aegis of the remnants of the welfare state (Lefebvre, 2008). Their engagement with these issues shapes their subjective selves and the attitude that they come to possess towards representative bodies—most notably the trade unions. The anti-unionist nature of the IT sector has worked against the unions as most workers in the private sector have come to believe that if they get recruited by a union then they might face potential unemployment. Under a welfare state or in public sector jobs, the workers can at times mitigate these issues because they are secured as far as their employment is concerned, which makes them relatively more empowered than their private sector counterparts. Most PSEs use payment structures independent of the efforts and productivity of the individual worker, thus reducing the risk that an individual worker possesses regarding wages and job security (Vickers & Yarrow, 1991). Such structures of job security however are not present in the private sector (Prasad, 2018), including the Indian IT sector.

It is of common knowledge that the workers in the Indian IT sector, like most other private sectors, are more exploited in nature than their public sector counterparts. The contours of exclusion include aspects such as job security, retirement benefits, and long working hours—which lead to a complex relationship between employment and upliftment and contribute to the creation of atomised individuals, the impacts of which are an important point for the arguments presented in the book. The IT workers differ significantly from the public sector workers. Previous research in different contexts has pointed out that the public sector employees are more pro-social than their private counterparts because they enjoy more socio-cultural capital and are less likely to perform menial jobs (Macbeath, 1979; Gill-McClure, 2007; Torin & Vlasspoulos, 2015). They also differ in terms of their ideology and motivation because a 'private enterprise is animated purely by consideration of profit, while social purpose and welfare are supposed to be the dominant motives of public enterprise' (Lokanathan, 1957, p. 9). The differences between the sectors play a significant role in determining the ways in which the trade unions function among them. In the public sector, the issues that the trade unions take up are usually more political than the private sector. This is because the public sector itself works on a premise that is highly political in nature as it draws its socio-political legitimacy from the state. The private sector necessitates

1 THE IT SOCIETY IN INDIA, ITS INHABITANTS, AND THEIR LIVES... 13

that trade unions work outside the domain of mainstream politics because its associated processes remain outside the mainstream frameworks of labour protests.

The kind of middle class that the IT sector employs are ones who can be referred to as being the professional managerial class (PMC) as defined by Barbara Ehrenreich and John Ehrenreich (1979). According to them, the PMC are a distinct class in themselves composed of individuals who work in mid-level and lower managerial positions and who do not own the means of production but rather further the capitalist reproduction acting as a component of the broader process of capitalist social control. Ehrenreich and Ehrenreich (1979) suggest that in every society, the term 'class' has been more often than not addressed through an economistic lens and analysed as a relationship between labour and capital, but in the contemporary times, it has evolve taking into cognisance various factors like control and coercive domination which may or may not be completely economic in nature. Class, according to Ehrenreich and Ehrenreich (1979), is not a social entity which can be determined purely on economic terms because it contains significant amount of cultural and social implications as well. The book agrees with this argument and extends the argument in the case of India.

In the case of India, certain unique features have to be taken into consideration. One of them is the existence of uneven development in India. The scale of uneven development in India has been unprecedented in recent years, which has not only affected the financial situation of the people, but also affect them psychologically by increasing the general anxiety levels in the society (Mezzadri, 2021; Baruah, 2023). The uneven economic development in India has resulted in the ideological construction of tendencies such as sub-nationalism, poor resource management and an uneven distribution of the effects of capitalist development causing widespread disparity and inequality, especially among the marginalised section of the populace (Sarma, 1966; Baruah, 1999). Individuals in precarious circumstances take up various methods to elevate themselves from those precarious situations such as the usage of achieved education and attributed social capital, both of which have been used for the construction of individuals who are highly atomistic in nature and often psychologically distanced from the broader society (Giroux, 2014; Carter, 2017). The dissolution of structures and networks of solidarity often play a critical role in this regard, and the Metro Middle Class (MMC) is one of the major results of the same.

The second unique nature of the Indian Professional and Managerial Class (PMC) is its relationship with migration and the urban space that it comes to inhabit in the IT Hubs. The Indian IT Hubs have often been developed in a manner which have resulted in significant changes in the local economy and social fabric altering the ways in which the local inhabitants define themselves and the space around them (Vasudevan, 2013; Oldenburg, 2018). The idea of space, as Lefebvre (1991) mentions, is a highly political one because space forms the basis of one's social existence and social relations under capitalism when it acts alongside other aspects such as temporality and capitalist alienation. The idea of space, and the lack of spatial restrictions, also forms one of the most important aspects of contemporary forms of labour that produces the conditions under which forms of resistance are often supressed by multiple means of socio-economic deprivation and cultural marginalisation (Harvey, 2009, 2016).

The IT sector by its very nature remains opposed to trade unionism because of the perceived role that trade unions play with regard to deterring the hyper-productive nature of work that often overlooks the well-being of the workers as an unnecessary addendum to their finances (Punekar et al., 1978; Bisht, 2010). Unlike the public sector where trade unions have historically been a highly visible and effective force (Crouch, 1979), they were found wanting in the private sector because they failed to come to terms with the subjective aspects of privatisation and neoliberalism that has created newer conceptions of class identity among the workers. The ways in which the workers define a good lifestyle, often run in opposition to the processes that generate of a working-class consciousness critical to which are the ability to articulate a working-class identity, an opposition to exploitation, along with the possession of a conceptualisation of an alternative to the present society (Mann, 1973). The creation of such a consciousness is greatly affected by the kind of work that the individual workers are involved in because class formation occurs through the everyday interactions that individuals have with the space and people around them (Thompson, 1963).

The involvement of workers in trade unions and other such representative bodies has a close connection with the nature of their inhabited space. In India, the private sector has often functioned as an autonomous body distinct from the mainstream socio-political processes. It has usually been left outside the domain of politics and has enjoyed a considerable autonomy as far as its practices regarding recruitment, promotions, and retrenchments are concerned. Fuelled by the autonomy granted to the private sector, different kinds of structures enable the exploitation of the workers through different methods. The bourgeoning IT sector in India is no different as well—as the subsequent chapters will exhibit. The class consciousness among IT workers has come to be defined by their relationship with the casteist, majoritarian and gendered structure of social production. Such processes of secondary class consciousness often drive them towards a state of class confusion—something that is one of the core aspects of this particular book. Class confusion is driven by a process of alienated class belongingness that deters them from gaining a working-class consciousness but rather makes them gain a consciousness that makes them further subservient to the power of capital.

The book is a result of fieldwork conducted, both in person and virtually, from 2020 to 2023 in seven major IT hubs in India: Bengaluru, Hyderabad, Pune, Gurugram, Noida, Kolkata, and Chennai. It is mainly based on ethnographic observations and in-depth interviews conducted with more than 200 IT and IT-enabled services (ITeS) workers, IT support workers, and union activists. In the context of the IT workers, to understand the marginalities that they face as an individual part of a social totality, it is critical to realise the differences between the IT, IT-enabled services (ITeS), and the support sector workers, that is, the invisible IT workers. While software-based workers traditionally are referred to as IT workers, other workers who work in knowledge processing outsourcing activities (KPOs), or in business process outsourcing activities (BPOs), call centres, and so forth are usually referred to as IT-enabled services (Hussain & Dutta, 2014). For the purpose of the present book however, the term IT Workers will be used to refer to both these categories.

The book is divided into eight chapters, including the current one. This chapter has provided a basic premise upon which the book is based upon speaking about the IT Hubs, the social composition therein, and the critical factors that one needs to consider while analysing the IT workers. However, much of the discussion in the first chapter has been at a general level, speaking about universal modes of exploitation in these spaces. Chapter 2 will speak of the IT workers who come from marginalised sections of the society, primarily Muslims, Dalits, and women. While the general state of exploitation in the IT sector have been widely referred to in various journal papers and books, it is the specific kinds of exploitation meted out to workers from the socially marginalised sections that has often evaded much critical academic attention.

16   S. DEB ROY

Chapter 3 speaks specifically about the women IT workers, especially about their lives as *women*. The chapter delves into the reproductive labour that women IT workers perform and analyses the relationship between their selves as women and their selves as IT workers. Reproductive labour in the context of the book encompasses housework, care work, emotional labour performed within domestic spaces, and the labour of people-reproduction. By household labour, the chapter refers to the daily chores within households, such as cooking, laundry, and so forth. Care work, on the other hand, includes the work, both psychological and physical, performed as a mother, sister, or a nurse. Housework emphasises the activity while care work focuses more on the relational aspect of the work performed. 'People-reproduction' refers to the activities that result in the reproduction of labour power in the society, including giving birth to children.

Chapter 4 speaks about the well-being strategies that are employed by most of the IT firms. The chapter speaks about the processes through which well-being strategies are being used by the IT sector to propagate a sense of the all-encompassing happiness among the IT workers resulting in what Marcuse (1964) had referred to as being the capitalist 'conquest of the unhappy consciousness'. The chapter critiques the neoliberal emphasis on happiness as an objective factor and argues about the centrality of particular subjectivities that workers imbibe within themselves. Chapter 5 mainly brings forward the plight of the indivisible IT workers. As against the popular belief, the IT sector does not only employ engineers and other kinds of software professionals. Rather, these workers, usually employed directly, form only a part of the total IT workforce in the country. The IT sector employs a host of different kinds of outsourced and contractual labour usually as janitors, security workers, delivery personnel, and so forth as support service workers to aid the jobs of the formal IT workers. This chapter analyses the kind of exploitation that these workers face and the processes which determine the kind of relationships that they share with the formal IT workers, or the direct employees.

Chapter 6 speaks in terms of the class composition that is emerging in the IT Hubs. The book takes reference to Barbara and John Ehrenreich's 'Professional Managerial Class' (PMC) and extends their argument keeping in mind the peculiar conditions provided by the Indian IT sector, mainly speaking in terms of gentrified urban spaces and the psycho-social impacts of the same. The chapter evokes the term, 'Metro Middle Class' (MMC) referring to the distinct nature of the IT workforce in India's IT hubs. Chapter 7 draws upon the state of trade unions in the Indian IT sector. It talks about how different IT unions in India are addressing the concerns of the IT workers, and the processes through which trade unions are subverted by the sector. The book uses the words 'worker' and 'employee' interchangeably until it reaches the conclusion where the sociological and political implications of the two terms are made explicit through an analysis of the arguments made in the previous chapters.

REFERENCES

Baruah, M. (2023). *Slow Disaster: Political Ecology of Hazards and Everyday Life in the Brahmaputra Valley, Assam.* Routledge.

Baruah, S. (1999). *India Against Itself: Assam and the Politics of Nationality.* Oxford University Press.

Berry, C. (2022). The Substitutive State? Neoliberal State Interventionism Across Industrial, Housing and Private Pensions Policy in the UK. *Competition and Change, 26*(2), 242–265.

Bhalla, G. S. (1987). *Indian Agriculture Since Independence.* National Book Trust.

Bisht, N. S. (2010). Trade Unions in Indian IT Industry? An Employees' Perspective. *Indian Journal of Industrial Relations, 46*(2), 220–228.

Carter, L. (2017). Neoliberalism and Stem Education: Some Australian Policy Discourse. *Canadian Journal of Science, Mathematics and Technology Education, 17*(4), 247–257.

Chadchan, J., & Shankar, R. (2012). An Analysis of Urban Growth Trends in the Post-Economic Reforms Period in India. *International Journal of Sustainable Built Environment, 1*(1), 36–49.

Chakraborty, I. (2021). *Invisible Labour: Support Service Workers in India's Information Technology Industry.* Routledge.

Chandrasekhar, C. P. (2003, July 4). ITeS and Hard Facts. Frontline, pp. 127–29. Retrieved April 5, 04, 2023, from https://frontline.thehindu.com/columns/article30217711.ece

Chandrashekhar, C. P., & Ghosh, J. (2019, July 29). The Withering Trend of Public Employment in India. *Business Line.* Retrieved April 5, 04, 2023, from https://www.thehindubusinessline.com/opinion/columns/the-withering-tren-of-public-employment-in-india/article28750003.ece

Crouch, H. (1979). *The Indian Working Class.* Sachin Publications.

Dekker, S. (2022). *Compliance Capitalism: How Free Markets Have Led to Unfree, Overregulated Workers.* Routledge.

Desai, A. R. (1975). The Myth of the Welfare State. In *State and Society in India: Essays in Dissent.* Bombay: Popular Prakashan.

Desai, A. R. (1984). *India's Path of Development: A Marxist Approach.* Sangam Books.

Didimishe, S. (2023, December 2). *IT Companies Emerge as Top Employers in India*. Financial Express. Retrieved April 5, 04, 2023, from https://www.financialexpress.com/business/industry-it-companies-emerge-as-top-employers-in-india-2898225/

Ehrenreich, B., & Ehrenreich, J. (1979). The Professional—Managerial Class. In P. Walker (Ed.), *Between Labour and Capital*. Boston: South End Press.

Fernandes, L. (2006). *India's New Middle Class: Democratic Politics in an Era of Economic Reform*. University of Minnesota Press.

Gera, I. (2022, June 15). Job at Hand: India Far Behind Other Nations in Public Sector Employment. *Business Standard*. Retrieved April 5, 2023, from https://www.business-standard.com/article/current-affairs/job-at-hand-modi-govt-aims-to-increase-workforce-by-a-third-in-18-months-122061401358_1.html

Gilbert, M. R. (1998). "Race", Space, and Power: The Survival Strategies of Working Poor Women. *Annals of the Association of American Geographers, 88*(4), 595–621.

Gill-McClure, G. (2007). Fighting Marketization: An Analysis of Manual Municipal Labor in the UK and the US. *Labor Studies Journal, 32*(Spring), 41–59.

Giroux, H. (2014/2020). *Neoliberalism's War on Higher Education* (2nd ed.). Haymarket Books.

Goldthorpe, J. H. (1982). On the Service Class, its Formation and Future. In A. Giddens & G. Mackenzie (Eds.), *Social Class and the Division of Labour*. Cambridge University Press.

Gopalakrishnan, K., Dayasindhu, N., & Narayanan, K. (2022). *Against All Odds: The IT Story of India*. Penguin.

Gordon, J., & Gupta, P. (2003, November 14–16). *Understanding India's Services Revolution. International Monetary Fund*. Paper prepared for the IMF-NCAER Conference, A Tale of Two Giants: India's and China's Experience with Reform, New Delhi.

Hardt, M., & Negri, M. (2000). *Empire*. Harvard University Press.

Harvey, D. (2005). *A Brief History of Neoliberalism*. Oxford University Press.

Harvey, D. (2006). *Spaces of Global Capitalism: A Theory of Uneven Geographical Development*. Verso.

Harvey, D. (2007). Neoliberalism as Creative Destruction. *The Annals of the American Academy of Political and Social Science, 610*, 22–44.

Harvey, D. (2009). *Rebel Cities*. Verso.

Harvey, D. (2016). *Social Justice and the City*. University of Georgia Press.

Hussain, Z., & Dutta, M. (2014). *Women in Kolkata's IT Sector: Satisficing between Work and Household*. Springer.

Huws, U. (2017, December). A New Bill of Workers' Rights for the 21st Century. *Think Piece*, p. 92. Retrieved April 5, 2023, from https://www.compassonline.org.uk/wp-content/uploads/2017/11/A-new-bill-of-Workers-Rights.pdf

Katz, C. (1993). Karl Marx on the Transition from Feudalism to Capitalism. *Theory and Society, 22*(3), 363–389.

Khan, S. (2019, March 15). The Casteist Underbelly of the Indian Private Sector. *The Wire*. Retrieved April 5, 2023, from https://thewire.in/caste/the-casteist-underbelly-of-the-indian-private-sector

Lefebvre, H. (1991). *The Production of Space*. Basil Blackwell.

Lefebvre, H. (2008). *Critique of Everyday Life: Volume 3, From Modernity to Modernism*. Verso.

Lokanathan, P. S. (1957). The Public Sector in India. *Indian Journal of Public Administration, 3*(1), 9–15.

Macbeath, I. (1979). *Votes, Virtues, and Vices: Trade Union Power*. Associated Business Press.

Majid, N. (2001). The Working Poor in Developing Countries. *International Labour Review, 140*(3), 271–291.

Mann, M. (1973). *Consciousness and Action among Western Working Class*. London: Macmillan.

Mansoor, K. (2021). Status of Employment and Occupations of Muslims in India: Evidence from a Household Survey—2011–2012. *Journal of Muslim Minority Affairs, 41*(4), 742–762.

Marcuse, H. (1964). *One Dimensional Man*. London: Routledge.

Mehta, H. (2022). *The Maverick Effect: The Inside Story of India's IT Revolution*. Harper Collins Publishers India.

Mezzadri, A. (2021). Marx's Field as Our Global Present. In A. Mezzadri (Ed.), *Marx in the Field*. Anthem Press.

Ministry of Electronics and IT. (2022, August 3). Number of Employees in IT. New Delhi: Government of India. Retrieved April 5, 2023, from from https://pib.gov.in/Pressreleaseshare.aspx?PRID=1847841

Murthy, N. R. N. (2010). *A Better India: A Better World*. Penguin.

Nair, J. (2007). *The Promise of the Metropolis*. Oxford University Press.

Oldenburg, V. T. (2018). *Gurgaon: From Mythic Village to Millennium City*. Harper Collins Publishers India.

Paul, S. (2014). Special Economic Zones and the Exploitation Underneath. *SSRN Journal*. Retrieved April 5, 2023, from https://papers.ssrn.com/sol3/papers.cfm?abstract_id=2359449

Phadnis, S. (2023, March 2). Indian IT Sector to Touch $245 Billion in FY23: Nasscom. *Times of India*. Retrieved April 5, 2023, from http://timesofindia.indiatimes.com/articleshow/98344616.cms?from=mdr&utm_source=contentofinterest&utm_medium=text&utm_campaign=cppst

Prasad, A. (2018). *Private Regulation and Workers' Rights in India*. Winshield Press.

Prasad, P. H. (1988). Roots of Uneven Regional Growth in India. *Economic and Political Weekly, 23*(33), 1968–1992.

Punekar, S. D., Deodhar, S. B., & Sankaran, S. (1978). *Labour Welfare, Trade Unionism and Industrial Relations*. Himalaya Publishing House.

Reddy, B. V. R. M. (2022). *Engineered in India: From Dreams to Billion-Dollar CYIENT*. Penguin.

Sarma, J. N. (1966). Problems of Economic Development in Assam. *Economic and Political Weekly, 1*(7), 281+283–286.

Sengupta, A. (2007). *Report on the Conditions of Work and Promotion of Livelihood in the Unorganised Sector*. National Commission for Enterprises in the Unorganised Sector.

Shah, H. (2023, November 7). *Why Indian Engineers Are Unemployable & What's the Solutions*. LinkedIn. Retrieved April 5, 2023, from https://www.linkedin.com/pulse/why-indian-engineers-unemployable-whats-solutions-harshad-shah-atfqf#:~:text=As%20of%202021%2C%20India%20annually,for%20a%20%24%203.7%20trillion%20Economy.&text=India%20boasts%20the%20distinc-tion%20of,engineering%20education%20institutions%20and%20infrastructure

Smith, N. (1979). Toward a Theory of Gentrification: A Back to the City Movement by Capital, Not People. *Journal of the American Planning Association, 45*(4), 538–545.

Telangana Today. (2024). *Hyderabad ranks among world's top 10 fastest-growing cities, predicts massive GDP surge*. April 12, https://telanganatoday.com/hyderabad-ranks-among-world-stop-10-fastest-growing-cities-predicts-massive-gdp-surge [Accessed 04.05.2024]

The Economist. (2022, October 27). India's Regional Inequality Could Be Politically Explosive. Retrieved April 5, 2023, from https://www.economist.com/asia/2022/10/27/indias-regional-inequality-could-be-politically-explosive

Thompson, E. P. (1963/2013). *The Making of the English Working Class*. London: Vintage.

Torin, M., & Vlasspoulos, M. (2015). Are Public Sector Workers Differently? Cross-European Evidence from Elderly Workers and Retirees. *IZA Journal of Labor Economics, 4*(11). https://doi.org/10.1186/s40172-015-0027-3

Tronti, M. (1962). *Factory and Society*. Operaismo in English. Retrieved April 5, 2023, from https://operaismoinenglish.wordpress.com/2013/06/13/factory-and-society/

Tumbe, C. (2018). *India Moving: A History of Migration*. Vintage.

Vanaik, A. (2001). The New Indian Right. *New Left Review, 1*(9). Retrieved April 5, 2023, from https://newleftreview.org/issues/ii9/articles/achin-vanaik-the-new-indian-right

Vasudevan, V. (2013). *Urban Villager: Life in an Indian Satellite Town*. SAGE.

Vickers, J., & Yarrow, G. (1991). Economic Perspectives on Privatisation. *Journal of Economic Perspectives, 5*, 111–132.

Wainwright, J. (2013). *In Marx's Laboratory: Critical Interpretations of the Grundrisse*. Brill.

Weiss, H. (2019). *We Have Never Been Middle Class*. Verso.

World Economic Forum. (2019, October 1). *What the Private Sector Can Do for India's Economic Growth*. Retrieved April 5, 2023, from https://www.weforum.org/agenda/2019/10/private-sector-investment-in-india/

CHAPTER 2

The Exploitative Nature of the IT Spaces

Introduction: Numerous Marginalities, One Sector

The IT workforce in India is not a homogeneous entity, but rather a diverse one—something that it has come to inherit from the diversity that India possesses as a country itself. In inheriting India's diversity, the IT sector has also inherited the numerous levels of social exclusion and marginalisation that the Indian society possesses. Among the different kinds of marginalised identities that characterise contemporary India, three have assumed prominence in recent times—Muslims exploited and excluded on the basis of their religious identity; Dalits exploited because of their caste identity; and women, who despite the large strides of feminist political philosophy and activism continue to be oppressed and exploited because of their gender identity. Muslims, Dalits, and women form an important part of the workforce in India's IT sector—either as the formal IT sector workforce or as invisible workers. Their social marginalisation often become the major fulcrum around which they form their social identity that plays a role in the formation of their class, caste, gender, and religious consciousness. The development of the software industry in India has been the subject of numerous studies over the last couple of decades (Srinivas, 1998; D'Costa & Sridharan, 2004). With an ever-increasing and differentiated population, the cities which harbour these industries have

© The Author(s), under exclusive license to Springer Nature Switzerland AG 2024
S. Deb Roy, *The Rise of the Information Technology Society in India*, Dynamics of Virtual Work,
https://doi.org/10.1007/978-3-031-58128-1_2

21

been bringing forward societal alterations both at macro and micro levels. These alterations are again, intimately related to the production of commodities and information, which today is not only about simple production, but rather, entails within itself, aspects of consumption which are equally important for the sustenance of the overall system. Contemporary society is about the management of the entire process in which capital is reproduced (Tronti, 1973). This in turn creates a condition where the organic and dynamic relationship between living and dead labour exists in a form widely different from the industrial age (Tronti, 1962).

Most historical accounts of the growth and development of the IT sector in India have ignored the internal contradictions that characterise the lives of the working class in the IT sector. They have portrayed the IT sector workers as a homogenous workforce one who are radically different than other sections of the working class in the country. One of the major markers of distinctions that the IT sector 'boasts' of is the kind of meritocracy that has been at the centre of gate-keeping processes in the sector. In the absence of any affirmative policy specifically for oppressed communities, the vast gap that exists between the human capital and employment within marginalised communities with regard to access to capital assets or income generating opportunities continues to increase (Thorat, 2004). Most accounts often portray the IT workforce as a homogeneous workforce, one which is predominantly male, harbour a middle-class upbringing, caste-conscious, and Hindu. However, the Indian IT industry is located in a country where there is a widescale diversity in terms of class, caste, race, ethnicity, and gender. The Indian society consists of around six major organised religions, innumerable castes (and sub-castes), a diverse array of languages and dialects, along with a huge variation in terms of geographical landscapes and cultural forms. Among all the different categories of individuals, certain categories stand out to be the most exploited of them all: Muslims, Dalits, and women. The treatment extended towards Muslims, Dalits, and women in their workplaces has an effect on their social consciousness. The social consciousness that the workers from these categories possess is drastically affected by how they get treated in their workplaces. The IT sector in India is often accorded to be a hyper-meritocratic sector where factors such as caste, class, and gender become dormant and non-effective components of the social reality. Such perceptions are theoretical ones fuelled by a belief in an ideal meritocratic society where structural inequalities have become redundant and exist only in the domain of theory.

2 THE EXPLOITATIVE NATURE OF THE IT SPACES

In the real world, however, exploitation is not a theoretical concept, but rather is a social reality that is faced by individuals on an everyday basis. The everyday life of workers from marginalised socio-economic and cultural backgrounds is a critical part of the lifestyle that cities such as Bengaluru, Hyderabad, and Gurugram promote. Taking their marginalisation into cognisance, this chapter problematises and speaks about three such sections of the society: Muslims, Dalits, and women in India's IT sector. The first section speaks about the Muslim workers and the ways in which their exploitation takes place in a multifaceted way in contemporary IT spaces, while the second section talks about Dalits in IT workplaces and IT hubs in the country. The third section takes cue from the arguments presented in the two sections and moves towards analysing the conditions faced by women in the IT sector.

Liberal Islamophobia in Action

Workers coming from marginalised communities and oppressed sections of the populace form an important part of the working populace in most Indian cities. Because of the social composition in place, the workers in the IT sector as well, like their counterparts in other sectors of the Indian economy, get affected by the broader contours of exploitation that function in the society. Marginality is a multifaceted reality of the Indian society, one which creates the social conditions for various ways of exploitation to exist in the society. Exploitation in the case of the IT workers who come from marginalised sections of the populace have to be analysed through two interrelated frameworks: their direct exploitation as workers one which places them at an equal pedestal with other workers, and their social exploitation as citizens and human beings that makes them subservient to other workers.

A significant section of the marginalised workforce of the IT sector are migrants to cities that harbour the major IT hubs. Different cities harbour different kinds of social spaces and compositions. Because of widescale migration, the diversity in terms of the population has been on a steep increase since the past few decades. In Bengaluru alone, around 50 per cent of the city's entire population of around 4.5 Million was composed of migrants in 2019, that is, during the pre-Covid era (Times of India, 2019). In 2023, around 42 per cent of the city's population originated from outside the city (Kumar et al., 2023). Gurugram, on the other hand, has witnessed a rise of around 29 per cent in its migrant population between 2001 and 2011 (Das

Gupta, 2017). However, even though the percentages might seem tremendously high, there are wider class differences that exist within these percentages. Gurugram has around 800,000 migrant unskilled workers, while Bengaluru's total migrant populace is composed of around 50 per cent mainly unskilled construction workers (Viswanath, 2023; Rao, 2020).

Migrant workers form a significant corpus of the middle-class Muslims that these cities take pride in. Migrant Muslim workers might not face direct exploitation in their workplaces or in the urban centres, but they continue to face exploitation of a multifaceted nature that focuses on the social nature of their existence. Their economic selves remain relatively protected by the financial benefits that the IT sector provides, but their social ontologies remain exploited as human beings and as citizens. They get affected by the broader social processes that continue to affect their working selves. Such issues range from them remaining worried about the incidents that take place in the society at large, to those that 'might' have been occurring near their homes. The effects of such fears go beyond the mere workplace and influence their social well-being. The exploitation of such individuals takes place through a multifaceted framework that makes economic well-being subservient to social well-being.[1] They continue to live as subservient human beings because they remain psychologically worried about their native places—which often remain entrenched with Islamophobic violence that has been rendered mainstream by the contemporary society. Muslims in India have become to feel insecure both socially and personally because of the increased attacks on their lives and lifestyles (Ellis-Petersen & Hasan, 2023).

Instances of structural and material violence against Muslims have been on the rise across the nation (Citizens against Hate, 2021; Jacob, 2022). Muslims also are more likely to be convicted and comprise the largest proportion of the prison populace of the country (Tyagi, 2023). The crimes and structural violence that the Muslims of India have found themselves engulfed in has made it extremely difficult for them to lead a 'mainstream' life in contemporary India—even if they are employed in well-paying and dignified jobs. The situation has been further worsened by the constant attack on their religious beliefs and styles of life that has been a regular feature in the working principles effected by the contemporary government in the country (Deb Roy, 2022). The attacks on their ways of life have not left the Muslim IT workers untouched as well with

---

[1] Chapter 5 engages with the idea of well-being and its limitations among India's IT sector workers.

religious riots becoming a common issue in cities such as Gurgaon and Bangalore (Kumar, 2023; Srivastava, 2023). While it is true that such incidents usually do not materially affect the middle-class Muslims, these incidents definitely have a psychological effect on them. In situations such as those, the idea of them coming from the middle class assumes a complicated position in comparison to their religious identity. Such incidents of majoritarian violence on Muslims have influenced the kind of urban experience that the IT workers from minority communities have been facing in contemporary India. Two Muslim IT workers from Bengaluru narrate:

> Muslim workers in the IT sector in cities like Bangalore and Gurgaon are very scared of what might happen to them. For starters, many of them today fear that they might be lynched. It is a difficult time for us. The problem with most of us is that we cannot question the way in which the society and politics is run in the country. (Muslim IT Worker, Bengaluru)

> It is very difficult to work in the sector today. With what is going on in the country, there is a general state of fear in the society, and that is true for the IT workers as well. On the face of it, everything is so far so good, but if you just scratch the surface, you will see the insecurity and prejudices that still reign in the society. (Muslim IT Worker, Bengaluru)

The fears of the Muslim employees referred to in the statements reproduced above are not unique to these particular individual employees, but are rather a social phenomenon now, one which finds cognisance with many Muslim IT workers. As many employees revealed, Muslim workers today have been increasingly preferring to work from home (WFH) because they find their workplace environment to be unsuitable to their social, cultural, professional, and human development. Such issues are usually evaded to in mainstream reports and documents regarding the IT sector in the country because the desired ideological construction of the IT workforce in the country is one that disregards any internal contradictions between them (Shakthi, 2023). While the conditions of Muslim workers in most other sectors remain dismal, the fact that even in a sector such as IT that was formed in India with the promise of providing not just economic benefits but also prospects of vertical social mobility to the workers speaks volumes about the relative stagnancy that certain pre-capitalist forms of exploitation continue to enjoy in a fast-changing world.

In recent times, India has witnessed the rise of majoritarian Hindu nationalist form of governance fuelled by the inefficiency of the liberal discourse in the Indian society (Bhargava, 2002). It also received impetus from the fact that the discourse that existed in India following independence in 1947 was one dominated by industrial growth, rather than a growth of employment opportunities (Prasad, 1994)—which has played a key role in the proliferation of marginality in the post-colonial Indian society. Amidst such a scenario, the landowning and middle classes had come to dominate the bureaucracy and the state, resulting in the formation of 'feudo-capitalism', an Indic form of the Asiatic mode of production, denoted by a situation where groups of individuals from certain privileged backgrounds have come to dominate the annals of state bureaucracy akin to a caste group, creating the avenues for the domination of the subaltern and marginalised classes creating and sustaining the characteristic features of State landlordism and State Monopoly Capitalism in India (Jal, 2018, p. 16). As time progressed, this same class of people and communities found themselves in control of the bourgeoning and deregulated private sector as well that came into being after the 1991 neoliberal reforms.

The development of the Indian state has been a process that intersected the rationalisation of both tendencies of overlordship based on attributes such as Caste, as well as the ideological and material establishment of the State as a sovereign body constantly (re)creating the subaltern classes as both surplus labour and surplus population (Jal, 2018). This constant creation and recreation are contingent upon the relationships those are shared between pre-capitalist social norms and mainstream capitalism in societies such as India (Krader, 1974; Jal, 2018), that remain entrapped within a constant struggle between oriental traditions and western modernity (Marx, 1974; Anderson, 2016). Every society, at the level of totality, has some peculiar characteristics, which impacts the relationship shared between the universal and the particular contradictions in the society.[2] The socio-political and cultural situation in any country has an indelible impact on the way in which the social consciousness is shaped in the society, acting both at the level of the totality and at the level of the individual.

Contemporary India, a result of such processes, is a culmination of the traditional value structures and the post-independent capitalist developmental processes which have been followed up by the structural adjustments that had been initiated in the country since 1991. Despite the neoliberal reforms, the conditions faced by the marginalised populace

---

[2] Examples here can be cited of the social hierarchy among Muslims, which often gets translated into a structure akin to the caste system among the Hindus despite the idea of caste not being a part of mainstream practices of Islam (P.C., 2017).

have not increased significantly. In the public sector, Muslims constitute less than 7 per cent of the workforce (Jaffrelot & Saini, 2023). The number of Muslims in the private sector remains abysmally low in comparison with their percentages in the total population of the country. As Ghazala Wahab writes:

> [E]ven in the private sector, among middle level to senior employees (from senior executives to director), only 2.67 per cent are Muslims. According to the [Economic Times][3] Intelligence Group Analysis of 2015, of 2,324 senior executives in BSE-500 listed companies, only 62 were Muslims. Even more worrying was the finding that in places where Muslims were employed in very senior positions, their remuneration was comparatively lower than that of their peers. (Wahab, 2021, p. 389)

This is in synchronisation with the broader labour process in the country where employment of Muslims has decreased significantly since 1947, and they constitute the worst paid and most vulnerably employed religious community in the country (Sanghi & Srija, 2014). They constitute the poorest of all the religious communities in the country with significantly lower assets and consumption levels than even most of the lower-caste Hindus (Jha & Kishore, 2023). Because of their lower asset possession, the propensity of Muslims becoming poorer increases manifold during times of financial crises. The spaces that the IT workers inhabit are also not distinct from the broader socio-cultural and economic tendencies in the country. They get affected by the structural and ideological changes taking place in the broader society and constantly get modified by the various ways in which the ruling class and political formations determine the ideological fabric of the country. The multinational companies' functioning cannot escape the general state of affairs in the country. As a senior trade unionist working with an IT union and who is also a member of the Communist Party of India (Marxist) stated:

> How can you think that the tech park is separate from the society? That is a laughable claim, but unfortunately most of the IT workers believe that. They think that they are the middle class, so the growth of the far-right, the constantly growing radicalisation does not affect that. That is not true at all. The government gives constant freedom and licenses to the corporates, and the corporates fund the government. And, the IT workers are trapped right in the middle of the process.

[3] More details available at Karunakaran (2015).

The idea of being from the middle class plays a critical role in the lives of these IT workers from Muslim communities. The construction of the middle-class Muslims has been based on their acceptance of modern education and technological advancement that has increased their access to routes of vertical social mobility (Wahab, 2021). However, that being said, the historical marginalisation accorded to the Muslims continues to play a major role in the lives of Muslims even in contemporary India. The Sachar Committee Report (2007) that brought forward the plight of the Muslim citizens of India stated that out of all the different communities living in India, Muslims in India constitute not only the most financially vulnerable section of the population, but are also forced to live through patterns of social exclusion. The IT sector workers also are no different from the same. Muslim workers in these spaces continue to face similar kinds of exploitation and modes of exclusion like their counterparts in the informal and unorganised sectors. While in terms of their class position, these workers might locate themselves at an advantageous position than other Muslim individuals, but the constantly changing dynamics between their religious affiliations and their class positions creates a confusing social existence for them, as two Muslim workers revealed:

> It is very confusing for us. Sometimes, we are techies, sometimes we are Muslims, and sometimes, when some of our colleagues are drunk, we are Pakistanis. It's a problem, but then everybody has got to earn a living, right? That is the reason, I have stopped going to these office and house parties altogether. It has harmed my career growth, but I cannot take that risk anymore. I might laugh it off at that point, but the insecurity lingers on. (Muslim IT Worker, Gurgaon)

> The problem is not so much with the middle management people and those from the higher positions. It is usually a problem for the new entrants. They are the ones who get harassed more often than not. Some people get constantly reminded that they are Muslims. It is true that they might get the most prestigious award at their office, but it is also true that they are also the ones who get most exploited because of their religious identity. (Muslim IT Worker, Bengaluru)

The internal contradictions that dominate the lives of the IT workers contradict their imagery as a homogenous workforce that generates a public perception of the IT workers being a section of the workforce where differences due to religion, caste, gender, and race get relegated by their appreciation for and expertise in science and technology. However, science and technology have a distinctly political and socio-economic character, one which determines the effects that it has on the vulnerable populace within any social context (Mackenzie & Wajcman, 1999; Deb Roy, 2022). The introduction of new technology affects the various methods through which individuals interpret their possibilities of upwards or downwards by changing the overall income distribution and the cost of labour in a society, especially in countries of the Global South (Harriss-White, 2011).

The growth of technological interventions in the workplaces, most of which are employed to increase the productivity of the workers through either co-operation or coercion under contemporary capitalism, cannot be negated, especially after the technological dependence rendered mainstream by the Covid-19 pandemic (Hodder, 2020; Rasool et al., 2022). The introduction of technology often does not affect the wages of the workers lower down the hierarchy in a positive manner (Lee & Clarke, 2019). Technology alters the production mechanisms and creates the conditions under which new and low-skilled workers suffer considerably (Lee & Clarke, 2019). The rise of technology in the labour process has contributed tremendously to the growth of the middle class and the white collar workers. Technology affects different workers depending on the hierarchical structure to which they belong, creating segregations within the erstwhile working class in advanced industrial societies (Dunayevskaya, 1958). Technological development in India received praise because of its perceived role in the creation of a classical class-based segregation in the Indian society relegating forms of pre-capitalist modes of exclusion. But as Desai (1984) had argued, the development of capitalism in India follows a path which appropriates pre-capitalist modes of exclusion. For people belonging to the marginalised sections in India, technological development and their embracement of the same has been unable to counter the social perceptions that exist regarding them. In doing so, the social structure in place has ensured that while technology and its associated impacts on the labour process have not been critiqued and have rather been embraced, it has continued to fulfil the classical trajectory of technological development albeit in a modified manner in India: sustaining a cultural underdevelopment of the marginalised sections (Stewart, 1977), and furthering segregations within the relatively affluent middle-class workforce (Dunayevskaya, 1958; Cleaver, 1979).

The appreciation and expertise with regard to technology and scientific development that Muslim tech-workers possess fail to counter the social perception that is generated by the popular media that paints Muslim individuals as being anomalies in India. The kind of assault that Islamophobia has inflicted upon the Muslim citizen has not even spared the affluent Muslims, leave alone the ones who lie at the bottom of the social hierarchy. Muslims in India today have come to be challenged to such an extent by the majoritarian violence that the question of them being citizens has come under contestation, and 'citizenship, as a concept and as it is experienced on the ground by millions of vulnerable people, has come under challenge—which is to say, pressure, intimidation, threat, and assault—in the time of Hindutva' (Ram, 2021, p. 37). The attack on Muslims in India has had an indelible effect on Muslim IT workers because it has changed the nature and their perception of the social reality that exists around them. The urban space that IT workers live through in their everyday lives is constructed out of various practices pertaining to profit accumulation that are rendered mainstream by capitalist structures in place. The exploitation that is inflicted upon these workers constructs their consciousness as workers and has an effect on their consciousness as citizens as well. Their continued exposure to modes of structural and material exploitation based on their religion and caste constructs these workers as subservient human beings who enable the construction of a more productive and vulnerable citizenry for capitalism to exploit and manipulate.

The Social Stagnancy of Dalit Techies

Muslims constitute around 15 per cent of the population in India.[4] However, while Muslims constitute the largest percentage of minorities in the country, the Indian society does not function strictly in terms of religious segregation. The more prevalent method of segmentation that one finds in India is the caste structure. While caste as a system of stratification is intrinsic to the Hindus, the ideological effect of the caste structure in India is such that even various forms of Abrahamic religious structures—which traditionally did not harbour the idea of internal segregation among themselves—developed their own notions of caste-based segregation when they were propagated in India (Sebastian, 2016). The prevalence of

[4] The data is from 2011—the last census done by the Government of India. Further details are available at the Census website: https://www.census2011.co.in/religion.php [Accessed 04.12.2023]; and through Pew Research Center Data at: https://www.pewresearch.org/religion/2021/09/21/population-growth-and-religious-composition/ [Accessed 04.12.2023].

caste-based segregation thus can be taken to be one of the most basic aspects of the Indian society, which occupies an important part in different sectors of work and employment in the country. Bhimrao Ambedkar had realised the importance of the role of caste in the Indian society, and had stated:

> The caste problem is a vast one [...] It is a local problem, but one capable of much wider mischief, for 'as long as caste in India does exist, Hindus will hardly intermarry or have any social intercourse with outsiders; and if Hindus migrate to other regions on earth, Indian caste [will] become a world problem'. (Ambedkar, 1916/1973, p. 2)

Technology firms, the tech parks, workplaces, and their associated urban spaces are parts of this broader socio-political and cultural structure in place. And like elsewhere, Dalits continue to be exploited in the IT sector as well. In the previous section, the book analysed the experiences of the Muslim workers that highlighted their plight and the constant exclusion that they face both within their workplaces and within the society in general as well as the relationship between these two sites of exploitation. It highlighted that Muslims in the IT sector continue to be exploited because of their religious identity in a myriad of different ways, many of which contribute to their direct dehumanisation, while some contribute to a more nuanced process of dehumanisation *but dehumanisation, nevertheless.*

The conditions of life are not that different for the Dalit workers as well. Dalit workers in the IT sector often come to work in the IT sector with the hope that they would be able to escape the conditions of exploitation that is meted out to them in their respective native places. Their engagement with the IT sector comes through the supposedly liberatory nature of the sector that can potentially counter the effects of the social evils that the traditional caste-structure-based functioning of the Indian society presents to them. Dalit individuals come into the IT sector with the hope that being a part of an upwardly mobile capitalist workforce would allow them to escape the feudal modes of exploitation prevalent in their native communities or places. Their expectations from the sector remain focused on its ability to uplift them financially and provide them with a dignified lifestyle. The importance of financial stability in the lives of Dalit workers in the IT sector is akin to middle-class Dalit individuals in the public sector.

It is very important to have financial stability in today's day and age. We did not grow up in the traditional sense of the term being engaged in our ancestral occupations. I am a *chamar* by caste but my father worked as a clerk in an office in a small town in Uttar Pradesh. Even though he did not do any of the ancestral tasks, we still received casteist slurs from the society. From there, I went to an engineering college, got a degree, and finally have travelled to Hyderabad to make a life of my own. So, yes, I will do anything to have a financially secure future. It took me a lot of hard work to get here, and the job pays me well. I have no issues. (Dalit IT Worker, Hyderabad)

However, the process through which one can get engaged with the IT sector is a path ridden with multiple and multifaceted exploitative contours. Dalit workers come into the IT sector after suffering through years of exclusion and exploitation in higher education—a crucial part of their transformation as subservient workers. Within higher education, Dalits have remained one of the worst sufferers of the structural violence that the Indian society renders mainstream in the society. Speaking about the exploitation of Dalits in education in a recent work, Bharat Rathod states:

The change has shaken the historical hegemony of the privileged castes in Indian higher education, and they feel a decline in their cultural capital hegemony and the loss of their control over higher education. Therefore, caste hierarchies, feudal mindsets, and exclusionary cultural representations are infused into institutional life. Further, due to the conglomeration of social identities of students, Indian universities are facing diversity, social justice, and discrimination issues. Moreover, caste-based discrimination in higher education [...] has been neglected for decades and is now pervasive and institutionalized across institutions in India. (Rathod, 2023, p. 2)

The exploitation that is meted out to Dalit individuals as students continues to influence them as workers. As students, Dalits face numerous hurdles, many of which remain entrenched with pre-capitalist modes of exploitation and continue to haunt them throughout the trajectory of their working lives. Because for most IT professionals, their time as students creates the basis of their working selves, any exploitation meted out to them as students has a lasting impact on them. Their experience during their student lives continue to affect them as workers influencing the choices that they make in their lives as working individuals and the kind of life that they lead as citizens and human beings. On the issue, two Dalit IT workers spoke at length about their experiences in their respective engineering colleges and how that experience continues to shape their lives, even after they have left those spaces a long time ago:

> Engineering colleges are the most insensitive spaces you can find in the country. Yes, reservation policies and directives are followed there, but do they make effective and democratic citizens? Absolutely Not. There is a general lack of political consciousness in those colleges that is bolstered by the restrictions put on political and social activism on the campuses. (Dalit IT Worker, Bengaluru)

> The problem is with the way in which the government speaks of reservations. Now, we all know that the seats in any government college is limited and only limited students can be accommodated there, but the only people who get blamed for a general unreserved person not getting into a college are the backward castes and other reserved categories. These people then keep on humiliating us saying that we are reserved category people and do not deserve to be here. (Dalit IT Worker, Hyderabad)

The above statements reveal that the inhumane exploitation and harassment that the students faced during his student days had a drastic impact on the experiences that he had in the workplace. Dalit workers and their issues in the IT sector get relegated or fail to get resolved adequately even if they are brought to the attention of the higher authorities, because of the kind of human resource management practices that the IT sector in India possesses. This can again be better explained if one takes the example of the management of the IT sector during Covid-19. While many have prided themselves in the fact that the Indian software industry did not get *stopped in its tracks* by Covid-19, it cannot be denied that even with Working from Home, there are forms of social exclusion and exploitation that have continued unabated. Two women IT workers' statements can be referred to in this context:

> The organisation does not understand that I might have my own set of problems, which might be different than others. For example, a few months ago, they said that I should start working Sundays and take two days off during the weekdays. Now ideally, some people would not have issues with that. But I have a child who has school during weekdays and Sundays are the only days that I can spend some time with him. Plus, on Sundays there are additional responsibilities as well, so it is difficult for me. (Woman IT Worker, Bengaluru)

The organisation does not do much for my personal growth. Although I know that some of my colleagues have been able to learn new skills and manage their work-life balance very well, it has been difficult for me, very difficult actually because I have the additional responsibility of domestic work. I stay with my in-laws, so that is also a problem in my context. Earlier, it took me a few minutes to get assistance for a problem. Today, it takes me a few hours. It not only hampers my own productivity but also impacts the overall performance of my team. The organisation has to look into these aspects while talking about well-being, which it does not. For men, it is easier because they do not have an additional pressure on. (Woman IT Worker, Kolkata)

The basic ideas presented in the statements above is the kind of differences that one can see with regard to the behaviour that the human resource team and the company exhibits towards their specific problems, which might often be about the issues that they face as human beings and citizens and not as workers per se. One potential solution to the issues faced by Dalits and Muslims is to employ more individuals coming from these communities in positions of power in the IT firms. However, such solutions do not question the implications of power ideologically, but rather prepare the ground for a more class-based exploitation of the workers coming from marginalised backgrounds. Alterations that work on the basis of replacing an individual at a position of power by another individual do not contradict the fundamental issues that arise from that position of power (Fraser et al., 2019). Exploitation of the workers from marginalised communities is a ramification of the social processes of exploitation that go far beyond the issues presented by mere workplace management. They affect the workers not only as workers but also as citizens and above all, as human beings. The exploitation meted out to marginalised workers in the IT sector restricts their social capacity as effective citizens curtailing their freedom to become participatory citizens of the society—one of the major hallmarks of the Nehruvian vision of a democratic India that was institutionalised in 1947 (Ram, 2014).

The problems caused by such issues within the IT sector—a sector that employs a 100 per cent educated and graduate workforce because of the kind of work that it has to perform—reflect the state of affairs in India, where literacy rate stands at 78 per cent overall, with women literacy rate being about 65 per cent. The literacy rates for Dalits and Muslims are 66 per cent and 57 per cent, respectively, with Dalit women and Muslim women literacy rates being 56 per cent and 52 per cent, respectively

(Raghavendra, 2020; Siddiqui & Khan, 2022). It is true that with the coming of neoliberalism, certain sections of the marginalised communities have come to enjoy various modes of vertical mobility (Sheth, 1999)— which is reflected by the growth of the Muslim and Dalit middle class as have been depicted by Wahab (2021) and Teltumbde (2018). But while neoliberal capitalism does benefit certain individuals in obtaining social mobility, even if they are from oppressed communities (Teltumbde, 2018; Masoodi, 2019), the kind of social mobility that it promotes creates the conditions for a subsequent privileging of certain kinds of knowledge determined by the kind of social practices in place. Science and technology greatly affect the job structure of any economy. Technological develop-ment 'tends to eliminate the individual "jobs" [and] ... the need for skill in the hands and strength in the muscles and replace them by a require-ment for knowledge and control' (Macbeath, 1979, p. 114). And both knowledge and control socially are often placed disproportionately at the hands of the already privileged which increases the propensity of further exclusion and marginalisation of the already marginalised. One can take the example of women here to further substantiate this point. The situa-tion of women globally in professional degrees, such as medical, engineer-ing, and law, is worse with women lagging far behind than their male counterparts with a higher drop-out ratio for women as well (Salve, 2016a, 2016b). Similar conditions exist for Dalits and Muslims as well. For exam-ple, out of all the Muslim women, only around 2 per cent reach pre-university levels and 0.14 per cent receive some form of technical education (Siddiqui & Khan, 2022). Dalits also exhibit excessively high drop-out ratios among all the different communities in India with some estimates suggesting it to be more than 20 per cent (Nagarajan, 2022; Rathod, 2023).

Women, Muslims, and Dalits thus naturally find it difficult to find jobs in the sector, not only because of the higher rates of exploitation meted out to them as students (Silbey, 2016; Rathod, 2023) but also because of how various tech firms have now begun to specifically instruct their human resource personnel to refrain hiring people from these social groups because of the increased costs and regulations associated with devising mechanisms surrounding caste and gender discrimination in the work-places. One IT worker working as a recruiter states:

> These days, certain companies are constantly telling their recruitment teams to not employ women, Muslims, and Dalits. They say that employing these people increases the responsibilities and costs associated with the day-to-day

36   S. DEB ROY

functioning of the company because of the increased risk of complaints, maintaining sexual harassment investigation committees, etc. So, there is a general propensity towards not employing many of them. (Male IT Worker, Pune)

Workers from marginalised communities often remain entrapped within job descriptions that do not satisfy their capabilities. Muslims, Dalits, and especially women face considerable hurdles in getting employed in job descriptions that suit their professional eligibility. There is a tendency of underemployment in the formal sectors for workers coming from marginalised communities. Marginalised individuals find it particularly difficult to get promoted and find representation in higher bodies. They suffer from the underemployment that neoliberalism produces at a mass scale in developing societies because the very nature of everyday life has changed with an increase in insecurity for women (Navarro, 1998; Filiz, 2020). Even when they do get employed, they are often underemployed despite being highly qualified, which then subsequently leads to underrepresentation in higher bodies and committees (Livingstone, 2004).

PATRIARCHY AND THE IT WORKERS

Muslims and Dalits, as the chapter exhibits, have to live through various kinds of exploitative frameworks in their everyday lives as IT workers. However, while analysing the exploitation of Dalits and Muslims, it cannot be denied that one is still speaking from a largely male-worker perspective. Social categories have more often than not been formed on the basis of the effects that they have on the male workers. But social spaces—and more so, urban spaces—are a creation of the unpaid gendered labour of millions of women. The IT landscape is no different. The ways in which the male IT workers lead their private and professional lives is drastically influenced by how their female counterparts are located in the society. This has become particularly prominent with the coming of the Covid-19 pandemic when many male IT workers in India had to face the burden of increased domestic work and household labour entrusted upon them. At the same time, women face risks of sexual harassment in their workplaces, which constitutes a deplorable state of existence for them within the workplace, which in turn is also complemented by the socio-cultural marginality that they face in the society and within their families in general.

The way in which the urban space in India has been structured, especially in the major IT Hubs in the country, is such that the gendered nature of urban society becomes explicit in the manner in which the individual lives of the IT workers are structured in India. The lived experience of Muslim and Dalit IT workers exhibit that the gentrified urban spaces have failed to consider the specific nature of the exploitation that is meted out to them. Semi-feudal and other forms of pre-capitalist modes of exploitation continue to have an effect on the workers coming from marginalised backgrounds, especially the women therein. The IT sector works on the principle of a normalised Indian citizen assuming that *all of its employees* conform to the dominant narrative of *the ideal working human being* in India—a cisgender-heterosexual Hindu male. Because Muslims, Dalits, and women do not conform to this standard imagery, their social existence as IT workers itself is often put under question through such processes of patriarchal, majoritarian, and misogynist normalisation. The exploitation of the women workers however occurs within a complex circuit of exploitation and repression that encompasses various aspects of their everyday lives. Urban spaces, more often than not, have been developed in a manner that are unsuitable to fulfil the specific requirements of women. Women in urban spaces often have to make changes to their everyday social and individual practices to make themselves at home in the city that includes making changes to their routine activities and their behavioural patterns (Massey, 1994; Kern, 2020). Such changes mostly are brought forward with the intention of protecting them from issues such as sexual harassment and molestation, many of which are common in the lives of the women IT workers. The evolution and the subsequent normalisation of such norms have a drastic effect on the lives of women workers.

While both Muslims and Dalit men face similar issues, their methods of engagement with the issues presented to them are different than how women do it, even if they are Muslims or Dalits themselves. Dalit and Muslim men face greater social exclusion in the society, but even then, the conditions of life that they face continues to get determined by the privilege that they can exert as being men. One can here take the example of shifts, especially the graveyard shifts. For the men, even if they are marginalised as citizens in the society, they do not face equal risks in terms of sexual harassment or molestation that makes even marginalised men more empowered than women. The risks that women face also get increased because of the ways in which the urban space is structured that makes it difficult for women to possess security and express their own individuality (Massey, 1994; Kern, 2020), both economically and socially. The everyday life that women live through is very different than men. The social practices that women come to inhabit make them distinct from other sections of the population. It is the social practices that deter individuals from having an alternative conceptualisation of the urban space that they occupy (Lefebvre, 1991). Women workers of the IT sector suffer from the disproportionate reproductive work bestowed upon them that affects the social practices that they come to embody within themselves. Social practices, though primarily autonomous in their unalienated forms, get routinised under capitalism. The domination that capitalism brings forward in the society under neoliberal globalisation creates forms of routinisation in the social and psychological lives of the workers, especially if they come from marginalised social backgrounds. Modes of routinisation enable these workers to create a certain state of ontological security within their lives, which helps them shroud the fact that they lead a life that is detrimental to their existence as individual human beings but rather conforms to the lives that their partners or children lead. This has a direct impact on the kind of experiences that women have, because the social space and the work environments that they find themselves does not allow them to voice their concerns openly, particularly due to the lower representation of women in effective positions of power. One woman worker from Chennai recounted:

> Having a woman as a HR helps a lot in our case. I can speak to them regarding issues that concern strictly woman employees. For example, menstrual leaves, the issues with maternity leaves, women's health, or the problems that I face when I am on my periods, all these issues are difficult to be discussed with a male HR. Even if I earn equal to my husband, most of my life revolves around home. There are issues at home which affect my work life, these are things that only a female boss or a female HR will understand. (Woman IT Worker, Chennai)

For most women who live as per the schedules and lives of other members of their families, the burden of reproductive work increases manifold and vice versa. Motherhood plays an important role in this context because it often becomes the determining factor behind the kind of social practices that a woman worker can embody within herself. When children come into the families of IT workers, their lives change drastically. Changes are not only restricted within the structure of the family, but also within the lives of the individuals therein affecting their professional and personal lives. For people who do the entirety of the requisite reproductive labour, it becomes increasingly difficult to maintain a daily life rigidly based on their professional schedule, more so in the case of women. The exploitation that is meted out to women is multifaceted in nature, one that encompasses diverse aspects of a woman's social status in the society as a worker, as a citizen and as a human being. Many of these aspects do not get adequate representation within the sector and get bolstered by the fact that women and other marginalised workers have fewer people to speak to regarding the problems as the human resource personnel usually employed are upper caste men.

Marriage in the context of India has widespread effects, especially for the women. Marriage often results in women having to move away from their native places, getting detached from their known environment. Detached from their native places and entrapped within reproductive chores, most women often have no option but to frame structures and networks of solidarity with those with whom they share a space. Even those employed in the IT sector, who enjoy a certain advantage with regard to their class positions, cannot escape the constant exploitation meted out to them as women in the form of conservative discourses constructed out of social dogmas regarding marriage, childbearing, unequal property relationships, and so forth (Bumiller, 1991; Ahmad, 1999). For the women workers of the private sector, exploitation is not only economic in nature but is rather highly social in form and content. The intersectional nature of their exploitation makes them subservient to the internal disciplining processes of their respective companies. The private sector substitutes public accountability with its own internal mechanism by forcibly making the workers accountable to their higher officials such as HR managers and employment co-ordinators. Performance reviews in the private sector are usually associated with increasing domestic tensions, accelerating stress and anxiety among the women workers. Two narratives from IT workers can be referred to here to substantiate this point. The first narrative is from an IT worker in Pune and the second from her counterpart in Kolkata. Both these workers work in junior level positions in their respective companies. The only factor that segregates them is the status of their husbands, the effects of which can be analysed from these narratives:

40   S. DEB ROY

During appraisals, there is a lot of pressure on us. Our family lives get very complicated during that time. If husband is in same sector it does become a bit easier but otherwise it is very difficult. My husband is a PSE worker, he does not understand what I am going through. If I must match his salary, I need regular appraisals. That is the only way that works. That is the only way in which I can justify my odd working hours to somebody who goes at 9 and comes back at 5 on point every day. (IT Worker, Pune, August 2022)

Appraisal Time is a difficult period. Both me and my husband work in IT so it kind of rubs off on both of us. At that time, there are so many issues. Both of us turn cranky. It is usually 15 days of total chaos, and after that if one of us do not get the increment that we had hoped for then there are different issues altogether, where I have to take the lead often. (IT Worker, Kolkata, December 2022)

These narratives bring forward the difficult conditions that women face at home during the time of the year when their appraisals are due. There are different factors that contribute to the contesting times that the struggle for appraisals produce for women workers. The contradictions that exist between the formal sector women workers are based on both class and gender. The class confusion that becomes characteristic in the ways in which the middle-class constructs differences between their individual and their social positioning. While on an individual level, the workers remain entrenched into the ideology of consumerism that provides them with a certain level of social empowerment; their social positioning continues to remain subverted by men. This reflects the way in which the Indian society has traditionally been constructed in a way where the burden of personal responsibility has befallen upon the women more harshly than it has on the men. This point has been noted by women from both the public and private sectors. Two workers argue:

When me and my husband come back from our offices, it is usually I who has to take the initiative to finish up the work needed at home. Call his parents, call my parents and all that. I understand that it is not his fault, it is just how the society is. Women are supposed to do those kinds of work. It is not the fault of men, but of the system. (Woman IT Worker, Kolkata)

Some of the people think that we are living a very good life. You see all the glamour and lifestyle which comes with living in a city like Bengaluru, but it is also imperative that you also see the struggle that we must do. We do not get anything readymade here. With the increasing pressures of the city life, it is a guarantee that it will impact your personal life, more so as a woman because you need to manage the family. (Woman IT Worker, Bengaluru)

These narratives highlight the exploitation at the domestic level that women face regardless of their employment conditions and social status. The private and intimate lives that women live through on an everyday basis become the foundation upon which they construct their working lives. For many women, even the maintenance of their work schedules proves to be extremely difficult. The control which the system exerts on the partners of these women has a direct implication on the lives of these women. Working mothers suffer more because childcare remains one of the critical responsibilities that is often accorded to them, especially when they have non-compliant and patriarchal partners. The routinisation of everyday lives for these women act as a tool to render invisible the disproportionately balanced relationship between reproductive labour and professional responsibilities. A working woman managing both the household and the official duties constitutes one of the central subjects of oppression in the contemporary urban society, which makes them distinct from other categories of marginalised populace. Dalit and Muslim women continue to be harmed by the various trajectories of exploitation and oppression that is institutionalised upon them by the dominant social ideology in place. A combination of all these factors creates a situation where even efficient and well-performing workers from the marginalised communities face difficulties in getting promotions or regular pay hikes and continue to suffer from various forms of pay-gaps. Three women workers from Bengaluru, Kolkata, and Noida spoke at length about the issues:

The chances of a woman getting promoted is lesser than others. The same goes for Muslims or Dalits. Promotions in the sector are often seen to be one of the major ways in which women can improve their social standing, but the chances are very low. Most of the women are put in customer centric kind of jobs because those are seen to be better suited to women. And those jobs often pay less. (Woman IT Worker, Bengaluru)

Women are often employed in job descriptions that are more customer oriented in nature. One of the major reasons is that engineering, or specifically speaking coding, is still considered a male job, so obviously women cannot do it. We are purposefully kept in jobs such as customer service, client management, etc., where pay and status within the company is low. (Woman IT Worker, Kolkata)

The problem is that most IT companies do not think that women can function equal to men. So, for example, whenever there is a function at the office they will put us into management. No man is made a chairman there, but a woman is. Likewise for application management or maintenance, since it requires a regular and sustained time where I have to sit in front of the computer, it is usually given to the men. Before Covid, the excuse was that women are often bad coders, now the excuse is that women cannot often give time to such things. But then why do you give more hikes to those who do that kind of work? (Woman IT Worker, Noida)

Being a Muslim or a Dalit, or a woman within the Indian society is a tougher job on most days. Muslims, perhaps face the worst impacts of chauvinism that is so rampant in the Indian society in the contemporary times. They are made to undergo a process of *othering* whereby their very existence in India has been rendered to conditions of exoticism and backwardness (Naqvi, 2016). For Dalits, life has become more difficult under the rule of the far-right. Brahmanism has become a dominant force; in fact it always has been, in the contemporary society under the BJP. The rise of the far-right in India is a direct result of the way in which the secular forces of the country have been unable to resolve the many issues that this country faces, with caste oppression being one of the most important ones. As Suraj Yengde assertively states: 'The Indian state-society is an entity of Brahmin supremacy. Every major enterprise in India functions under the strict dictums of Brahmins and other dominant castes' (Yengde, 2019, 'Being a Dalit'). The fault-lines which exist in the society have increased manifold and have explicitly been made visible by the different 'events' which have shaken the country in the past few years such as the continuous attack on the country's reservation system designed to uplift the marginalised communities, demonetisation, and the disastrous way in which the COVID-19 pandemic was handled in India.[5]

Being part of a paid employment relation is a critical part of any individual's life, one that often engulfs diverse aspects of an individual's social construction—physically and mentally. With the coming of the post-industrial society, the concept of work has undergone a radical transformation from the industrial era in the sense that one does not 'do work' anymore but rather 'has work' creating a situation where the social meanings of the terms, 'work' and 'job', have become interchangeable reducing

[5] Deb Roy, S. (2024). *Covid-19 and Social Change: Arguments from and for India.* Abingdon: Routledge (Forthcoming).

the concept of 'work' exclusively to waged labour, that is, labour which results in some form of financial gain for the worker (Gorz, 1982). Such conceptions of work are the primary force behind Dalits, Muslims, and women joining the IT sector of the country. However, it would not be justified to analyse all the marginalised sections of the populace as being equally affected by social processes of exclusion that operate within the domains of contemporary waged labour. Women—including the Hindu women—constitute the worst victims of such processes, mainly because of the unpaid and disproportionately managed reproductive labour processes in the society. Contemporary capitalism attempts to compensate such processes through the creation of atomised individuals providing the individuals with a false sense of empowerment and individuality by destroying the traditional networks of community and solidarity.

The management of the reproductive labour of women has implications for the broader industrial and social processes, as Chap. 3 will speak about in further details. The dynamics of reproductive labour and the intimate spaces of the IT workers determine and get determined by the internal dynamics of social space and practices. The reproductive labour that women perform is mainly composed of three parts: care work, household labour, and people-making labour. Be it within Hindu, Muslim, or Dalit families, women in families always share a disproportionate burden of the reproductive labour. The next chapter speaks specifically about the social reproduction labour that women perform and the dynamic relationship that it shares with their exploitation as IT workers. In speaking of women in general, it is also essential to take cognisance of how caste and religion intersect with the exploitation of women through the contemporary usage of spatiality and temporality.

The urban space, the social practices that they come to embody, and social reproduction labour share an intimate relationship with each other. The analysis of unwaged reproductive labour as unproductive work is not a recent process but has been the basis of the historical opposition towards the conceptualisation of household labour as actual work (Vogel, 2013), which is also related to the distinction between wage-labour and self-determined activity, the dialectical relationship between which forms the basis of the idea of 'productivity' itself under capitalism. And, productivity, as has already been mentioned, is one of the core philosophical vantage points of the Indian IT sector.

REFERENCES

Ahmad, I. (1999). Religion in Politics. In S. Tomar (Ed.), *Eqbal Ahmad Reader: Writings on India, Pakistan, and Kashmir.* Retrieved December 4, 2023, from https://archive.org/details/eqbal_ahmad_reader_2017

Ambedkar, B. R. (1916/1973). *Castes in India: Their Mechanism, Genesis and Development.* Awami Press.

Anderson, K. B. (2016). *Marx at the Margins: On Nationalism, Ethnicity and. Non-Western Societies.* University of Chicago Press.

Bhargava, R. (2002/2010). Liberal, Secular Democracy and Hindu Nationalism. In *The Promise of India's Secular Democracy.* Oxford University Press.

Bumiller, E. (1991). *May You Be the Mother of a Hundred Sons: A Journey Among the Women of India.* Penguin India.

Citizens against Hate. (2021). Submission to SR on Freedom of Religion or Belief on His Report on Anti-Muslim Hatred and Discrimination to the 46th Session of the Human Rights Council. Retrieved December 4, 2023, from https://www.ohchr.org/sites/default/files/Documents/Issues/Religion/Islamophobia-AntiMuslim/Civil%20Society%20or%20Individuals/CitizensAgainstHate.pdf

Cleaver, H. (1979/2014). *Reading Capital Politically.* Phoneme Books.

D'Costa, A. P., & Sridharan, E. (2004). *India in the Global Software Industry.* Palgrave Macmillan.

Das Gupta, M. (2017, February 6). Delhi, Gurgaon, Gautam Buddh Nagar Favourite with Migrants: Economic Survey. *Hindustan Times.* Retrieved December 4, 2023, from https://www.hindustantimes.com/india-news/delhi-gurgaon-gautam-buddh-nagar-favourite-with-migrants-economic-survey/story-d1i4C0zMJfA8HMjDfptyyK.html

Deb Roy, S. (2022). *Mass Struggles and Leninism.* Phoneme Books.

Desai, A. R. (1984). *India's Path of Development: A Marxist Approach.* Sangam Books.

Dunayevskaya, R. (1958). *Marxism and Freedom.* Humanities Press.

Ellis-Petersen, H., & Hasan, A. (2023, August 4). 'How Will Any Muslim Feel Safe?' Spate of Attacks Increases Tensions in India. *The Guardian.* Retrieved December 4, 2023, from https://www.theguardian.com/world/2023/aug/04/how-will-any-muslim-feel-safe-spate-of-attacks-increases-tensions-in-india

Filiz, A. (2020). Underemployment, Unemployment, Gender and Changing Conditions of (Non) Work Under Neoliberalism. *Journal of Economy Culture and Society, 61,* 341–353.

Fraser, N., Bhattacharya, T., & Arruzza, C. (2019). *Feminism for the 99%.* Verso.

Gorz, A. (1982). *Farewell to the Working Class.* Pluto Press.

Harriss-White, B. (2011). Revisiting "Technology and Underdevelopment": Climate Change, Politics and the "D" of Solar Energy Technology in Contemporary India. In V. Fitzgerald, J. Heyer, & R. Thorp (Eds.), *Overcoming the Persistence of Inequality and Poverty* (pp. 92–126). Palgrave Macmillan.

Hodder, A. (2020). New Technology, Work and Employment in the Era of COVID-19: Reflecting on Legacies of Research. *New Technology, Work and Employment, 35*(3), 262–275.

Jacob, N. (2022, June 21). Data Dive: Sixfold Rise in Cases Filed under Hate Speech-Related Law in 7 Years. Fact Finder. Retrieved December 4, 2023, from https://www.factchecker.in/data-dive/data-dive-sixfold-rise-in-cases-filed-under-hate-speech-related-law-in-7-years-822966#:~:text=Cases%20filed%20under%20this%20section,Crime%20Records%20Bureau%20(NCRB)

Jaffrelot, C., & Saini, M. (2023, January 20). A Workforce Less Diverse: Muslims in Public and Private Sector. *The Indian Express.* https://indianexpress.com/article/opinion/columns/a-workforce-less-diverse-muslims-in-public-and-private-sector-8094176/

Jal, M. (2018). *In the Name of Marx: Aakar Books.*

Jha, A., & Kishore, R. (2023, June 30). Muslims are the Poorest Religious Group in India. *Hindustan Times.* Retrieved December 4, 2023, from https://www.hindustantimes.com/india-news/muslims-in-india-the-poorest-religious-group-with-high-inequality-and-limited-opportunities-data-analysis-reveals-101688097160955.html

Karunakaran, N. (2015, September 7). Muslims Constitute 14% of India, But Just 3% of India Inc. *Economic Times.* Retrieved December 4, 2023, from https://economictimes.indiatimes.com/news/politics-and-nation/muslims-constitute-14-of-india-but-just-3-of-india-inc/articleshow/48849266.cms

Kern, L. (2020). *Feminist City.* Verso.

Krader, L. (1974). Introduction. In *The Ethnological Notebooks of Karl Marx.* Van Gorcum and Company.

Kumar, C. (2023, March 9). Communal Cases on the Rise in Karnataka, 122 Since 2019. *Times of India.* Retrieved December 4, 2023, from https://timesofindia.indiatimes.com/city/bengaluru/communal-cases-on-the-rise-in-karnataka-122-since-2019/articleshow/98503792.cms

Kumar, S., Malik, A., & Attri, V. (2023, May 10). Securing the Migrant Vote. *The Hindu.* Retrieved December 4, 2023, from https://www.thehindu.com/opinion/op-ed/securing-the-migrant-vote/article66830797.ece

Lee, N., & Clarke, S. (2019). Do Low-Skilled Workers Gain from High-Tech Employment Growth? High-Technology Multipliers, Employment and Wages in Britain. *Research Policy, 48*(9), 103803.

Lefebvre, H. (1991). *The Production of Space.* Basil Blackwell.

Livingstone, D. W. (2004). *No Room at the Top: Underrepresentation and Underemployment of Highly Qualified Women and Minorities.* Paper presented at the Maximising Existing Talent Conference. Center for Work-Life Policy.

Macbeath, I. (1979). *Votes, Virtues and Vices: Trade Union Power*. Associated Business Press.

Mackenzie, D., & Wajcman, J. (1999). *The Social Shaping of Technology*. Open University Press.

Marx, K. (1974). *The Ethnological Notebooks*. Van Gorcum and Company.

Masoodi, A. (2019, January 24). *Joining the India Story: Rise of the Muslim Middle*. Mint. Retrieved December 4, 2023, from https://www.livemint.com/politics/news/joining-the-india-story-rise-of-the-muslim-middle-1548262657277.html

Massey, D. (1994). *Space, Place and Gender*. University of Minnesota Press.

Nagarajan, R. (2022, July 5). 1/4th of Tribals, 1/5th of Dalits Quit Class IX & X in 2019–2020. *The Times of India*. Retrieved December 4, 2023, from https://timesofindia.indiatimes.com/india/1/4th-of-tribals-1/5th-of-dalits-quit-class-ix-x-in-2019-20/articleshow/84161197.cms?from=mdr

Naqvi, S. (2016). *Being the Other: The Muslim in India*. Aleph.

Navarro, V. (1998). Neoliberalism, "Globalization", Unemployment, Inequalities, and the Welfare State. *International Journal of Health Services, 28*(4), 607–682.

P. C., S. (2017). Muslim Social Organisation and Cultural Islamisation in Malabar. *South Asia Research, 37*(1), 19–36.

Prasad, P. H. (1994). *Gandhi, Marx and India: An Alternative Path of Progress*. Aakar.

Raghavendra, R. H. (2020). Literacy and Health Status of Scheduled Castes in India. *Contemporary Voice of Dalit, 12*(1), 97–110.

Ram, N. (2021). In B. Karat & V. Prashad (Eds.), *Delhi's Agony: Essays on the February 2020 Communal Violence*. Leftword Books.

Ram, R. (2014). Jawaharlal Nehru, Neo-liberalism and Social Democracy: Mapping the Shifting Trajectories of Developmental State in India. *Voice of Dalit, 7*(2), 187–210.

Rao, H. S. R. (2020, May 19). *Bangalore's Informal Labour Markets*. Indian Institute of Management Bangalore. Retrieved December 4, 2023, from https://www.iimb.ac.in/turn_turn/bangalore-informal-labour-markets.php

Rasool, T., Warraich, N. F., & Sajid, M. (2022). Examining the Impact of Technology Overload at the Workplace: A Systematic Review. *SAGE Open, 12*(3).

Rathod, B. (2023). *Dalit Academic Journeys: Stories of Caste, Exclusion and Assertion in Indian Higher Education*. Routledge.

Sachar, R. (2007) *For More Details, Refer to the 2006 Sachar Committee Report Which Can Be*. Retrieved December 4, 2023, from https://www.minorityaffairs.gov.in/show_content.php?lang=1&level=0&ls_id=14&lid=14

Salve, P. (2016a, July 28). *More Indian Women are Going to College but Fewer are Working*. Scroll. Retrieved December 4, 2023, from https://scroll.in/article/812591/more-indian-women-are-going-to-college-but-fewer-are-working

Salve, P. (2016b, July 28). *More Girls Studying, But 84% Drop Out After Graduation.* India Spend. Retrieved December 4, 2023, from https://www.indiaspend.com/more-girls-studying-but-84-drop-out-after-graduation-16526

Sanghi, S., & Srija, A. (2014). Employment Trends Among Religious Communities of India. *Economic and Political Weekly, 49*(17), 22–24.

Sebastian, A. (2016). Matrilineal Practices Along the Coasts of Malabar. *Sociological Bulletin, 65*(1), 89–106.

Shakthi, S. (2023). Corporate Brahminism and Tech Work: Caste in a Modern Indian Profession. *South Asia: Journal of South Asian Studies.* https://doi.org/10.1080/00856401.2023.2215137

Sheth, D. L. (1999). Secularisation of Caste and Making of New Middle Class. *Economic and Political Weekly, 34*(34/35), 2502–2510.

Siddiqui, Z. S., & Khan, A. S. (2022). Educational Status of Muslim Women in India: A Comparative Study. *International Journal of Creative Research Thoughts, 10*(6).

Silbey, S. S. (2016, August 23). Why Do So Many Women Who Study Engineering Leave the Field?. *Harvard Business Review.* Retrieved December 4, 2023, from https://hbr.org/2016/08/why-do-so-many-women-who-study-engineering-leave-the-field

Srinivas, S. (1998). *The Information Technology Industry in Bangalore* (TBDPU Working Paper No. 89). The Bartlett Development and Planning Unit. Retrieved December 4, 2023, from https://www.ucl.ac.uk/bartlett/development/sites/bartlett/files/migrated-files/WP89_0.pdf

Srivastava, S. (2023, January 15). Communal Violence in Gurgaon: Mono-Religious Cosmopolitanism. *Indian Express.* Retrieved December 4, 2023, from https://indianexpress.com/article/opinion/columns/communal-violence-in-gurgaon-mono-religious-cosmopolitanism-8875183/

Stewart, F. (1977). *Technology and Underdevelopment.* Macmillan.

Teltumbde, A. (2018). *Republic of Caste: Thinking Equality in the Time of Neoliberal Hindutva.* Navayana.

Thorat, S. (2004). On Reservation Policy for Private Sector. *Economic and Political Weekly, 39*(25), 2560–2563.

Times of India. (2019, August 14). *Bengaluru's Migrants Cross 50% of the City's Population.* Retrieved December 4, 2023, from https://timesofindia.indiatimes.com/city/bengaluru/bengalurus-migrants-cross-50-of-the-citys-population/articleshow/70518536.cms

Tronti, M. (1962). *Factory and Society.* Operaismo in English. Retrieved December 4, 2023, from https://operaismoinenglish.wordpress.com/2013/06/13/factory-and-society/

Tronti, M. (1973). Social Capital. *Telos, 17*, 98–121.

Tyagi, M. (2023, April 14). Statistics Show More Muslim Convicts than Hindu, But What's Behind These Numbers?. *The Wire*. Retrieved December 4, 2023, from https://thewire.in/rights/statistics-show-more-muslim-convicts-than-hindu-but-whats-behind-these-numbers

Viswanath, K. (2023, March 15). Time to Recognize Migrants' Role as Builders of Our Cities. *Hindustan Times*. Retrieved December 4, 2023, from https://www.hindustantimes.com/gurgaon/time-to-recognise-migrants-role-as-builders-of-our-cities/story-siBfBqehCGzqLzEo9DdxaO.html

Vogel, L. (2013). *Marxism and the Oppression of Women: Towards a Unitary Theory*. Brill.

Wahab, G. (2021). *Born a Muslim: Some Truths About Islam in India*. Aleph Book Company.

Yengde, S. (2019). *Caste Matters*. Penguin Random House India.

CHAPTER 3

Social Reproduction and the IT Women

INTRODUCTION: THE IMPORTANCE OF SOCIAL SOLIDARITY STRUCTURES

Exploitation is not a theoretical concept, but rather is an everyday affair for most of the IT workers. While the previous chapters have often spoken at length about issues that mostly concern the workplace, this chapter delves into the personal spheres of the IT workers. Having a more nuanced analysis of the intimate lives of workers is critical under contemporary capitalism because capitalism today has infiltrated the everyday lives in a far more destructive manner than it ever has in history. The everyday life is of supreme importance in the contemporary urban society because it is within the realm of everyday life, where one confronts reality as lived experience and constitutes for oneself a sense of ontological security (Giddens, 1991). It is also the space where one not only acquires individual and group identities but also comes into contact with structures forming the same. The social space that individual workers occupy is an important part of their overall identity as workers. The social space inhabited and lived by people as part of their everyday lives is an intrinsic part of the human ontology that 'subsumes things produced and encompasses their interrelationships in their coexistence and simultaneity' (Lefebvre, 1991, p. 73) determining one's public and private lives.

© The Author(s), under exclusive license to Springer Nature Switzerland AG 2024
S. Deb Roy, *The Rise of the Information Technology Society in India*, Dynamics of Virtual Work,
https://doi.org/10.1007/978-3-031-58128-1_3

Urban spaces that have been formed as IT hubs in India are parts of the gentrified social reality that reinforces gendered notions of patriarchal subsumption. For the women, such kinds of gendered urban spaces become highly exploitative in nature making them amenable to patriarchal domination (Massey, 1994; Kern, 2020). Within such gendered urban social spaces, the everyday lives of women get determined by contradictions such as class and caste that get intertwined with their gendered subordination producing a subpar and exploitative state of existence for the women. The life of women is determined by the state of the sexual division of labour, most elaborately and explicitly noticed in the reproductive labour performed by women and its distribution both within the domestic space and in the society in general. The effects of such influences on the lives of working women are mediated through diverse networks of patriarchy and contemporary capitalism. The destruction of modes of social solidarity constructs an important part of such networks of exploitation. Social solidarity still remains a non-commodified and 'Wedded to the belief that the market should be the organizing principle for all political, social, and economic decisions, neoliberalism wages an incessant attack on democracy, public goods, and non-commodified values' (Giroux, 2005, p. 2).

Contemporary urban social lives remain at a perennial risk of being engulfed by the bourgeoning neoliberal and capitalist individualisation that actively promotes alienation (Lefebvre, 2014). But, human beings are inherently social in nature, and it is in the innate nature of human beings to progress towards a social mode of living. In the context of India, modes of living have been mediated through the structure of communities or kinship bonds based on nativity, caste, or gender. It is these structures of fraternity within and among the communities that enable the exploitation of women creating the cultural legitimacy that is required to subvert them. For women, networks of solidarity thus become extremely important because the exploitation of women takes place through the utilisation of culture that makes certain modes of exploitation of women universal in nature (Narayan, 2018). Since the women in the society are often directly linked to the structures of the community, their struggle begins from the level of the community or any such structure—of which the family is also a part and manifestation—from which it extends towards struggling for individual autonomy.

Solidarity or community-based living has the potential to make any species, human or otherwise, react unitedly towards oppression of any kind thus putting them at an advantageous position both quantitatively as well as qualitatively (Pannekoek, 1912/2018). Communities are extremely important to social lives, in both urban and rural spaces. Urban Communities are typically characterised as communities of place, where the segregation between communities is often performed with the help of built environment rather than naturally occurring entities as in rural spaces (Farahani, 2016). Communities of place (Hillery, 1955) in urban spaces (Farahani, 2016) have not received much attention as far as its relationship with household labour and social reproduction is concerned. Unlike rural spaces, where household labour and social reproduction are divided substantially within the community, urban spaces are characterised by spatially alienated nuclear families which make such division increasingly difficult to be brought into effect.

Despite the fact that a direct interrelationship might be difficult to be brought forward, the existence of an indirect relationship between these important aspects of urban everyday life cannot be denied. In this regard, one of the purposes of the current chapter is to exhibit that even within urban spaces, reproductive labour shares a relationship with community-based living, albeit in a different manner than rural spaces. Effective communitarianism has an effect on the populace's well-being and their general outlook about the society influencing the decisions that they take and the choices that they make in terms of their lifestyles, employment, and social allegiances (Holland et al., 2011). The concept of the 'community' and its importance in India can be felt with regard to the IT sector as well. While the ideas concerning the meanings and implications of the 'community' have been continuously subjected to alterations historically, its importance cannot be denied in a context such as India. The structure of social solidarity that is most persistently visible in the Indian society is that of the community, which has a tremendous effect on the social and individual consciousness of human beings (Dube, 1990). The transformation of the Indian society under neoliberalism has depended upon the ways in which neoliberal capitalism has changed the structure of the communitarian social relations in the country affecting the caste, class, and gender relationships therein (Patnaik, 2017). For simplicity, the chapter uses the words 'community', 'structures of social solidarity', and 'social solidarity networks' interchangeably specifically keeping the Indian context in mind. References to special circumstances, wherever necessary, however have been clarified in the text.

The kind of community or social solidarity network that an individual becomes a part of determines the kind of engagement that the individuals have with the society in general. However, the concept of 'community' within the Indian society has been used, mostly, to refer to caste and class-based social clusters. Different factors like place, space, and interests have been deemed to be primordial factors of constructing a community at different points of time (Farahani, 2016). In the context of the present chapter however, the focus will be on communities of interest (Wellman, 2005) or consumption-oriented communities (Nethercote & Horne, 2016) that have increased profusely with the growth of gentrified urban spaces. The urban spaces that IT hubs construct often encourage the formation of contrived spaces that are formed in a manner that increases the productivity of the workers without delving into the nuances of the effects of industrialisation and loss of the idea of one's own subjectivity within contemporary societies that produces a sense of 'community loss' (Kempers, 2001; Lyon & Driskell, 2011). The implications of community loss are worse for women than the men, because the subjugation of women occurs both as a social category and as individuals. The exploitative space and temporality that engulfs them works through the unpaid reproductive labour that women perform that is traditionally devalued as unproductive labour (Bhattacharya, 2017).

Taking cue from the points made above, the current chapter speaks about the social reproduction labour of women IT workers and analyses its relationship with their identities as workers. It provides a framework through which one can begin to look afresh at the community building activities within India's urban neighbourhoods, mostly populated by white-collar workers. This chapter will analyse processes in which gender and community formation processes are related within India's urban spaces. The chapter challenges the perennialism, at times associated with the idea of 'community lost' by analysing the loss of 'place' to be in a dialectical relationship with the overall social space and its associated structures of exploitation. Social reproduction labour performed by women, plays a critical role in this context because of the role of gender in formulating the very foundations of the urban space. The reproductive labour that women perform makes them a distinct part of the IT workforce within the IT hubs. Reproductive labour usually has three components, household labour, care work and the labour of people-making. The current chapter that begins from problematising the processes through each and every aspect of one's everyday life becomes a potential source of profit accumulation and oppression. The chapter then looks at the phenomenon of social practices and their routinisation under contemporary capitalism and the relationship which it shares with the dynamics of reproductive labour.

TIME, SPACE, AND SOCIAL REPRODUCTION

Working lives are always structured around time and space. Both these aspects remain intertwined with each other in the production of the IT lives that the book speaks about. Time has both a concrete and abstract nature related to the use value and abstract value of the commodities. With the development of capitalism, abstract value dominates over the use values as Marx (1976) had exhibited because abstract labour comes to dominate over concrete labour through 'the existence of a socially valid system of time-reckoning comprising abstract-time-units, and ... the commodification of labour and the market mediation of human reproduction in society' (Martineau, 2015, p. 118). Likewise, Lefebvre (1991) talks about two kinds of space—the absolute and the abstract. While the former represents the space produced for the appropriation of use values, the latter represents the space produced for the realisation of exchange values. The peculiarity of reproductive labour is that while it is performed primarily within the absolute space, it has wide ramifications within the abstract space as it creates the necessary conditions for the very sustenance of the abstract space itself. The liberation of women workers, within these circumstances, is intimately related to a reconceptualisation of reproductive labour because while most of men's labour directly accounts for 'productive' work, most of women's labour get relegated as unproductive work— making them look like unnecessary components within the social factory. One of the reasons for the same is the dominant understanding of the concept of 'work', which restricts it to only financial value producing activities in the post-industrial society (Gorz, 1987). Women's reproductive labour repaid mostly by non-material entities like '*love*' and '*care*' (Fraser, 2016) have made it further difficult to think of them as productive labour. This can be countered by reconceptualising household labour and people-reproduction activities (Fraser et al., 2019) as directly productive labour as they contribute to the maintenance of the overall social labour power (Dalla Costa & James, 1975).

54   S. DEB ROY

Time plays a crucial role in this regard, because under contemporary capitalism time has become one of the core areas through which a neoliberal way of life is brought into existence destroying networks of social solidarity and subsuming human existence within a cycle of productive activities. The lack of time for many of the IT workers constitutes the basis of their social existence as individual human beings in the society. The fast-paced life that the IT sector prides itself in is a manifestation of the domination of abstract time over concrete time, whereby the increase of the domination of abstract time over concrete time creates the social circumstances for a generalisation of hyper-productivity in the society. The capitalist domination over time was explained by Postone (1993) through his differentiation of time into concrete and abstract time whereby the former was designated to be time understood through 'natural cycles and the periodicities of human life as well as particular tasks or processes' while the latter understood as '"empty" time ... independent of events' (Postone, 1993, pp. 201–02). The domination of abstract time over concrete time produces the idea of time as an independent variable, constitutes the way in which capitalism identifies the time for the working class—that is often divorced from natural time cycles or human subjectivity—and is based on the idea of enhancing productivity. The lifestyle that the IT sector promotes is one that leaves the workers with little time for their personal well-being. Speaking on the issue, two IT workers from Kolkata and Bengaluru respectively stated:

> It is a fast-paced life, we do not have much time to give to ourselves. Most of us have EMIs, loans, etc. If somebody is done with all that, then they will have some form of aspiration or a dream vacation that they want to go to. All of these thigs make us work harder. Sometimes, it pays off, but sometimes it is just very difficult. (Woman IT Worker, Kolkata)

> Time is very important. Our shifts are in the morning, so nobody has the time to do anything else. We get up, rush through the morning chores, and then run for the office. Most of the times, I have to do certain jobs before I leave for work, including setting up my son's school box, his bag, keep something in the refrigerator for the evening, etc. (Woman IT Worker, Bengaluru)

'Work', of all kinds, shares an intrinsic connection with time. But, while this relationship in the past was based upon the concept of working-hours or the working-day (Marx, 1976), today, it is based upon the complete colonisation of time (Shippen, 2014). The idea of an individual's time being completely colonised by social forces draws from the intimate nature of contemporary capitalism that ensures that it can spread its circuit of exploitation within the most intimate and personal spaces of the workers (Negri, 2003). The household has often been seen as being outside the direct influence of capitalism. Contemporary capitalism does not desire only a dominated workforce, but rather require a subservient workforce to exploit. Patriarchy and capitalism shape the relations of production attempting to reinforce the belief that the primary responsibility of women is towards their families. Such modes of ideological domination were critical to industrial capitalism because it could not directly control the household that prompted it to create a sexual and gendered division of labour that allows it to exert a form of indirect control (Hartmann, 1981). Under neoliberal capitalism, however, capital has been able to influence the household as well. The domination over the household does not generate out of a vacuum but is rather shaped by the social reproductive work that women perform in general in the society. Such changes within the nature of contemporary capitalism are intimately related to how the dominant social forces shape the 'lived' social reality, especially for the most vulnerable sections of the society. Time becomes an instrument of altering the spatial dynamics of women's lives putting them in a position where they often end up sacrificing potentially more humane forms of social life that do not further alienate them (Lefebvre, 2014). In the contemporary society, where *'time is money'*, it has become important to understand how 'time' as a concept intersects with processes like household labour and community formation under capitalist globalisation.

The devaluation of time is associated with the devaluation of reproductive labour and the labour power that it produces on a daily basis, which forms the very material basis on which the world sustains itself (Fraser et al., 2019). To theorise household labour as an essential part of the social structure, the people-reproduction activities have to be seen as socially necessary and productive labour (Dalla Costa & James, 1975; Vogel, 1983/2013). Gender here plays an important role, because the daily reproduction of life, which is the most important aspect of the sustenance of any form of society, is heavily dependent upon the sexual division of labour, where women are supposed to perform the entirety of the labour associated with people-reproduction (Fraser et al., 2019). The quantity of labour, which is performed by women within their homes, contributes to the surplus capacities or collective energies of the society, that is, 'the collective fund of social energies exceeding those required to reproduce a given form of life and to replenish what is used up in the course of living it' (Fraser, 2014, p. 58). The ways in which a society spends its surplus capacities, in turn, determine how a society is functioning, both ethically and economically (Fraser, 2014), because they influence the delicate relationship between the monetised 'productive' work and the un-monetised domestic labour.

In pre-modern societies, all the different forms of labour were considered to be 'productive'—albeit in their own ways because the concept of 'productive' labour itself was a creation of capitalist development. 'Productive' labour, as Gardiner (2000) notes, was an integral part of the daily life in pre-modern societies, where no rigid distinction existed between productive and unproductive forms of labour. The sexual division of labour, which in its modified form creates a distinction between productive and unproductive labour, in the post-industrial society has important impacts on the surplus capacities (Fraser, 2014) of the society, as well as on the quality and dynamics of everyday social life in general. As four IT workers narrate:

> My husband shares some of the household chores, but more often than not, I have to do bulk of the work. There is no doubt about that. It is frequently the case that he does not even know how to put the rice on the cooker, how would I expect him to do all the household work? Simply not possible. He does most of the work which he can do like sweeping the floor, cleaning the bathroom, etc. (Woman IT Worker, Bengaluru)

> We have a maid who does most of the work. So, it usually does not come to any of us. The only household job that we have to do is to cook the dinner. She takes a lot of money though. But we do not have much choice. Without a maid, it is difficult to sustain the kind of life that we have. (Woman IT Worker, Noida)

> My wife does most of the household work. I cook sometimes, but that is mostly on weekends. But it is compensated because I earn more. My salary is much more than my wife's salary. I do not mean to say that it is her responsibility to do all the work, but both of us have to contribute to the household and the family in some way or the other. (Male IT Worker, Noida)

> I live with my girlfriend, and we share household work, most of the times. Sometimes, when she has work, I do the work, and vice versa. I understand that situations can change. For example, if we marry and have kids, then obviously her responsibilities might increase. (Male IT Worker, Bengaluru)

The narratives reveal that among the formal IT workers, there is an increasing propensity to share the housework between themselves, even for unmarried couples. However, for men in general, such labour is often performed as a form of recreation that helps them recuperate, while for women, it is usually a responsibility. The difference between responsibility and recreation plays a key role in the narratives above. The former symbolises a kind of compulsion, a necessity to engage in a certain kind of work, while the latter denotes a certain notion of choice—one can choose to either do that or not engage in that at all. The compulsion to perform certain forms of work produces a form of alienation that contributes towards the alienation of these workers from the society around them (Fromm, 1961). The differences between compulsion and choice are manifested through the quantity and quality of interactions that one has with the public sphere. Historically, urban spaces have been designed in a manner which restricts women's mobility within the public sphere (Massey, 1994). Mobility and engagement with the public sphere are markers of a vibrant and participatory public and social life—one which is often the reason for large-scale migration to these IT hubs in the first place for many of the IT workers. Men enjoy more freedom in terms of maintaining a vibrant social life and their private life, even if they do most of the household work. This is because the urban spatiality allows them to manipulate the sexual division of labour according to their own will, which again leads one back to reiterate the claim about urban spaces being inherently gendered in nature. This is reflected in the two statements reproduced below:

> I cannot go out much during the weekdays. It is usually during the weekends because it is only during the weekends that I can get that much time. Plus, there is also the issue about women going out at night, which is basically the issue with weekdays. My shift is over at 10 or 12 at night, after that it is not possible to go out. There is no time for me. I have very specific shifts, and I have to adhere to them. Yes, sometimes, I do deviate, but more often than not, it is the same. I can maintain a routine of personal well-being but mostly it has to be focused upon the workplace. (Woman IT Worker, Pune)

> The job pays well. If it demands us to sacrifice certain things, we should not crib about that. I migrated from my town to earn money. Well-being and all can wait. Even if I do household labour, I can still maintain a healthy lifestyle. I think it all depends upon the individual. I go to the gym in the morning, take my kids to school, and then go to the office. When there is a night

shift, my wife does all of this. I always help with household chores. In fact, doing household chores makes me relax. (Male IT Worker, Bengaluru)

Men can live a healthy life even if they maintain strict schedules because the social space that they find themselves in makes it more conducive for them. For example, one can analyse the statements made above by the male workers who said that do not any household work mandatorily, because that allows them to maintain a very professional daily schedule. The sharing of some household chores actually benefits working men because it helps them in recuperating from the pressure that they face within their workplaces revealing the relationship between one's style of life, one's gender and the social reproductive work that the individual performs. Increased reproductive labour increases the propensity of women to get entrenched within the domestic or household space. The style of life that an individual is able to practise in one's everyday life is influenced by the social space that one finds around oneself, the quality of everyday life, and the totality of the social labour performed by an individual (Lefebvre, 1991; Gardiner, 2000). Reproductive labour and the style of life share an intrinsic, often inversely proportional, relationship with each other. The more reproductive labour that a woman worker is made to perform, the more subsumed style of life that she can possess. In countries like India, where women are traditionally exploited in terms of their sexuality and people-production capacities, the propensity of them being entrenched more within reproductive labour increases manifold (Bumiller, 1991). The social fabric that one finds in India is dominated by the traditional style of life that finds relevance till date in urban India. The effects that reproductive labour has on woman corporate workers are different than the kind of effects that they have on the informal workers who serve the corporate workers.[1]

The institutional separation between 'productive' and 'unproductive' labour accentuates the restrictions over women's labour within the private sphere, making it difficult to conceptualise reproductive labour within a general socio-political framework (Vogel, 1983/2013) integrating reproductive labour with various other social processes. It is a paradoxical scenario, both psychologically and sociologically, because while it is broadly accepted that the society today has become a post-industrial one (Gorz,

---

[1] The details of this point will be engaged with in Chap. 4, which speaks about the invisible IT sector workers.

1987), the remnants of the sexual division of labour, which in some ways, even precedes the industrial society (Engels, 1884/1941), continue to persist and impact the daily social life in the twenty-first century, by affecting the relationship between the distribution of reproductive labour, social life and gendered identities. Most new modes of exploitation get reinforced through constantly evolving ideological structures which reproduce 'in a purposive manner a selective version/vision of the past (or its fragment) in order to contest the proposal of modern, globalised, cosmopolitan and liberal culture and society' (Benczes et al., 2020, p. 5). And since capitalism 'has grown out of the economic structure of the feudal society' (Godelier, 1967, p. 99), so it is not surprising that it has often come to reproduce them in the contemporary times, albeit in a different form and differing contents (Harvey, 2010). Capitalism in its contemporary form depends upon the extraction of relative surplus labour from the workers along with the extraction of absolute surplus value because relative surplus value extraction contributes to heightened productivity more effectively. And heightened productivity is one of the basic fulcrums around which the IT sector of the country functions, as one women employee stated:

> The question is of productivity and how you describe it. For us, productivity means getting work done quicker than it usually is by others. So, if somebody can sacrifice a weekend to do some office work, it is usually praised in the office. It is an unhealthy practice that few HR managers consider. The sacrifice of a weekend puts a lot of additional pressure. It is only an example, other examples might include working overtime, taking up more work than what one can handle, etc. These are common practices because it increases the chances of getting promoted. (Woman IT Worker, Hyderabad)

The question of reproductive labour is a central one for the contemporary times and has been an important question for organisations and political arguments (Arruzza, 2017). Some of them have highlighted that the more a person is engulfed by reproductive work, the less time one has to lead to healthy and satisfying 'style of life':

> It is a difficult life you know. Some of the work is done by the maid, but sometimes, I do have to cook. You cannot eat food cooked by the maid every day. Sometimes, when my husband's friends come over, I have to cook some special meals. Even on holidays, it is difficult, but it is more difficult on working days if I have to do that after I come back from work. These are

issues that nobody can check or verify. If you would not have asked me about this particular case, I would not have said that as well. (Woman IT Worker, Gurgaon)

The time taken by the woman worker to cook 'special' meals, impacts the available time left at her disposal to maintain her social relationships outside the domestic space, albeit in varying proportions in different contexts. The sexual division of labour uses the idea of 'time' as an instrument of oppression and by creating and sustaining the conditions through which women get relegated into a restrictive private sphere. The restrictions are put by engaging women within a non-negotiable relationship with the social structure in place that subsumes them under familial responsibilities leaving them little time for any social life or engagement with the public sphere. Contemporary capitalism thrives by manipulating the processes in which the various social classes utilise their time and social space (Massey, 1994; Shippen, 2014). It is an integral part of the formation of the capitalist 'social factory' (Tronti, 1962). The social factory under capitalism—a situation where the entire society begins to act like a means of production—makes use of both capitalism and patriarchy to construct an exploitative 'totality' harbouring within itself a continuous dialectical struggle between the particular and the absolute (Lefebvre, 2016) and between the spatial and the temporal (Massey, 1994), simultaneously.

SOCIAL PRACTICES, REPRODUCTIVE LABOUR, AND THE GENDERED URBAN REALITY

The world of business today is far more complicated than it ever was in human history. The ethics and tactics through which businesses are conducted in contemporary world have undergone significant changes, especially with the growth of the service sector and the IT sector. The service industry involves both knowledge and information-based work, is highly demanding of its workers, both physically and psychologically—for the employees and the organisations involved therein (Pradhan & Hati, 2019). The complexity within the world of business and global capitalist structures have complemented and have been complemented by a growing social complexity caused by capitalist development that play important roles in the determination of an individual's success within the industry

(Panda & Rath, 2017; Pradhan & Hati, 2019). The patriarchal colonisation of the social space that women inhabit within the IT hubs constitutes one of the most important aspects that determine the social and personal practices that women IT workers come to embody. Social practices are an integral part of human lives. Be it the primitive societies described by Engels (1884/1941), or the more recent theories about the post-industrial society (Bell, 1976), social practices are an important aspect of the everyday lives of all the classes, castes, genders, and races. Social practices exhibit the state of freedom in a particular society, and the kind of social status that an individual or a group possesses.

Social practices, in their natural unalienated forms, are triggered primarily by the spontaneous needs arising out of basic human sensibilities. But under a regime induced control, be it psychological or material in nature, these are triggered by a sense of alienation (Lefebvre, 2014) and a complete mechanisation of urban life (Benjamin, 2002). Within this sociopolitical milieu, Gorz (1987) argued that even if the radical dream of the abolition of work is successful, it will only be emancipatory in nature if it allows autonomous practices to grow and flourish. The very understanding of autonomous practices by Gorz (1987) was based on liberatory social practices being self-determined in nature, such that an activity is the end in itself and not a means to an end (Gorz, 1987), which is significantly different from the highly routinised forms of social practices under capitalist modernity. The domination over social practices constitutes the common sensical nature of neoliberal control over the society. As David Harvey notes:

> For any way of thought to become dominant, a conceptual apparatus must be advanced that appeals to our intuitions and instincts, to our values and our desires, as well as to the possibilities inherent in the social world we inhabit. If successful, this conceptual apparatus becomes so embedded in common sense as to be taken for granted and not open to question. (Harvey, 2005, p. 5)

The routinised form of everyday life that most women workers adhere to makes it easy for neoliberal capitalism to achieve a common sensical status in the society. The effects of neoliberalism becoming a way of life manifests itself in the ways in which human beings shaping them as consumerist individuals doing with structures of solidarity (Navarro, 2007). However, in countries such as India, neoliberal capitalism, or any form of capitalism, does not operate along the classical lines. Capitalist development in India had integrated pre-capitalist and feudal norms of exploitation within itself. Capitalism in India is a unique combination of the pre-capitalist modes of exploitation and their relationship with contemporary mainstream capitalist modes of exploitation (Desai, 1984).

The lives of women, even if they are engaged in professions such as IT, are determined by the traditional understandings of honour, chastity, and modesty that determine the kind of work that one does, and the labouring processes associated with it. A significant part of such an ideological conditioning is because of the perceived economic dependence that women have had in general on men, which created the idea of 'the dependent woman'—that provided a tremendous impetus to the public-private dichotomy. The so-called economic dependence on men that most women possess as parts of their everyday lives, and the morality associated with the cultural construction of domesticity and chastity has resulted in women being institutionally subverted in the society (Kalpagam, 1994). In the IT sector, women workers are as much empowered financially as the male workers—at least on pure theoretical terms as Chap. 2 has put forward—but they still remain subservient to the male members of the society, because the social structure in place creates a sense of dependency within them not in the economic sense but in a socio-cultural sense whereby they continue to remain dependent on the male members for validating their honour and modesty—which often become critical parts of their financial empowerment as well.[2] One woman IT worker who is herself a victim of harassment in a tech firm in Bengaluru states:

> The question of protecting the modesty of women is still an important one. I cannot go out in the open if it is widely known that I have been harassed in the office. I have lodged a complaint to the internal complaints committee, that is fine but I cannot make it known to the general public in the workplace. That is because once it is widely known, then they will look at me differently, it will also affect my chances of promotion because to many, I might have shown the company in a bad light. Also, whenever a harassment occurs, or at least the ones that I have seen, occurs between a male employee at a higher position and a woman employee at a lower position. So, if ever there is a complaint made, it is usually the women who has to face the other colleagues because no one dares speak against the seniors. (Woman IT Worker, Bengaluru)

[2] Chapter 2 has dealt with this point in details.

The fact that such processes continue unabated points one towards a complete patriarchal colonisation of social space, that gives rise to certain social practices that are inherently gendered in nature, evading processes of upliftment through mere economic empowerment. Honour and modesty for women in the context of South Asia is often related to the concepts of 'public esteem and private shame' which are manipulated to exert control on women's sexuality and movement to ensure obedience and chastity (Coomaraswamy, 2005, p. 35). Jobs such as cleaning in bars or in places which are frequented by men, or sex work are often associated with the notion of ideal womanhood in India, which is based on chastity and the protection of communal honour (Coomaraswamy, 2005). Neoliberal capitalism makes it difficult to critique such changes because it converts itself into a common sensical mode of analysis. The fear of losing one's modestly often makes many of these workers succumb to structures of exploitation.

The difficulties that women face in maintaining their personal and professional well-being forms the core of the urban life that women IT workers lead in most of the major IT hubs of the country. Conversations with women IT workers reveal that most of the reproductive labour in IT spaces is still performed by women. The disproportionate burden of reproductive labour not only affects their social life but also has an impact on how women construct an identity and a space of their own within the society. The identity and social belongingness that women experience in the society is affected by the strategies of surplus value put in place by the dominant social order. Contemporary capitalism is not about solely extracting surplus labour from the workers and dominating them, but rather it is about inflicting total social control (Hardt & Negri, 2000) and the household, though an important part of the capitalist structure, is the only space, where capitalist influence has traditionally not been exerted directly (Hartmann, 1981). The household constitutes an important part of the capitalist circuit of social control because it forms the most intimate and private space that a human being occupies and a control over the same ensures that capital can control the dynamics of people production and nourishment in the society.

Mainstream forms of industrial capitalism have however struggled to do that directly, until the arrival of consumerist capitalism—a point that will be taken up in Chap. 6. However, with the coming of COVID-19, the social dynamics surrounding intimate spaces has changed drastically. COVID-19 has enabled the sustained usage of the household space for waged activities, and as such has changed the dynamics of reproductive labour that is performed within homes—and constructs the basic character of *the home*. With the coming of Work from Home, the home has become an extension of the office or rather it has mutated into becoming the 'office' itself—reiterating the view that contemporary labouring processes are no longer constrained within the physical boundaries of a factory (Negri, 1989; Hardt & Negri, 1994). Locked within their homes, working from home completely subsumed them within the digital spaces, where many of them have lost access to modes of direct communication with their peers. Under such circumstances where the employee also loses his/her channels of direct communication, the individual employee is at a greater risk of being alienated from his/her work because they tend to lose their decision-making autonomy along with their task identity (Shantz et al., 2015). In such situations, the employees do not get to exert their spontaneous human instincts while interacting through digital modes of communication, which not only affects the entire labouring process but the psychological state of the employee that has a significant effect on one's well-being and social ontology, as a worker stated:

> It is difficult to speak with a computer you know. The entire point about well-being is that we are human beings. The company makes us work like machines and to a certain extent, it also takes cognisance of that point. There are people for whom face-to-face conversation is very important for effective performance. The expectation from the organisation that everybody can manage their performance equally from home results in additional pressure. I have to manage a household of five, does everybody have to do that? (Woman IT Worker, Bengaluru)

Industrial capitalism has traditionally not been able to directly influence the household, which made it necessary for it to institutionalise a sexual division of labour that constructed a separation between the public sphere of waged work and the private sphere of unwaged reproductive labour (Hartmann, 1981; Fraser, 1994). If the influence of capitalism has to penetrate the entire society on a psychological as well as a material basis, it is essential for capitalism to have a strong control within the household. This necessitates the control over social practices because it is through them that spaces get constructed and keeping them in order would also mean keeping the entire system, including the sexual division of labour, intact. As reproductive labour plays an important part in the reproduction and sustenance of capitalism, any alterations within the household labour and the associated sexual division of labour has a direct impact on the entire structure of the society itself. The gendered nature of operational power relations in the society acts as one of the basic foundations of the sexual division of labour. This is, in turn, related to the processes through which the ideas of masculinity are produced (Campbell & Bell, 2000) and the effect which these ideas have on the disproportionate relationship between household labour and gendered social practices.

An economistic understanding of reproductive labour fails to analyse the nuances of reproductive labour because it is rarely financially reward-ing—unless relatively in the case of paid domestic workers. A holistic understanding of the importance of the reproductive labour thus needs to consider the various aspects of productivity (Vogel, 1983/2013; Fraser, 2016), space (Lefebvre, 1991; Massey, 1994), time (Gorz, 1987; Shippen, 2014), and everyday-social practices (Lefebvre, 1991). The work that male workers do, even when they do household labour, is ascribed a higher dignity than those of women workers. Male workers, even if they come from marginalised backgrounds, possess certain distinct advantages over their women counterparts. Because of the way in which the society is structured, male workers usually have more freedom in terms of forming communities of support for themselves. Being a part of a collective or hav-ing a communitarian group makes one better equipped to engage with the issues of everyday life. A sense of community or social solidarity is essential for developing not only a sense of belonging, but also a sense of safety (Kusenbach, 2006) and camaraderie (Wellman, 2001). Women workers in the IT sector lack in both these aspects, as two women IT workers have stated from Bengaluru and Gurgaon:

> The problem is that because of the way in which the society has been struc-tured, women tend to be highly competitive among themselves as well as in general. One of the major reasons for this is that we have been neglected so much and subjected to so much social pressures that we actually want to excel a lot more than others at our jobs. So, we are more competitive in nature. That is natural. (Woman IT Worker, Bengaluru)

> I have come here to make a career, and not make friends. But at the same time, it is true that there is a lot of office politics that goes in within the offices, so doing anything also is very difficult. Everybody is worried about their careers, so almost nobody wants to do anything that goes against the

interests of their own careers. It is a problem. We wanted to form a community space, and that did get formed as well with the help of the HR but now it is largely defunct. (Woman IT Worker, Gurgaon)

Being a part of a collective or any form of structure of solidarity greatly enhances human potential. Being part of such structures helps in countering the degrading quality of everyday life that one enjoys that has an effect on the kind of community that one becomes or desires to become a part of. A community in this context can be said to be characterised by the allegiance or sense of belonging that one enjoys towards a particular place, the fraternal relations therein, and the interactions that they have within that space (Hillery, 1955). However, any community is also not completely independent of the power relations that capitalism renders mainstream in the society. Within the communities of place formed by the women IT workers as well, power relations manifest themselves through a variety of ways based on one's employment, domicile or based on the financial standings of their partners. Those who are more secured in their financial lives usually exert a significant influence on how such communities function. One woman worker, who is herself a member of a neighbourhood collective in Pune, states:

> Your professional standing determines a lot of the behaviour that is shown towards you in the residential spaces. Since most of the people live with others who work in the IT sector, it ultimately comes to you—the competition, social status, professional hierarchies, all of it. There occurs a class-based segregation in these communities as well. If somebody works as an HR, then that person naturally will hold a greater social capital in the community. (Woman IT Worker, Pune)

The construction of such communities by effecting internal segregations among the non-capitalist classes are a manifestation of neoliberal capitalism's effects on the community formation processes of human beings, which has changed the nature of communities from being dominated by pre-capitalist and feudal caste relations to newer forms of communities constructed out of the transformation of pre-capitalist forms of social relationships to capitalist ones that substitute their community-based identities into a working-class identity (Patnaik, 2017). A major part of such transformation, however, is because of the widespread mobility that contemporary forms of labour has achieved (Huws, 2014)—which often robs the women workers of any options that they might have in terms of choosing their immediate communities.

The formal IT sector workers' ideas of a community usually are characterised by an idea that conforms to community being a space that they construct within gated societies excluding those who cannot afford to live in those spaces or a space within their workplaces that harbours individuals performing similar jobs as them. Such spaces in the context of the formal IT workers are usually gated communities of residence or their workplace—which are strongly rooted in an idea of exclusion bolstered by capitalist gentrification (Stein, 2019). Effective communities, however, are formed on the basis of 'space' and not merely based on the location or a 'place', locality, or other forms of physical territoriality (Farahani, 2016). The contradictions that result because of such issues become apparent in the case of the married IT sector women workers for whom reproductive labour often becomes the basis of social existence.[3] The oppression of women as invisible workers cannot be negated by mere activism but requires a new idea of philosophical intervention itself because the exploitation of reproductive labour is a framework of existence itself (Dunayevskaya, 1973; Fraser et al., 2019). This exploitative framework of existence based on the complete subjugation of women's labour becomes the dominant factor when women enter low-paying informal jobs. It determines their social identity and the organisational forms that *they think* will contribute towards their emancipation. Often alienated from their native spaces, women tend to form their own kinds of communities to negotiate with the gendered nature of the space that they inhabit. The availability of meaningful time and the unequal distribution of reproductive labour are inter-related and significantly impact each other. These factors work together in the everyday lives of women to restrict women within the private sphere, if not completely materially then ideologically. Being restricted within their private lives, these women have little option but to form fraternal and solidarity-based ties with their neighbours. Two women workers narrate:

> With whom will I mix? After office, it is very difficult for us. I am so tired after office that I cannot even take care of my own self. At that time, is it possible for me to socialise with others. There are also issues with the family. They also have reservations with regard to caste and gender so no options for me. (Woman IT Worker, Kolkata)

[3] See Chap. 2 for some details on marriage and its effects on women workers.

Most of my family and friends are back home. But I have friends here, but most of those friends are only superficial friends because we did not really choose them. When I got married, we bought a house here, and they were the only other sociable families here. Because at the end, you do have to maintain certain cordial relationships with your neighbours. My husband does not mix much, but I do because it does help me better equipped to deal with the pressure. The reason why we are able to do that is because we can manage our household labour more effectively than others. There are women who do not have time to go out of their homes. We are lucky in that respect. (Woman IT Worker, Bengaluru)

The narratives reveal that women are more likely to form friendly, or even familial, terms with their neighbours. Their tendency to transcend kinship-bonds provides them with a certain sense of autonomy and bestows upon them a potential of organising themselves spontaneously while negotiating with the unequal distribution of reproductive labour. The point that women tend to show more likelihood to share co-operative ties with their neighbours proves that women share more potential than men in terms of organising the space around them provided they are able to negotiate with the reproductive labour accorded to them. These communities of place, imbibed with the positive potential of women, both as individuals and as a social 'class', have the capacity to enable women to struggle against the oppressive sexual division of labour within the private sphere and steer them towards socio-political emancipation by struggling against other social and economic issues. These communities or structures of solidarity, since formed by the women themselves, can enable them to exert their social potential on their own, free from the heretical restrictions imposed upon them by patriarchal socio-political spaces.

Women can form effective communities that enable the construction of broader structures of social solidarity, only if they can negotiate with the sexual division of labour sustained by the gendered spaces and power relations therein. The meaningful time available to an individual forms the basis of such manipulations that women workers can potentially perform in their everyday lives. For men, the creation of communities is relatively easier because they enjoy more freedom in fulfilling their necessary needs. The women workers, however, suffer from the relative curtailment of such unrestricted freedom, because the dominant social structure and the ideology in place completely subsumes the meaningful time available to them. The availability of meaningful time allows women to have an everyday life that is focused on their personal well-being and their ability to live spontaneous lives, which in turn makes them able to form effective fraternal ties despite performing most of the housework.

In situations where women have been able to manipulate the responsibilities which are traditionally entrusted upon them, they have been able to disassociate themselves from the traditional gendered patterns of everyday life. This, in turn, enables them to progress towards forming heterodox communities of place even if they have limited control over the social attributes of the people with whom they are forming the communities with. The relative control that women exert over such community or solidarity formation processes does not help them in exerting more control over the space that they inhabit, but rather merely make them more comfortable with the exploitation that they face. Such a mode of ideological re-structuring is a quintessential part of the alienated social existence that capitalism produces where individuals lose all control over their social activities and forcing them to relegate their human existence to be subsumed by the all-encompassing nature of one's activities and their consequences (Marx, 1844; Fromm, 1961).

The more spontaneous a lifestyle maintained by the women workers, or the more focused that they are regarding their own personal well-being, the more progress can the woman make towards constructing a community, even if they are within alienated urban social spaces. The everyday spontaneity of the women can only be maintained if they can destroy the heretical restrictions put in place by their private sphere and the disproportionately balanced reproductive labour. This process entails within itself the undertaking of co-operative activities and formation of fraternal ties, both of which are discouraged if they are relegated strictly within a patriarchal private space controlled by the men in the household. The situation becomes extremely difficult for those workers who are seeking low-waged work while being less educated than their counterparts (Kletzer, 1998)— the ramifications of which are usually found in the lives of workers who do not directly work for the technology firms as formal workers but rather *work as outsourced, contractual, or work for the formal IT workers.*

NEOLIBERAL CONTROL OVER THE IT WOMEN

Societies differ from each other greatly in terms of how people, especially women, come into social relationships with each other during the everyday production of the necessities of life-sustaining entities (Dalla Costa &

James, 1975). Based on the civilisational characteristics of a particular society or country, women come into diverse kinds of relationships with the space around them. However, regardless of the social structure that women find themselves in, the importance of community or structures of social solidarity cannot be discounted for women workers. Structures of social solidarities can have wide-ranging effects on human beings, especially for women because the exploitation of women takes place as a social category.

An effective solidarity structure, brought into existence during and through these interactions, can initiate processes of liberatory social psychology among the women, but that can only be done if the women have sufficient time on their hands to form the community, which effectively means disrupting the gendered paradigm of reproductive labour. The greatest strength of contemporary capitalism has been its ability to manipulate the concept of 'necessary' labour time and the transformation of leisure-time into a commodity with profit making abilities (Shippen, 2014). A significant part of the process is achieved through the implementation of restrictions put on social interactions, either directly or indirectly. A society that restricts social interactions among women by manipulating their *temporal realities* and restricts the creation of independent spaces that suit their demands and needs. Such restrictions affect the social status and psychological well-being of women, more so in a society that is heavily reliant upon the extraction of relative surplus value. The disproportionate and gendered distribution of reproductive labour becomes a crucial aspect of social dynamics, because it helps in increasing the amount of free labour available in the society for usage by men and powerful women alike. The routinisation of the everyday life is an essential aspect of the entire process of extraction of relative surplus value because it helps to construct the basis of a model of invisible oppression under advanced capitalism, by shrouding oppression under the rubric of 'routine everyday life' (Marcuse, 1964/2002). The routinisation or mechanisation of everyday life and systemic social structures results in the colonisation of time (Shippen, 2014) and exterminates the human social autonomy and spontaneity, which is an intrinsic requirement for liberation (Lefebvre, 1991; Tronti, 2019).

One's autonomous existence as a subjective human being becomes important in situations where social practices are alienated from their human roots and converted into sources of profit accumulation, and because it argues about discarding the negativity imposed by the routinisation of everyday life and embraces the positive potential within individuals and the class as a whole. The generation of the positive autonomous potential of human beings, especially if they come from marginalised communities, becomes critical because of the kind of employment avenues that the IT sector provides them with. Such modes of employment conform to the growing middle-class values in India that are constructed out of the western bourgeois value-systems, which do not align themselves to the traditional communitarian principles of India that are often based on the ideas of care and community (Chakrabarti, 2010).

In doing so, neoliberalism results in the complete erosion of individual freedom. The ways in which the IT space functions is that it creates the conditions through which models of community formation become the foundations of further exclusion in the society as is witnessed in most urban centres of India especially within the gated communities (Kamath & Vijayabaskar, 2009). Through the usage of various kinds of informal workers, the gated communities that the IT workers inhabit make the IT workers analyse the society through a veil, one that makes them further alienated from the actually existing material reality—a point that was put forward by Kosík (1976). By creating such segregations in the society, the neoliberal social reality ensures the generation of a compliant workforce, one which not only provides it with economic benefits but also social support—and Muslims, Dalits, and women are an important part of this social restructuring. They have remained an important part of the neoliberal project because they come to represent the most compliant and subservient subjects under neoliberalism. The communities or solidarity networks that most women form outside their workplaces often are composed of individuals who remain within the ideological restrictions imposed by the same social reality that they themselves are a part of.

Control over women ensures a control over the process of social reproduction that ensures a disciplinarian control over the working populace that ensures the continued reproduction of neoliberal capitalism and patriarchy. The reproduction of capitalism through patriarchy produces contradictory class locations for women workers by providing them with certain degrees of freedom enabling vertical social mobility but also dictating the terms of how they use their newfound freedom by controlling the social space around them. There is a constant social disciplining that determines the processes through which the women workers frame their subjective and objective experiences. The liberation of women cannot be seen as a complementary result of economic liberation, as was the case with the Engelsian vision, but rather it has to be analysed as an essential component of women's liberation (Dunayevskaya, 1970; Vogel, 1996). The alienated empowerment that women in the IT sector enjoy reflects the processes through which capitalism inflicts a technological rationality upon the society capturing the consciousness of the individuals therein (Marcuse, 1955, 1964). Most of these processes are mediated through the construction of processes within which despite being economically empowered, women continue to remain subverted by structures that refuse to treat them as visible beings with autonomy and self-subjectivity.

Women serve a very important purpose for the sector as a whole. For the IT sector, whose basic premise is often based upon the fetish of productivity, it is necessary that the worker has a 'caring', compliant and 'loving' family and household, which can not only replenish the worker but can also, if the need arises, dive into the market as a reserve army of labour (Kabeer, 2000) to enable further accumulation of profits as can be witnessed in the case of women's participation in the digital small-scale commercial ecosystems and platform labour structures. The idea of an ideal womanhood plays an important role in this regard. The construction of womanhood in India is based on traditional patriarchal values which when fused with neoliberal value structures constitutes a social order enabling a wilful compliance towards structures of authority, which is often analysed by the IT workers as being the prime movers behind their potential vertical social mobility. Such uncritical and wilful compliance of the middle classes towards structures of bio-political control and domination are often mediated through management structures which are formed to complement the broader socio-political and cultural structures that capitalism produces.

REFERENCES

Arruzza, C. (2017). From Social Reproduction Feminism to the Women's Strike. In T. Bhattacharya (Ed.), *Social Reproduction Theory*. London: Pluto Press.

Bell, D. (1976). *The Coming of the Post-Industrial Society*. Basic Books.

Benczes, I., Kollai, I., Mach, Z., & Vigvari, G. (2020). Populist Rebellion Against Modernity in 21st Century Eastern Europe: Neo-Traditionalism and Neo-Feudalism. In J. Kubik & R. Mole (Eds.), *POPREBEL Working Paper Series*.

Benjamin, W. (2002). *The Arcades Project*. Harvard University Press.

Bhattacharya, T. (2017). Introduction. In T. Bhattacharya (Ed.), *Social Reproduction Theory*. Pluto Press.

Bumiller, E. (1991). *May You Be the Mother of a Hundred Sons: A Journey Among the Women of India*. Penguin India.

Campbell, H., & Bell, M. M. (2000). The Question of Rural Masculinities. *Rural Sociology, 65*, 532–546.

Chakrabarti, D. (2010). D. P. Mukherji and the Middle Class in India. *Sociological Bulletin, 59*(2), 235–255.

Coomaraswamy, R. (2005). Identity Within: Cultural Relativism, Minority Rights and the Empowerment of Women. In I. Jaising (Ed.), *Men's Laws, Women's Lives: A Constitutional Perspective on Religion, Common Law and Culture in South Asia*. New Delhi.

Dalla Costa, M., & James, S. (1975). *The Power of Women and the Subversion of the Community*. Falling Wall Press.

Desai, A. R. (1984). *India's Path of Development: A Marxist Approach*. Sangam Books.

Dube, S. C. (1990). *Indian Society*. National Book Trust.

Dunayevskaya, R. (1970/2015). The WLM as Reason and Revolutionary Force. In *Women's Liberation and the Dialectics of Revolution: Reaching for the Future*. Aakar.

Dunayevskaya, R. (1973/1982). *Philosophy and Revolution: From Hegel to Sartre, and from Marx to Mao*. Humanities Press.

Engels, F. (1884/1941). *The Origin of the Family, Private Property and the State*. Lawrence and Wishart Limited.

Farahani, L. M. (2016). The Value of the Sense of Community and Neighbouring. *Housing Theory and Society, 33*(3), 357–376.

Fraser, N. (1994). After the Family Wage: Gender Equity and the Welfare State. *Political Theory, 22*(4), 591–618.

Fraser, N. (2014). Behind Marx's Hidden Abode. *New Left Review, 86*, 55–72.

Fraser, N. (2016). Contradictions of Capital and Care. *New Left Review, 100*, 99–117.

Fraser, N., Bhattacharya, T., & Arruzza, C. (2019). *Feminism for the 99%*. Verso.

Fromm, E. (1961/2004). Marx's Concept of Man, Continuum.

Gardiner, M. (2000). *Critique of Everyday Life*. Routledge.

Giddens, A. (1991). *Modernity and Self-Identity*. Polity.

Giroux, H. A. (2005). The Terror of Neoliberalism: Rethinking the Significance of Cultural Politics. *College Literature, 32*(1), 1–19.

Godelier, M. (1967). System, Structure and Contradiction in "Capital" (Trans. B. Brewsters). In R. Miliband & J. Seville (Eds.), *Socialist Register: Volume 4*. Merlin Press.

Gorz, A. (1987). *Farewell to the Working Class*. Pluto Books.

Hardt, M., & Negri, A. (1994). *Labor of Dionysus: A Critique of the State-Form*. University of Minnesota Press.

Hardt, M., & Negri, A. (2000). *Empire*. Harvard University Press.

Hartmann, H. (1981). The Family as the Locus of Gender, Class and Political Struggle: The Example of Housework. *Signs, 6*(3), 336–394.

Harvey, D. (2005). *A Brief History of Neoliberalism*. Oxford University Press.

Harvey, D. (2010). *The Enigma of Capital: And the Crises of Capitalism*. Profile Books.

Hillery, G. A. (1955). Definitions of Community: Areas of Agreement. *Rural Sociology, 20*, 111–123.

Holland, S., Burgess, S., Grogan-Kaylor, A., & Delva, J. (2011). Understanding Neighbourhoods, Communities and Environments: New Approaches for Social Work Research. *The British Journal of Social Work, 41*(4), 689–707.

Huws, U. (2014). *Labor in the Global Digital Economy: The Cybertariat Comes of Age*. Monthly Review Press.

Kabeer, N. (2000). *The Power to Choose: Bangladeshi Women and Labour Market Decisions in London and Dhaka*. Verso.

Kalpagam, U. (1994). *Labour and Gender: Survival in Urban India*. SAGE.

Kamath, L., & Vijayabaskar, M. (2009). Limits and Possibilities of Middle-Class Associations as Urban Collective Actors. *Economic and Political Weekly, 44*(26/27), 368–376.

Kempers, M. (2001). *Community Matters*. Rowman and Littlefield.

Kern, L. (2020). *Feminist City*. Verso.

Kletzer, L. (1998). Job Displacement. *Journal of Economic Perspectives, 12*, 115–136.

Kosík, K. (1976). *Dialectics of the Concrete: A Study on Problems of Man and World*. Routledge.

Kusenbach, M. (2006). Patterns of Neighboring: Practicing Community in the Parochial Realms. *Symbolic Interaction, 29*(3), 279–306.

Lefebvre, H. (1991). *The Production of Space*. Basil Blackwell.

Lefebvre, H. (2014). *Critique of Everyday Life*. Verso.

Lefebvre, H. (2016). *Metaphilosophy*. Verso.

Lyon, L., & Driskell, R. (2011). *The Community in Urban Society*. Waveland Press.

Marcuse, H. (1955/1986). *Reason and Revolution*. Routledge, Kegan and Paul.

Marcuse, H. (1964/2002). *One Dimensional Man*. Routledge.

Martineau, J. (2015). *Time, Capitalism and Alienation: A Socio-Historical Inquiry Into the Making of Modern Time*. Brill.

Marx, K. (1844/1975). Economic and Philosophical Manuscripts of 1844. In *Marx Engels Collected Works: Volume 3*. Lawrence and Wishart.

Marx, K. (1976). *Capital: Volume 1*. Penguin.

Massey, D. (1994). *Space, Place and Gender*. University of Minnesota Press.

Narayan, D. (2018). *Chup: Breaking the Silence About India's Women*. Juggernaut.

Navarro, V. (2007). Neoliberalism as a Class Ideology; or, the Political Causes of the Growth of Inequalities. *International Journal of Health Services, 37*(1), 47–62.

Negri, A. (1989). *The Politics of Subversion*. Polity.

Negri, A. (2003). *Time for Revolution*. Bloomsbury Academic.

Nethercote, M., & Horne, R. (2016). Ordinary Vertical Urbanisms: City Apartments and the Everyday Geographies of High-rise Families. *Environment and Planning A, 48*(8), 1581–1598.

Panda, S., & Rath, S. K. (2017). Modelling the Relationship Between Information Technology Infrastructure and Organizational Agility. *Global Business Review, 19*(8), 424–438.

Pannekoek, A. (1912/2018). *Marxism and Darwinism*. Trieste Publishing.

Patnaik, P. (2017). Caste, Community and Belonging: The Indian Case. *Social Scientist, 45*(1/2), 73–79.

Postone, M. (1993). *Time, Labour, and Social Domination: A Reinterpretation of Marx's Social Theory*. Cambridge University Press.

Pradhan, R. K., & Hati, L. (2019). The Measurement of Employee Well-being: Development and Validation of a Scale. *Global Business Review*. https://doi.org/10.1177/0972150919859101

Shantz, A., Alfes, K., Bailey, C., & Soane, E. (2015). Drivers and Outcomes of Work Alienation: Reviving a Concept. *Journal of Management Inquiry, 24*(4), 382–393.

Shippen, N. M. (2014). *Decolonising Time*. Palgrave.

Stein, S. (2019). *Capital City*. Verso.

Tronti, M. (1962). *Factory and Society*. Operaismo in English. https://operaismoinenglish.wordpress.com/2013/06/13/factory-and-society/

Tronti, M. (2019). *Workers and Capital*. Verso.

Vogel, L. (1983/2013). *Marxism and the Oppression of Women: Towards a Unitary Theory*. Brill.

Vogel, L. (1996). Engels's Origin: Legacy, Burden and Vision. In C. J. Arthur (Ed.), *Engels Today*. Palgrave Macmillan.

Wellman, B. (2001). Physical Place and Cyberplace: The Rise of Personalised Networking. *International Journal of Urban and Regional Research, 25*(2), 227–252.

Wellman, B. (2005). Community: From Neighbourhood to Network. *Communications of the ACM, 48*(10), 53–55.

CHAPTER 4

The Social Construction of Managerial Solutions to Political Problems

INTRODUCTION: PRODUCTIVITY ENHANCEMENT MEASURES AND THE WORKERS

The question of productivity is a central concern for contemporary capitalism. For any corporation or institution to function, the productivity of its employees forms the most important part. Productivity, on the other hand, under contemporary forms of capitalism has evolved from being managed purely by abject domination but has rather become something that is often ensured through modes of biopolitical control. Contemporary capitalism has come to realise that the question of well-being and mental health is a central concern for the organisation of work in the twenty-first century (Meister, 2021). Debjani Ghosh, the president of NASSCOM, says:

> In the tech sector, the most VALUABLE assets are its PEOPLE. Unlike physical assets, humans have feelings and we all have our good days and the not-so-good ones too. The idea of holistic employee wellness (physical & mental) has been a focus area for the industry for many years and companies have put in place definitive structures to roll out employee engagement initiatives and also measure their impact.[1]

---

[1] The quote is available at the official NASSCOM employee wellness webpage: https://nasscom.in/employee-wellness/ [Accessed 02.12.2023].

© The Author(s), under exclusive license to Springer Nature Switzerland AG 2024
S. Deb Roy, *The Rise of the Information Technology Society in India*, Dynamics of Virtual Work,
https://doi.org/10.1007/978-3-031-58128-1_4

The well-being of employees is an important factor having grave relevance across organisations—both the publicly funded ones and the privately funded ones. It is because both of them share certain commonalities between them, one of which is the organisation of work and the drive for profits and revenue—fundamental characters associated with any corporation regardless of the nature of its funding under neoliberalism (Rowlinson, 1997). Be it a university or a multinational trading company, workers are the most fundamental components of the successful organisation of any workplace. That being said, despite the importance that they possess, the well-being of the workers has come under serious crisis under contemporary capitalism. With a constantly expanding range of operations, well-being is intimately associated with the mental and physical health-related costs incurred by the organisations (Grawitch et al., 2006) and the productivity and performance of the employees (Wright, 2010), both of which are important factors in the growth and sustenance of the organisations.

Within organisations, human resource practices play the role of coded messages which communicate the functioning philosophy of any organisation to the employees (Bowen & Ostroff, 2004). These practices make the employees aware of the organisation's core principles, methods of application, their policies, and the basic underlying philosophy of the organisation. The relationship between the employers and the employed forms the backbone of a successful corporation and is a critical aspect of organisational sustenance. The expertise that skilled employees possess and use, in the contemporary society, is an important resource for the organisations, which makes the research on human resource management in organisations extremely important—both for the employers and for the employees (Scarbrough, 1996). The problem however is that such research is usually aimed at solving the problems that organisations face, and not the employees (Watson, 1977). Employees in this milieu receive relatively lesser importance, and even when they do, their interests are often seen to be completely aligned with their employers.

Organisations usually analyse theories and practices by the supposed profits that these practices and theories would reap in if applied within their organisational framework. Such a drive towards profitability and higher revenue becomes highly exploitative for the workers. Any service sector industry is highly demanding and extremely consuming in nature, not only for the employees but also for the employing organisations (Pradhan & Hati, 2019). The well-being of employees becomes a critical factor in the growth of any organisation, especially in the service sector, especially in the privately funded service sector. Under such circumstances, organisations often resort to tactics such as providing material resources to their employees to increase the well-being quotient of their employees. These include distribution of commodities such as bags and jackets to their employees, funding their vacations, and so forth. However, whether such material benefits can enable the construction of a holistic employee well-being strategy remains to be seen. Employee well-being has become a complicated domain with the ushering in of neoliberal reforms globally. The market individualism, that neoliberalism advocates in favour of, seeks to establish the rules of the market as a natural order in the society whereby every member of an organisation was sought to have a mutual benefit in the growth of the organisation (Delbridge & Keenoy, 2010). Almost all the organisations, both globally and in India, have had to adopt policies which are in synchronisation with the neoliberal economic model of development, which has resulted in a further popularisation of mainstream models of well-being strategies.

This chapter argues that well-being strategies in the IT sector have to address the concerns raised by critically analysing the mainstream practices with regard to human resource management in specific organisations which include giving credibility to the marginalised voices both within organisational practice and within theory (Delbridge & Keenoy, 2010, p. 807). The chapter brings forward the relevance of relating human resource management practices to the broader social structure and dynamics caused by socio-political events and processes. The chapter reiterates the idea that there is a difference between how employees and managers perceive of and respond to existent human resource management policies and practices (Wang et al., 2020). A critical part of such strategies involves the processes through which adequate amount of consideration can be given to the social positions from which well-being strategies are devised and popularised (Adler et al., 2007), and the social positions of those that they are designed to affect and impact. The present chapter takes these issues into account and tries to provide a comprehensive account of the limitations of the various well-being strategies adopted by the IT sector. It has three sections which discuss various aspects of the well-being strategies employed within the IT sector, and the implications of the same for the workers therein, with a particular focus on workers coming from marginalised sections of the populace. It provides an outline of the basic causality behind the necessity of developing employee-oriented well-being practices.

WELL-BEING: A CONTESTED TERRAIN

Well-being becomes an important part of the sustenance of the organisation itself because it is related to the productivity of the employees and as such becomes directly related to the *profitable* sustenance of the organisation itself, especially within neoliberal economic systems. Human resource management practices do affect not only the performance of individual employees but also the organisations themselves (Van de Voorde et al., 2012). Contemporary employees are increasingly becoming aware of the benefits that an employee-centred well-being structure within their organisations can provide to them as can be inferred from the statements provided below:

> My HR manager is important, as he forms the basic link between the company and myself, but the HR is often the person who is the most problematic person in the office because he has to manage the workers there. The problem is that all these HR people they do not see themselves as being parts of the employees, but rather as being one of the bosses. (Male IT Worker, Bengaluru)

> What is the point of an HR if he or she cannot provide us with an employee-centred strategy and resources for ensuring our well-being. Some of the things that the company wants us to do as part of its well-being strategy is downright irritating. Sometimes it is okay, and some people might even enjoy it, but for me it is a problem. They want us to come to the office on Sundays as well for gelling sessions. (Muslim IT Worker, Gurgaon)

The importance of an employee focused well-being strategy possesses has been highlighted by scholars such as Watson (1977, 1986), Scott (1994) and Legge (1978, 1995). However, employee-centred well-being practices are difficult to be conceptualised within the narrow boundaries of mainstream management studies which often resorts to unitarist, and homogenously deduced well-being practices assuming that employees and employers are equal stakeholders in the growth of an organisation and as such share mutual interests (Watson, 1977, 1986, 2010; Delbridge & Keenoy, 2010). The previous chapters, especially Chap. 2, has shown in detail the insecurities that Dalit and Muslim workers have begun to face following the rise of the far-right in the country. Alongside Chap. 2, Chap. 3 has put forward the conditions faced by the women workers of the IT sector, especially focused on the situations that they face as women and as citizens in the society. The relationship between these two faces of exploitation cannot be analysed through data-driven well-being interpretation mechanisms that most IT firms have come to develop. The reliance on data is a typical nature of the kind of society that advanced stages of capitalism develop which remains contingent upon processes of quantification producing modes of being that can be expressed as mathematical structures (Marcuse, 1964/2002).

Well-being refers to a state of overall quality of an employee's experience and functioning at work (Warr, 1987; Grant et al., 2007). However, as it can be noticed, the definition of well-being presented here is a vague one that leaves out a significant amount of very specific issues that certain employees might come to face because of their social positioning or because of the ways in which their social status is analysed or engaged with by the management or other workers. Based on the social positions that a worker comes from, the needs and demands of a particular worker from the workplace vary greatly, which in turn also creates variations with regard to their responses towards the well-being strategies in their organisations. The definition of well-being in human resource management theory and practice ranges from vulgar materialistic ones focused on financial stability, and the ability to possess material goods as a sufficient marker of well-being to psychological ones emphasising social well-being. In recent times, there has been a considerable growth in data-driven quantitative methods in analysing the well-being of workers in various IT firms. However, the critical commonality between most of them has been the assumption of a continuum between the employer and the employee, focusing on the idea that a co-operative partnership between the workers, the management, and the state or the government is a mutually rewarding one (Kochan & Osterman, 1994). The creation of such a perception of mutual gains is however difficult to be communicated subjectively, which makes objective and quantifiable values more attractive forms of communication. Such a characteristic of contemporary human resource management whereby every aspect of human existence runs the risk of becoming a quantitative value to mainstream human resource management theorists and practitioners (Cheng & Hackett, 2019). These methods contribute to a gradual commodification of the workers and their well-being. In doing so, these practices tend to homogenise the workers in the IT sector and do not pay adequate attention to the various social contexts that exist in the sector:

82   S. DEB ROY

The HR practices are very problematic in the office. They mostly do not have any idea regarding the various different issues that we face as human beings. For example, take the example of *namaaz* offering times. It is widely known, everybody knows that, but they still do not devise any particular policy for the same. It is an essential part of my existence, but it finds no relevance to the organisation. (Muslim IT Worker, Hyderabad)

What will they do? They think that we can think and do like all others. They do not take into consideration that as Dalits we face numerous issues on an everyday basis that cannot be taken into consideration by regular HR people. Say for example the constant evocation of the fact that we are reserved candidates and that the private sector should be free from reservations. I went to a good government college on a reserved seat. Did I do something wrong? No. It is a mental pressure on us. (Dalit IT Worker, Bengaluru)

The problem is that we as woman cannot even voice our concerns to those put in place to hear us. Women face many issues in the IT sector, we are often paid less, put into job descriptions that we do not deserve or are not trained to work in. Then there are also certain restrictions on what we can or cannot do with freedom which the society puts on us. The strategies for well-being that they come up with, most of it at least, do not really apply to us. (Woman IT Worker, Chennai)

The well-being of employees is analysed through two mainstream perspectives: hedonic and eudaimonic approaches (Ryan & Deci, 2001). The hedonic approach mainly focuses on happiness along with the individual's own evaluation—both cognitively and affectively—of one's own social and individual life (Diener, 2000). The eudaimonic approach emphasises more complex factors such as human potential, individual growth, and its realisation (Jahoda, 1958; Ryff & Keyes, 1995). Unsurprisingly, the hedonic approaches are simpler to be implemented because they tend to restrict themselves to happiness and pleasure related factors, often measured in quantifiable approaches (Erdogan et al., 2012). Unsurprisingly, a significant number of technology firms employ hedonic principles not only because of their simplicity but also because of the technological rationality that gradually robs human beings of their spontaneity and humaneness (Marcuse, 1941).

The importance of the maximisation of pleasure or happiness and minimisation of pain that characterises hedonic methods of ensuring well-being (Feldman, 2004) does not question the mainstream alienating characteristic of happiness under capitalism that contributes to a gradual commodification of human existence. Under contemporary capitalism, the focus on happiness has become an important part of the productivity network that capitalism (Segal, 2017). Eudaimonic approaches, on the other hand, are relatively more complicated because they focus on individual growth of an employee which is also related to the social context (Ryff, 1989; Keyes, 1998). While such approaches seemingly provide better ways of analysing the well-being of the workers, it has to be taken into consideration that under capitalism, happiness also constitutes an important part of the alienating framework of existence. Contemporary capitalism, unlike the pure industrial mode of capitalism, functions through an all-encompassing mode of exploitation whereby emotional factors such as happiness and optimism have also become part of the capitalist complex of exploitation because of their role in productivity-enhancing processes (Negri, 2016; Illouz, 2007). The usage of emotions and consciousness of the workers by forces of capital to enhance the productivity of the workers coincides with the manipulation of the consciousness of the workers. The previous chapters have noted how technology firms manipulate the consciousness of their employees to suit their needs, providing them with a false consciousness through which they are able to generate a false sense of empowerment mediated through the illusion of their control over the dynamics of their own economic, personal, and social lives. If one goes by Erich Fromm (1961), then these conditions constitute the basis of an alienated sense of human existence among the workers.

There is an inversely proportional relationship between the meaningfulness of work and alienation. However, detailed studies into the concerns of the individual employees within the employee-employer relationship are extremely scarce (Shantz et al., 2014, p. 2350). The question of well-being becomes extremely critical in a situation like the present where the entire society has begun acting like a production unit taking within its fold, the entire human existence of the workers (Tronti, 1962; Negri, 1989). Thus, an effective strategy for ensuring well-being needs to encompass both the official workplaces and the non-workspaces that a worker inhabits including the most intimate spaces. The COVID-19 pandemic has been excruciatingly difficult for the IT workers, who have been living through numerous rapid mutations within their lives with little changes to the structural models of well-being within their organisations. With the fusion of the office and the home, the official workspace or the factory of the yesteryears has lost its special ascription within the society with no rigid segregation between them. With the massive digitalisation of

84 S. DEB ROY

the society and workplaces, with a significant amount of work being performed virtually, methods such as informal behavioural analysis and physical interactions—that formed the core of traditional well-being strategies—have ceased being the markers of an effective well-being strategy for most of the corporations as many IT workers inform.

Organisations employ multiple methods to keep their employees happy and resourceful. However, the critical point to be analysed here is the analysis of the emphasis on resourcefulness and happiness that most firms employ that in turn have frequently advocated in favour of bringing forward steps that homogenise all the workers, neglecting the subjective experiences of their employees (Diener, 1984, 2000). Such drives towards homogenisation are a characteristic feature of contemporary capitalism as these prepare the ground for a more open and favourable global structure of exploitation (Anderson, 2020). It is the homogenising drive of capital that makes hedonic approaches towards well-being, which tend to quantify, and simplify, the complicated and multi-dimensional relationship that an employee shares with the organisation so popular among IT forms. The relationship between the IT firms and the employee is one that is mediated through productivity—the more productive a worker is, the more valuable one is to the firm, and the more well-taken care of the worker will be. Human resource practices pertaining to well-being become an important part of the three-pronged relationship because these practices are usually the mode through which the firm establishes a socio-economic and cultural connection with the worker. Two IT workers spoke in detail about how their respective companies communicate with them through the kind of well-being policies that they devise:

> A company is not only a place or something that I work for. It might have been the case for public sector where people left the office at 5 PM but not for us. For us, the company is a part of our everyday lives. It is what we breathe in and breathe out. With work from home, this has only increased, Earlier there was issues with only the working hours, but now with work from home, the working day has increased beyond limits. The manager thinks he can call me at 12 at night, 7 in the morning—basically any time that he wishes to. The working day has increased beyond limits. The company wants to make us understand that we are all just slaves. (Male IT Worker, Bengaluru)

> The major issue is with the company's mode of communication. With these mechanical ways of letting us know what it thinks regarding us, the com-

4 THE SOCIAL CONSTRUCTION OF MANAGERIAL SOLUTIONS... 85

pany has rendered us completely helpless. It does not consider the household chores that we have to do neither does it consider the issues with motherhood and all that. All it cares about is the work that we do. A compassionate human-to-human communication would have been so much better than those emails telling us what we should or should not do regarding our mental health. (Woman IT Worker, Bengaluru)

From these statements, it can be identified that the relationship that a worker shares with a firm that one works in is not one that is determined purely in financial terms, but also one that is equally determined by the kind of attitudes that the firm possesses towards its employees—especially the workers coming from the marginalised sections of the population for whom the increase of productivity comes at a much greater cost than others.

Under contemporary capitalism, maintenance of productivity becomes a key concern for capital because that reflects the state of control over the society. The biopolitical control that contemporary capitalism desires to inflict upon the society ensures a constant subjugation of the potentially revolutionary subjectivity of the non-capitalist classes (Hardt & Negri, 2000)—a point that will be highlighted in Chap. 6. A financially well-to-do firm might prove to be financially rewarding but might not be as well-being oriented as other small firms, but small IT firms might prove to be better at negotiating with the social reality of the workers, especially if they come from marginalised communities:

The problem is that some of the big companies pay a lot of attention to well-being but the major issue that they see well-being from their own lens. I have to manage my own home, that is something that the company does not understand. It wants me to be on Zoom meetings with other employees or with new entrants for ice-breaking sessions but the major issue that I do not want to. It is too difficult for me to do all those things and manage my home at the same. Yes, it pays good, but it is just that. The society as a whole has become depressing and more demanding in nature. How can I work in peace knowing that I might be infected anytime, and that there is nobody to care for me and my family's health beside myself? (Woman IT Worker, Bengaluru)

My company is a good one. I was shocked to see that they had institutionalised a norm that it was compulsory to read current affairs and let other people know about what is going on in the world. It is actually a good practice. Being a Muslim, it gives me a good opportunity to bring up certain issues that I want to. The organization pays for my internet, but the maintenance costs like electricity and furniture, which come with working from home have to be borne by me personally. With a rising cost of living, I remain worried about those costs which would otherwise be borne by my organisation. (Muslim IT Worker, Kolkata)

Thus, as can be inferred from the statements made above, financial well-being often does not pave the way towards a more holistic approach towards workers' well-being, but rather only forms a part of it under contemporary capitalism. Economic measures often only affect individuals as workers but as Chaps. 2 and 3 have exhibited, the exploitation of workers coming from marginalised sections of the society often is focused on their identities as being individuals coming from a particular section of the populace, and not always by the amount of money that they earn.

Well-being strategies determine the kind of relationship that they share not only with their employers but also with the organisations or bodies that are often formed to represent them—including collectives focused on specific demands such as women's collectives, and most importantly, trade unions.[2] Most organisations believe that a focus on workers' well-being can offset the need of a union in the workplace. In fact, the entire theoretical trajectory of contemporary HR practices is focused on the decimation of the IR framework, which also indicate a shift from being a platform to ensure that workers' requirements are met to a framework to one that just effectively manages individuals. The drive towards HR from an IR perspective that dominated Indian industrial set-ups till the early 1990s implied a shift away from a conflict-oriented perception of the relationship between the employers and the employed (Saha, 2017). Some part of this transformation owed itself to the changes within the class nature of the employees that HR practitioners had to engage in. The growing influence of an apolitical middle class in these professions made it particularly difficult for trade unions to function within the sector which left a void that was duly filled in by the employers themselves, as has been further explained in Chaps. 6 and 7.

The organisation that an employee is a part of influences the social positioning and the dynamics of the social existence of the particular worker. Based on one's social class and social positioning, an employee might possess a different framework of evaluating their employment and

---

[2] Trade unions and the role that they can play or have been playing have been engaged with details in Chap. 7 and the Conclusion.

living conditions. The organisational understanding of a 'happy' and 'well off' employee can be significantly at odds with the employee's perception of happiness, satisfaction, and resourcefulness. Well-being to the employees, does not mean merely a greater financial stability, but rather means a holistic development of their selves. The previous chapters have engaged in detail with various kinds of social cleavages that function with the IT companies and the spaces that they develop, especially the social fault lines around Muslims, Dalits, and women. When firms employ hedonic methods to ensure well-being they frequently adopt a uniform well-being policy that works well in line with a particular section of the employees only, that is, the upper caste, middle class, cisgender heterosexual Hindu men.

> The HR practices usually in practices are synonymous with the majority of the society. So, we will have certain functions during Hindu festivals. Take for example, Holi. The festival of colours and all of that is fine, but it is a highly casteist festival where a lower caste woman was killed, and we celebrate that as a victory of good over evil. I am not going over whether it is justified or not, but do they even know the intricate details of the story that is behind the festival? I am a Dalit and I celebrate it; it is fine I understand that most of them are oblivious to the issue. But then why is there no celebration of Ambedkar's birth anniversary? That is the biggest festival for us, and we are a majority in the country. (Dalit IT Worker, Hyderabad)

Such approaches are prescriptive approaches towards human resource management practices focusing on the individual well-being of the employee neglecting the social dimensions of the employee's overall lived experience and conception of social reality that is based on political economy, industrial development, sexual division of labour, social inequality, and so forth (Watson, 1977, 2010). The devaluation of the lived experience of individuals results in firms adopting a de-humanised approach towards their social exploitation. Both approaches towards well-being focus more on talent management than actual human management basing their analysis and strategic actions upon the quantification of workers into productive units of exploitation. Most of these methods neglect the social and workplace reality as perceived by the employees themselves, which results in a complete subjugation of their subjective and multi-dimensional selves, which are critical to developing effective well-being strategies for them. It encapsulates processes of both the physical and psychological well-being of the employees (Warr, 1999; Juniper et al., 2011). Employees, especially in the contemporary society, remain highly susceptible to emotional and mental stress. And, hence their well-being depends to a large extent on their psychological well-being, which takes into cognisance the overall social personality of the employee including the employee's actions and state of mind in the workspace, as well as outside the workspace (Zheng et al., 2015). Organisations often face the dilemma caused by the relationship between and the objective determinants of a happy life, and the subjective factors related to a fulfilling human existence. Contemporary organisations often attempt to solve the conundrum by providing material benefits to their employees. While it cannot be debated that such benefits do help the employees and make them happy about their jobs, it is also simultaneously true that such material benefits make the organisations a perennial entity in the lives of their employees. The concept of a 'break' in the professional lives of the employees becomes almost non-existent in these scenarios because they remain connected to their organisations at a psychological level.

> My company gives me a jacket, and it has mandated that I wear it at all times when inside the campus. The jacket as a resource might help me by providing warmth during winters—it does actually—but at the same time, the jacket also becomes a means through which I wear the organisation quite literally. So, if there is an X company which is a rival, so the employee of X company also becomes my rival because my wearing of the jacket signifies that I am one with the company. The allotment of such provisions to employees, effectively, becomes a means through which the organisation becomes a part of the employees' life even outside the workspace. (Male IT Worker, Bengaluru)

> Financial aspect is important, nobody I think can deny that, but that is not all. There is something called work-life balance, there is also something called management of the human potential. If after working for eight hours a day, I cannot even spare half an hour for my own self, then that entire thing about payment goes flat and worthless because I cannot afford to be less productive. I am too tired by the time I finish work that I cannot do anything else. I straightway go to sleep. (Male IT Worker, Pune)

The narratives prove that for most of the employees, mere fulfilment of material pursuits does not contribute to an effective well-being strategy, because the social status that they enjoy is not affected only by their material wealth but also because of the communities or sections of the populace that they come from. In Chaps. 2 and 3, the conditions faced by workers who come from the marginalised communities had been analysed. It has been exhibited that workers from marginalised sections of the populace face exploitation and processes of exclusion not only within the workplace but also multiple modes of exploitation across the broader society. Even if the struggle between the controller and those being controlled is an inherent struggle of all industrial set-ups (Edwards, 1986; Blyton & Turnbull, 1994), the struggle does not manifest in the same way for all the workers. Employees are not static entities, and as such possess highly dynamic subjective interests, prominently embedded within the contours of their social existence (Hardt & Negri, 2000). These subjective interests provide meaning and a sense of purpose to the lives of the employees, which often get disrupted by the organisational policies (Legge, 1978). Critically analysing human resource management practices is an important aspect of management—both theoretically and practically. As Tony Watson states:

> It is particularly necessary to help counter the tendencies by human resource management academics to act, in effect, as 'best practice' advisors and legitimacy-givers to corporate interests (suggesting to employers which employment management practices to adopt in order to increase corporate 'competitive advantage', for example). (Watson, 2010, p. 915)

Such profit-seeking modes of well-being strategies can only be countered through a more sociological and social-justice oriented approach towards well-being that takes into cognisance the workers' perspective. Understanding the employees' perspective means taking note of the social space within which the employees find themselves in which can often be starkly contrasting in character (Mitter & Sen, 2000). The social and personal selves of individual workers are related to the broader social changes that determine the contemporary nature of human society. The state of human resources in any society depends on the social changes that the employees face in their everyday lives, which again is intimately affected by the changes occurring within the social space that the employee perceives, conceives, and lives through. In India, because of the kind of social spaces that the Indian society has come to generate, a homogenous strategy for ensuring well-being through a vulgar materialistic lens is bound to fail because the exploitative social relations in India are often outside the sphere of economic and material issues.

Strategies for Well-Being: Questioning Normality

Most technology firms, over time, have realised the centrality that workers occupy within their strive for profitability and sustenance. They have realised the immense importance that human beings carry as *human capital* (Blyton & Turnbull, 1994)—a term that has come to be equated with rising productivity in recent times.[3] The strive for a rising productivity has often been equated with a constant manipulation of the psychological conditioning of the workers whereby the workers have often been entrapped into a mode that conforms to the dominant mode of social structuring, as is usual under a society dominated by technocratic rationality that aids the construction of de-humanised and atomised subjects (Marcuse, 1941). The well-being industry has been criticised by many scholars because of its insistence towards the generation of a consciousness that enables a further commodification of the society. Critical to how contemporary forms of capitalism work is its usage of the subjective experiences of human beings to increase its profitability and further improve its strategies of accumulation. Mainstream management of personnel, which forms an important part of this corpus, realistically remains concerned with cost management, more than it remains concerned about human management. Watson defined *Mainstream Personnel Management* in the following words:

> Personnel Management is concerned with assisting those who run work organisations to meet their purposes through the obtaining of the work efforts of human beings, the exploitation of those efforts and the dispensing with of those efforts when they are no longer required. Concern may be shown with human welfare, justice or satisfactions but only insofar as this is necessary for controlling interests to be met and then, always at least cost. (Watson, 1986, p. 176)

The focus on the least-cost factor creates the conditions under which the complete subsumption of the worker within the capitalist structure in place takes place. With a social structure that is designed to marginalise the already marginalised, an approach towards ensuring well-being that is

---

[3] The World Bank maintains a Human Capital Index which can be found at: https://thedocs.worldbank.org/en/doc/db7f895796c12c71469bbc98330a0541-0140022023/original/Factsheet-HCP-Nov-2023.pdf [Accessed 02.12.2023].

prepared from the perspective of capital often assumes a complete homogeneity between the needs of the employee and those of the employer. In reality, however, such assumptions are based on flimsy grounds because they do not consider the fundamental contradictions between labour and capital. Hedonic approaches of well-being, which tend to label organisations as 'good' or 'bad' depending on the allocation of material benefits to their employees, thus remain restricted to unitarist frameworks whereby only the objective perspective reigns supreme. The dominant practice of human resource management has been to theorise the issues in a manner that often takes that the interests of the employee and the employer are aligned (Hannon, 2010). However, this one-dimensional perspective, fails to take into cognisance the inherent struggle between the two, which is a characteristic feature of all industrial relations. As Blyton and Turnbull argue:

> [W]ithin organisations a common interest between management and workforce cannot be assumed, willed, or 'managed' into existence. On the contrary, the nature of employment relations, and the basic relationship between profits and wages, authority, and compliance, creates a persistent (albeit often latent) tension between employers and employed, management and workforce. (Blyton & Turnbull, 1994, p. 4)

Within contemporary corporations however, the management uses various mechanism to theoretically obliterate these differences to the common workers, including steps such as consistent communication, mechanisms to increase employee-confidence, and allocating responsibilities that align with the personal interests of the employees (Tjan, 2009). The question of well-being has become extremely complicated with the coming of COVID-19. The emergence of COVID-19 caused a significant number of the IT offices to being shut down. However, the physical closure of offices did not deter the firms from making the workers work, *often for longer hours* as the first chapter has shown. With Work from Home becoming a widespread alternative mode of operations for organisations, newer issues pertaining to well-being have arisen. NASSCOM states:

> India Inc went into shutdown, along with the rest of the nation in March. [M]ajority of India's IT companies [continued] to work remotely. This [had], no doubt, helped keep infections in check. But it … spurred a series of unintended consequences. Despite restrictions on working in an office,

there are other ways to contract the virus. The levels of stress are exacerbated in India's workforce as they juggle multiple responsibilities, and steer clear of the virus in every imaginable way.[4]

This statement was made sometime during 2021, but the effects of the pandemic have continued to linger on in the lives of the IT workers. Organisations attempt to keep their employees happy by providing them with some extra funding through which they can carry on their professional activities outside the offices smoothly. These include providing funds for their computers, their entire work from home set-up, and so forth. Making and then subsequently keeping the employees happy under these circumstances can help the organisations in retaining them even when the situation becomes relatively normalised in comparison to rapid industrial disruptions caused by COVID-19. Happiness, and its maximisation, to most organisations, becomes a critical factor in employee retention and salary negotiations, especially in situations like the one caused by COVID-19. Under the contemporary social system, the very existence of non-workspace places is under jeopardy, and as a result the well-being of employees also has to go beyond the workspaces. Hedonic approaches do help in those, but only in a limited manner, because they do not approach happiness as a subjective element of human life but convert it to a quantifiable value or a tangible commodity (Segal, 2017).

The WFH process that was rendered mainstream due to COVID-19 has explicitly converted the intimate spaces and private lives of the IT workers into a highly efficient component of the production unit. The maintenance of employee productivity had become a critical question for many of the tech firms. The various steps that many companies had been taking to ensure the well-being of their workers often involved widespread usage of surveillance technology such as smart watches and beacons (Nagar, 2018, p. 3). Most of these tactics had been increased during the pandemic when the usage of everyday technological artefacts increased profusely within the domestic spaces of the IT workers. While official literature cites many of these procedures as being ensuring a continued well-being, the reality of the procedures as experienced by the employees themselves remains questionable, as the following statements reveal:

---

[4] The quote is available at the official NASSCOM employee wellness webpage: https://nasscom.in/employee-wellness/ [Accessed 02.12.2023].

> I am not very comfortable with the organisation knowing about the content of my interactions with my colleagues or my team, which are at times very personal in nature. At the same time, the problem now is that the manager thinks he can call me at midnight even though my shift ends in the evening because he can get the data regarding my whereabouts at any time. I have no issues with being told what to do but I don't like being under constant surveillance. The manager and the company do not understand the importance of communication within the work process. (Male IT Worker, Bengaluru)

> There are two aspects of any job. The first point is the technical aspect and the second is the human aspect. When one speaks of HR policies, it is important to understand that the HR has also become redundant in most offices now, at least in Kolkata. Today, most of these jobs are handled by the technical manager—whose first responsibility to handle the technical aspect of things. The technical manager cannot handle the humanitarian aspect of an employee's life because he or she is not trained to do so. The HR has been rendered powerless and that is affecting many employees as we cannot talk freely with technical managers. (Male IT Worker, Kolkata)

Such innovations have rendered mainstream the surveillance of everyday lives leading to the establishment of what Zuboff (2019) calls surveillance capitalism. Surveillance capitalism is, as Zuboff (2019) says, parasitic in nature. It enables the usage of digital connections to further the commercial profit: 'It revives Karl Marx's old image of capitalism as a vampire that feeds on human labour, but with an unexpected turn. Instead of labour, surveillance capitalism feeds on every aspect of every human's experience' (Zuboff, 2019, 'Home or Exile in the Digital Future'). Such modes of ensuring well-being assume a continuity between individual well-being and improvement of the work environment—an approach typical of mainstream well-being practices (Biggio & Cortese, 2013). Such attempts try to increase job-satisfaction in ways that do not cater to the employees' well-being but only alters the work environment of the employee—which often does not result in any direct change in levels of job satisfaction of the individual employee. One issue that comes out prominently in these narratives is the continued suppression of the workers' ability to voice their concerns to appropriate authority. The inability to voice concerns constitutes a critical part of becoming alienated from one's work, which has a negative impact on one's overall productivity (Shantz et al., 2014, 2015). Because of the inability to voice their issues and concerns, there has occurred a loss of control and 'ownership' over one's own labouring process—a crucial part of alienation (Marx, 1844/1975)—affecting multiple dimensions of organisational and employee relationship (Shantz et al., 2014, 2015). The loss of control indicates an erosion of the centrality of workers within a relationship of conflict that exists between the employers and those employed (Witheford, 1994). While the loss of control makes it difficult for an employee-centred human resource management practice to come, it is a paradoxical position because it is the loss of control that also requires the intervention of an employee-centred well-being policy. The growing alienation that usually results from such processes requisites a policy that understands the inherently conflicting nature of the employee-employer relationship and intervenes into processes which direct the functional operation of the organisations taking the conflicting nature of the relationship into account (Edwards, 1986, 2005).

The well-being of employees is a holistic matter that encompasses diverse aspects of human potential and subjectivity, including both the mental and physical aspects of a worker's life (Thanem & Elraz, 2022). Contemporary modes of ensuring well-being, instead of being a method of ensuring well-being of the workers, have enabled the organisations to enhance the productivity of the workers—one which has been consistently used during the COVID-19 pandemic. The realisation of human potential has suffered consistently because its realisation has been seen as a secondary objective to most mainstream human resource managers. The marginalisation of human potential leads to workers suffering through a state of extreme deprivation, especially in the services sector, which is particularly *cruel* on most of the employees. An IT job often entails long hours, graveyard shifts, and high-performance-oriented working hours—most of which contribute to lower levels of physical well-being, increased risks to health ailments, and higher levels of stress and anxiety (Ferri et al., 2016; Dun et al., 2020; Cannizzaro et al., 2020; Berge et al., 2023; Lingas, 2023). However, as Beck (1992) had noted long ago, such risks under contemporary forms of capitalism, are always unevenly distributed in the society, and the IT sector is no different.

One-dimensional approach towards well-being, fails to acknowledge the gradual evolution of the workers and the relation between existent social dynamics and well-being. The employees today, apart from their objective interests, also have their own distinctive subjective interests, prominently embedded within the conditions of their social and psychological existence, producing new forms of subjectivity everyday through their social and individual activities (Hardt & Negri, 2000). Employees today are possessors of multifaceted personalities, one which has become one of the major characteristics of the contemporary workforce. The multi-dimensional nature of their personalities makes them an extremely diverse workforce, where each and every part of their social existence—along with the interactions that they have—is determined by the specific sets of needs and desires that they come to possess, both as human beings and as workers. These needs and desires differ based on the way the particular employee's own reflexive understanding of the society, in addition to one's employment conditions. The reflections about the society that Dalits, Muslims, women, and workers from other marginalised sections possess are often much more robust and critical in nature than a worker conforming to the normalised imagery of an IT worker in India.

Eudaimonic approaches can become helpful in this aspect because they can help human resource management practices to take these social contexts into consideration and can help practitioners move beyond prescriptive and normative models of well-being developing a more critical and nuanced understanding of human behaviour, needs, and their own individual ways of analysing and experiencing the society. Such an understanding becomes critical to new employees, who shift jobs more frequently than experienced ones, work on relatively low salaries, and are often new entrants within the overall IT urban space. Frequent changes within and of jobs has a distinct effect on the employees that contributes to a growing need of subjective well-being strategies because of the altering dynamics of living and employment conditions constantly (Wright & Nishi, 2013). It is often the case, as many new IT workers narrates across cities, that one begins to evaluate and analyse the well-being practices in their present job through the lived experiences of their previous jobs. This analysis can also be related to the perceptions that an employee might possess with regard to one's current job and organisation. Such perceptions, if one follows the already existing critical literature focused on capitalist development and social changes associated with such development, can be related to the social interpretations that an individual employee draws from one's lived experience. These lived experiences and the interpretations which follow cannot be homogenous in nature because there would be different and varied subjective interests and viewpoints of various employees. Different human resource practices in such situations can have differential outcomes because they might be perceived differently by employees (Beijer et al., 2019; Boon et al., 2019; Wang et al., 2020).

Different employees, contingent upon their social status and positioning, harbour different ways of understanding their well-being. These differences in the ways of conceptualisation their own well-being cannot be recorded or evaluated through surveys that are often distributed to the workers for the purpose of evaluating their 'state of existence' aimed at analysing the individual employee's ratings of self-satisfaction and happiness (Erdogan et al., 2012) contain quantitative markers to indicate the state of an employee's well-being and happiness. Quintessential to hedonic approaches, they usually attempt to speak in terms of quantifiable entities, such as happiness quotient, job satisfaction quotient, and so forth, tending towards devising standardised methods which can be applicable across a diverse range of organisations and the employees therein. Eudaimonic approaches can enable well-being strategies to focus on human psychology and social contexts (Ryff, 1989; Keyes, 1998) that contribute to the subjective development of workers considering the social factors that construct their human selves overcoming the vulgar objectivist nature of hedonic models. This becomes a crucial component of contemporary well-being strategy because the employees today do not exist as a homogenous whole but get shaped by diverse patterns of existence both within and outside their workspaces affecting the psychological experiences of the employees (Zheng et al., 2015). Within a capitalist society, that is functioning akin to a factory, well-being strategies instead of focusing on particular temporalities only, has to take the entire social existence of the workers into account. The technical composition of working-class lives that determine the relationships between productivity and wage levels affects the division of labour within the organisation (Marks, 2012) and as such also influence the modes of communication within an organisation.

The focus on employee well-being stands on the foundational ground that employees form the backbone of any successful organisation. The nature of organisations under contemporary capitalism is such that they have emerged as social institutions whereby they have begun to use the society and its associated components as means of production (Tronti, 2019). Under such circumstances, well-being strategies cannot continue being based only upon the way in which employees behave within the offices or workspaces or the manner in which they get affected by factors related to work. Rather, well-being strategies have to evolve taking into consideration that the evolution of the society itself as a workspace. A contemporary and comprehensive strategy towards well-being demands the analysis of the composition of the employees as against the dominant model based upon the analysis of the composition of capital that contributes to an objective dehumanisation of the subjective selves of the workers in the IT sectors.

EMPLOYEE PERSPECTIVES MATTER!

Much of the ideological conditioning that well-being policies follow under contemporary capitalism is driven by the perception that a homogenised approach towards well-being paying only tokenistic importance to structural inadequacies is sufficient. At the same time, there is a consistent homogeneity within the well-being strategies employed by various companies, especially after COVID-19. For example, companies such as TCS, Infosys, and Accenture have all begun to pay special attention to a certain notion of lifestyle enrichment of their employees focused on exercises related to mental health, physical exercise sessions, and other forms of lifestyle-oriented strategies (TechGig, 2022). However, most of these strategies do not try to explicitly approach the subjective experiences of the workers, but rather work through a framework determined by a certain notion of homogeneity. In a society that is dominated by modes of homogenisation, the propensity of being alienated increases manifold, especially for workers engaged in the IT sector. In the IT sector, where meritocracy and hyper-productivity are highly valued aspects of one's status as an employee, the employees are encouraged to become akin with the larger homogenised. The perceptions that employees gain through their work is conditioned by the social contexts which they have experienced or continue to experience that determine their social status and their identity as human beings.

Perspectives which focus on the employee more than the employers cannot overlook the fact that for a majority of the employees who work in jobs which demand their continued focus and attention, work constitutes a dominant portion of their lives and as such their well-being as employees is directly related to their well-being as human beings which necessarily also means giving importance to subjective *human* factors. The dominant practice of human resource management has been to theorise the issues in a manner that often takes that the interests of the employee and the employer are aligned (Hannon, 2010). However, this one-dimensional perspective, fails to take into cognisance the inherent struggle between the two, which is a characteristic feature of all industrial relations. However, workers today possess a more sophisticated subjective self-analysis than the

98   S. DEB ROY

classical industrial working class because of the sophisticated role that it plays in the production process (Hardt & Negri, 2000). Thus, within contemporary society, there cannot be a well-being strategy which treats all employees as a single homogenous unit- either physically or psychologically. Watson (1977) argues that in order to bring forward meaningful and significant human resource management scholarship, it is necessary to relate these practices and theories to the existing socio-political reality which means taking into cognisance the political economic as well as sociological analyses of the society of which the employees are a part of. In situations such as the present, contrary to vulgar objectivist models, a multi-dimensional well-being model incorporating emotional, social, and psychological well-being can be much more helpful because they work from the perspective of the workers rather than those of the employers (Ryff & Keyes, 1995).

Comprehensive and holistic well-being strategies cannot be devised by economic theories alone but rather require a more nuanced and sociological approach aimed at understanding the problems that employees face within their workspaces as being a part of the broader social problems that the employees face (Mills, 1970; Watson, 2010). This often requires a pluralist approach which focuses on the contribution of factors such as trade unions and workers' associations (Watson, 1986; Legge, 1995; Delbridge & Keenoy, 2010), problematising concepts such as labour power and labour subjectivity, which often get overlooked by mainstream human resource management theories and practitioners because under any form of capitalism:

> [L]abour becomes a resource of a productive system and one of the major requirements which the employer has of this commodity is tractability. The employer [buys] labour power when [one] needs it, use[s] it in the way [one] requires to and dispose[s] of it when it does not yield the surplus which justifies its purpose. (Watson, 1977, p. 30)

A significant part of such dehumanisation tendencies owes itself to the complete entrenchment of the social reality under the aegis of the capitalist means, and relations of production, such that even anti-capitalist tendencies have tended to be influenced by the viewpoints—both material and ideological—that capital itself renders mainstream in the society. Such tendencies have made it normal for mainstream and dominant human resource management practices to assume that the interests of the employee and the employer are aligned (Watson, 1977; Hannon, 2010). These techniques are contingent upon how different organisations move towards the establishment of an employee-friendly social space—both within the workspaces and within the society in general. Eudaimonic approaches can help counter the objectivist and anti-subjectivist nature of the hedonic approaches but remain limited in scope because of their overtly psychological nature often neglecting the importance of material benefits—something which hedonic approaches essentialise. It is true that a comprehensive well-being strategy has to go beyond the issues faced by the employees within the workspace, but the issues concerning work cannot be neglected as well. It is essential to form alternatives to mainstream management theories and practices in such a way that the focus remains on structural changes which are required to effect fundamental alterations to the systemic exploitative structure that characterises industrial relations as they exist in modern organisations and corporations (Adler et al., 2007).

The employees' perspectives on well-being strategies are intimately related to the asymmetrical relationship between knowledge and power. Employees in general suffer from a low status in their respective organisations often lacking a general coherence about the kind of work that they are performing for their organisation (Legge, 1978). The ability to manage a work in accordance with their own individual subjectivities constitutes one of the most basic aspects of the generation of an effective well-being for the employees (Slemp & Vella-Brodrick, 2013). An employee-centred well-being strategy focuses on the employee as a subject oneself, devising strategies to theorise not only the objective contradictions of the workspace and the society, but also the subjective contradictions of human existence. Such a strategy is necessitated under contemporary forms of capitalism because of the constant attacks that both the IT sector and its well-being strategies have been mounting on the human nature of the IT workers causing them to look for managerial solutions to what are essentially socio-political issues.

References

Adler, P., Forbes, L., & Willmott, H. (2007). Critical Management Studies: Premises, Practices, Problems and Prospects. *Annals of the Academy of Management, 1*, 119–180.

Anderson, K. B. (2020). *Dialectics of Revolution: Hegel, Marxism, and Its Critics Through a Lens of Race, Class, Gender, and Colonialism*. Daraja Press.

100 S. DEB ROY

Beck, U. (1992). *Risk Society.* SAGE.

Beijer, S., Peccei, R., Veldhoven, M. V., & Paauwe, J. (2019). The Turn to Employees in the Measurement of Human Resource Practices: A Critical Review and Proposed Way Forward. *Human Resource Management Journal, 1*, 1–17.

Berge, L. A. M., Liu, F.-C., Grimsrud, T. K., Babigumira, R., Støer, N. C., Kjærheim, K., Robsahm, T. E., Ghiasvand, R., Hosgood, H. D., & Samuelsen, S. O. (2023). Night Shift Work and Risk of Aggressive Prostate Cancer in the Norwegian Offshore Petroleum Workers (NOPW) Cohort. *International Journal of Epidemiology, 52*(4), 1003–1014.

Beurden, J. V., Voorde, K. V. D., & Veldhoven, M. V. (2021). The Employee Perspective on HR Practices: A Systematic Literature Review, Integration, and Outlook. *The International Journal of Human Resource Management, 32*(2), 359–393.

Biggio, G., & Cortese, C. G. (2013). Well-being in the Workplace Through Interaction Between Individual Characteristics and Organizational Context. *International Journal of Qualitative Studies on Health and Well-being, 8.*

Blyton, P., & Turnbull, P. (1994/1998). *The Dynamics of Employee Relations.* Macmillan Business.

Boon, C., Den Hartog, D. N., & Lepak, D. P. (2019). A Systematic Review of Human Resource Management Systems and Their Measurement. *Journal of Management, 45*(6), 2498–2537.

Bowen, D. E., & Ostroff, C. (2004). Understanding HRM-Firm Performance Linkages: The Role of the "Strength" of the HRM System. *The Academy of Management Review, 29*(2), 203–221.

Cannizzaro, E., Cirrincione, L., Mazzucco, W., Scorciapino, A., Catalano, C., Ramaci, T., Ledda, C., & Plescia, F. (2020). Night-Time Shift Work and Related Stress Responses: A Study on Security Guards. *International Journal of Environmental Research and Public Health, 17*(2), 562.

Cheng, M. M., & Hackett, R. D. (2019). A Critical Review of Algorithms in HRM: Definition, Theory, and Practice. *Human Resource Management Review.* https://doi.org/10.1016/j.hrmr.2019.100698

Delbridge, R., & Keenoy, T. (2010). Beyond Managerialism? *The International Journal of Human Resource Management, 21*(6), 799–817.

DeNisi, A. S., Wilson, M. S., & Biteman, J. (2014). Research and Practice in HRM: A Historical Perspective. *Human Resource Management Review, 24*(3), 219–231.

Diener, E. (1984). Subjective Well-being. *Psychological Bulletin, 95*(3), 542–575.

Diener, E. (2000). *Subjective Well-being: The Science of Happiness and a Proposal for a National Index.* American Psychological Association.

Dun, A., Zhao, X., Jin, X., Wei, T., Gao, X., Wang, Y., & Hou, H. (2020). Association Between Nightshift Work and Cancer Risk: Updated Systematic Review and Meta-Analysis. *Frontiers in Oncology, 10*, 1006.

Edwards, P. (1986). *Conflict at Work*. Basil Blackwell.

Edwards, P. (2005). The Challenging But Promising Future of Industrial Relations. *Industrial Relations Journal, 36*(4), 264–282.

Erdogan, B., Bauer, T. N., Truxillo, D. M., & Mansfield, L. R. (2012). Whistle While You Work: A Review of the Life Satisfaction Literature. *Journal of Management, 38*(4), 1038–1083.

Feldman, F. (2004). *Pleasure and the Good Life: Concerning the Nature, Varieties and Plausibility of Hedonism*. Clarendon Press.

Ferri, P., Guadi, M., Marcheselli, L., Balduzzi, S., Magnani, D., & Di Lorenzo, R. (2016). The Impact of Shift Work on the Psychological and Physical Health of Nurses in a General Hospital: A Comparison Between Rotating Night Shifts and Day Shifts. *Risk Management and Healthcare Policy, 9*, 203–211.

Fromm, E. (1961). *Marx's Concept of Man*. Continuum.

Grant, A. M., Christianson, M. K., & Price, R. H. (2007). Happiness, Health, or Relationships? Managerial Practices and Employee Well-being Tradeoffs. *Academy of Management Perspectives, 21*(3), 51–63.

Grawitch, M. J., Gottschalk, M., & Munz, D. C. (2006). The Path to a Healthy Workplace: A Critical Review Linking Healthy Workplace Practices, Employee Well-being, and Organizational Improvements. *Consulting Psychology Journal, 58*(3), 129–147.

Hannon, E. (2010). Employee-focused Research in HRM. *The International Journal of Human Resource Management, 21*(6), 818–835.

Hardt, M., & Negri, A. (2000). *Empire*. Harvard University Press.

Illouz, E. (2007). *Cold Intimacies: The Making of Emotional Capitalism*. Polity.

Jahoda, M. (1958). *Current Concepts of Positive Mental Health*. Basic Books.

Juniper, B. A., Bellamy, P., & White, N. (2011). Testing the Performance of a New Approach to Measuring Employee Well-being. *Leadership and Organisation Development Journal, 25*(4), 344–357.

Keyes, C. L. M. (1998). Social Well-being. *Social Psychology Quarterly, 1*, 121–140.

Kochan, T. A., & Osterman, P. (1994). *The Mutual Gains Enterprise: Forging a Winning Partnership Among Labor, Management, and Government*. Harvard Business Press.

Lefebvre, H. (2014). *Critique of Everyday Life: One Volume Edition*. Verso.

Legge, K. (1978). *Power, Innovation and Problem-Solving in Personnel Management*. McGraw Hill.

Legge, K. (1995). *Human Resource Management: Rhetorics and Realities*. Palgrave Macmillan.

Lingas, E. C. (2023). A Narrative Review of the Carcinogenic Effect of Night Shift and the Potential Protective Role of Melatonin. *Cureus, 15*(8), e43326.

Marcuse, M. (1941/1998). Some Social Implications of Modern Technology. In D. Kellner (Ed.), *Collected Papers of Herbert Marcuse Volume 1: Technology, War and Fascism*. London: Routledge.

102 S. DEB ROY

Marcuse, H. (1964/2002). *One-Dimensional Society*. London: Routledge.

Marks, B. (2012). Autonomist Marxist Theory and Practice in the Current Crisis. *ACME, 11*(3), 467–491.

Marx, K. (1844/1975). Economic and Philosophical Manuscripts of 1844. In *Marx Engels Collected Works: Volume 3*. Lawrence and Wishart.

Meister, J. (2021, August 4). The Future of Work Is Worker Well-being? *Forbes*. Retrieved December 3, 2023, from https://www.forbes.com/sites/jeannemeister/2021/08/04/the-future-of-work-is-worker-well-being/?sh=724e95e84aed

Mills, C. W. (1970). *The Sociological Imagination*. Penguin.

Mitter, S., & Sen, S. (2000). Can Calcutta Become Another Bangalore? *Economic and Political Weekly, 35*(26), 2263–2268.

Nagar, N. (2018). Infosys: Employee Health and Safety Information. *Infosys*. Retrieved December 3, 2023, from https://www.infosys.com/industries/industrial-manufacturing/white-papers/Documents/employee-health-safety-solution.pdf

Negri, A. (1989). *The Politics of Subversion*. Polity.

Negri, A. (2016). *Reflections on Empire*. Polity.

Pradhan, R. K., & Hati, L. (2019). The Measurement of Employee Well-being: Development and Validation of a Scale. *Global Business Review*. https://doi.org/10.1177/0972150919859101

Rowlinson, M. (1997). *Organisations and Institutions: Perspectives in Economics and Sociology*. Macmillan Business.

Ryan, R. M., & Deci, E. L. (2001). On Happiness and Human Potentials. *Annual Review of Psychology, 52*(1), 141–166.

Ryff, C. D. (1989). Happiness Is Everything, or Is It? Explorations on the Meaning of Psychological Well-being. *Journal of Personality and Social Psychology, 57*(6), 1069.

Ryff, C. D., & Keyes, C. L. (1995). The Structure of Psychological Well-being Revisited. *Journal of Personality and Social Psychology, 69*(4), 719–727.

Saha, P. (2017, August 30). How and When 'Industrial Relations' Transformed into 'Human Resources'. *HR Katha*. Retrieved December 3, 2023, from https://www.hrkatha.com/features/how-and-when-industrial-relations-transformed-into-human-resources/

Scarbrough, H. (1996). Understanding and Managing Expertise. In H. Scarbrough (Ed.), *The Management of Expertise* (pp. 23–47). Macmillan Business.

Scott, A. (1994). *Willing Slaves?: British Workers Under Human Resource Management*. Cambridge University Press.

Segal, L. (2017). *Radical Happiness*. Verso.

Shantz, A., Alfes, K., & Truss, C. (2014). Alienation from Work: Marxist Ideologies and Twenty-first-century Practice. *The International Journal of Human Resource Management, 25*(18), 2529–2550.

Shantz, A., Alfes, K., Bailey, C., & Soane, E. (2015). Drivers and Outcomes of Work Alienation: Reviving a Concept. *Journal of Management Inquiry, 24*(4), 382–393.

Slemp, G. R., & Vella-Brodrick, D. A. (2013). Optimising Employee Mental Health: The Relationship Between Intrinsic Need Satisfaction, Job Crafting, and Employee Well-being. *Journal of Happiness Studies, 15*(4), 957–977. https://doi.org/10.1007/s10902-013-9458-3

TechGig. (2022, April 25). *How TCS, Accenture, and Infosys Are Ensuring Employee Wellbeing*. Retrieved December 2, 2023, from https://content.techgig.com/career-advice/how-tcs-accenture-and-infosys-are-ensuring-employee-wellbeing/articleshow/91077951.cms

Thanem, T., & Elraz, H. (2022). From Stress to Resistance: Challenging the Capitalist Underpinnings of Mental Unhealth in Work and Organisations. *International Journal of Management Reviews, 24*, 577–598.

Tjan, A. (2009). How to Align Employee and Company Values. *Harvard Business Review*. Retrieved December 2, 2023, from https://hbr.org/2009/08/how-to-align-employee-and-comp

Tronti, M. (1962). Factory and Society. *Operaismo in English*. Retrieved December 4, 2023, from https://operaismoinenglish.wordpress.com/2013/06/13/factory-and-society/

Tronti, M. (2019). *Workers and Capital*. Verso.

Van De Voorde, K., Paauwe, J., & Van Veldhoven, M. (2012). Employee Well-being and the HRM–Organisational Performance Relationship. *International Journal of Management Reviews, 14*, 391–407.

Wang, Y., Kim, S., Rafferty, A., & Sanders, K. (2020). Employee Perceptions of HR Practices: A Critical Review and Future Directions. *The International Journal of Human Resource Management, 31*(1), 128–173.

Warr, P. (1987). *Work, Unemployment, and Mental Health*. Oxford University Press.

Warr, P. (1999). Well-being and the Workplace. In D. Kahneman, E. Diener, & N. Schwarz (Eds.), *Well-being: The Foundations of Hedonic Psychology* (pp. 392–412). SAGE.

Watson, T. J. (1977). *The Personnel Managers: A Study in the Sociology of Work and Employment*. Routledge.

Watson, T. J. (1986). *Management, Organisation and Employment Strategy: New Directions in Theory and Practice*. Routledge.

Watson, T. J. (2010). Critical Social Science, Pragmatism, and the Realities of HRM. *The International Journal of Human Resource Management, 21*(6), 915–931.

Witheford, N. (1994). Autonomist Marxism and the Information Society. *Capital, and Class, 18*(1), 85–125.

Wright, T. A. (2010). More than Meets the Eye: The Role of Employee Well-being in Organizational Research. In P. A. Linley, S. Harrington, & N. Garcea

(Eds.), *Oxford Handbook of Positive Psychology and Work* (pp. 143–154). Oxford University Press.

Wright, P. M., & Nishi, I. H. (2013). HRM and Performance: The Role of Effective Implementation. In J. Paauwe, D. Guest, & P. Wright (Eds.), *HRM, & Performance: Achievements and Challenges*. Wiley.

Zheng, X., Zhu, W., Zhao, H., & Zhang, C. (2015). Employee Well-being in Organisation. *Journal of Organisational Behaviour, 36*(5), 621–644.

Zuboff, S. (2019). *The Age of Surveillance Capitalism: The Fight for a Human Future at the New Frontier of Power*. Public Affairs.

CHAPTER 5

The Invisible Information Technology Workers

INTRODUCTION

Urban spaces in India are home to a diverse group of individuals, coming from different castes, classes, races, ethnicities, genders, and religions. The kind of heterodox combination that most IT hubs construct creates a gentrified social reality for most of the inhabitants therein. Gentrified social realities under capitalism are usually constructed through a massive structural exclusion of the already marginalised (Stein, 2019). The informal workers play a critical role in the construction of such gentrified spaces in India, which is not surprising since the total workforce in India consists of around 93 per cent informal workers (Sengupta, 2007). IT companies in India do not only employ engineers and managerial staff but also other kinds of workers. These include security personnel, daily wage sanitation workers, drivers, cooks, maintenance staff, as well as delivery agents. Combined together, there are around 12 million such workers in the IT sector as of 2016–2017, with a high percentage of footloose labour among them (Chakraborty, 2021).[1]

Most of these services are outsourced to private companies and contractors—some national, but more often than not local. There is also a

---

[1] This number does not include domestic workers.

© The Author(s), under exclusive license to Springer Nature Switzerland AG 2024
S. Deb Roy, *The Rise of the Information Technology Society in India,* Dynamics of Virtual Work,
https://doi.org/10.1007/978-3-031-58128-1_5

105

massive involvement of the gig economy and the platform workers in the kinds of work which usually appear as outsourced jobs in the sector. These workers although work for the IT companies but do not do so overtly. In spite of being critical to the sustenance of the sector as a whole, they neither draw fair wages, nor are treated with the dignity that they deserve. These outsourced and platform workers form the core of the sixth chapter. The chapter engages with the lives of these workers and how different unions are taking them into consideration while devising their strategies as a whole. The chapter also talks about the relationship that unions in the gig economy and those in the IT sector share with each other and provides a framework through which they can be analysed as being parts of the movement of a new section of the working class, which brings forward certain critical discussions about contemporary class structure and its implications on the lives of the workers.

As of 2009–2010 'domestic workers, home-based workers, street vendors and waste pickers represented 33 per cent of the total urban employment (33 per cent of male and 24 per cent of female)' (Chen & Skinner, 2014, p. 223). In almost every kind of work that comes under the domain of informal work, issues concerning decent work, labour law regulations, and job security come to be important considerations. The contours of informal work arrangements are particularly harsh on women, Muslims, Dalits, people from other backward castes, and young people who either have to find work, either for sustenance or for fulfilling the responsibilities entrusted upon them by their ascribed or achieved social status. At the same time, some of these categories of individuals suffer from disproportionate responsibilities—such as caregiving and the labour of people-production in the case of women, sanitation work in the case of Dalits, and the social responsibility of finding a paid work in the case of young people—that is often entrusted upon such people, by the dominant social order (Blundell & Machin, 2020; Bell et al., 2020).

The creation of the invisible IT workers owes itself to the changes in the socio-economic structure of the country since the late 1980s. The constant decrease of publicly funded employment in the early 1990s, accompanied by a constant decrease in the funds allocated to programmes which used to directly benefit the poor and the marginalised, along with reduced public expenditure, rural development funds, and employment generation programmes (Patnaik, 2008; Shah, 2008). Following this, the state in India promoted the formation of 'primitive accumulation in an *anticipatory* sense as compared to actual dispossession' (Adnan, 2014,

p. 32). Primitive accumulation in India has produced the basis for the transition of the agrarian economy to a neoliberal one, and as such has decimated the agrarian relations of production in the country resulting in a growing reserve army of labour for capital in the urban spaces to exploit (Gopalakrishnan, 2009). The capitalist social structure demands that the workers are completely separated from all forms of property which makes them completely subservient to the means to which they can realise their labour. Capitalism thrives by actively reinforcing this distinction, and 'the so-called primitive accumulation, therefore, is nothing else than the historical process of divorcing the producer from the means of production. It appears as primitive, because it forms the prehistoric stage of capital and of the mode of production corresponding with it' (Godelier, 1967, p. 99).

The domination that scholars such as Tronti (1962) and others such as Negri (1989b) speak about cannot be exercised without the active consent of the middle class because of its control over the requisite resources, which are essential for capitalism to exercise control. The middle class has been placed at an advantageous position as far as its ability to use the avenues created by the neoliberal reforms to its own benefit are concerned. In India, it has been able to accumulate a considerable section of the wealth and income opportunities constructed out of the neoliberal reforms-based restructuring (Ahalya & Pal, 2017). The reforms have resulted in greater inequality, insecurity, unemployment, underemployment, casualisation, and informalisation (Das, 2015). The basic fulcrum of Tronti's idea was that once capitalism reaches a certain level of maturity within any society, it does not remain bound by the limits imposed upon it by the workspace but rather begins expanding it modes of domination over the entirety of the society. Both Tronti and then Negri had been speaking in the context of the Global North—specifically Italy—but with the development of capitalism on a global scale, the distinctions between the two have been constantly decreasing—especially for the workers employed in the IT sector. In an advanced stage of capitalism, the entire society takes up to be a means of production. While traditionally, the means of production have been theorised to be restricted to factories, the coming of age of a new kind of capitalism that does not remain bound by the confines of a factory or a workplace (Negri, 1989a, 1989b).

The chapter speaks about three major categories of informal work that remain critically important to the urban IT workers' sustenance of their desired or aspired lifestyle: domestic workers, security guards (security workers) and the sanitation and hospitality workers. These workers are parts of the social space that the IT sector develops in most major IT hubs in India. They are each prescribed a particular role, both materially and ideologically in the society, with many of them fulfilling multiple roles for the workers and the space in general. The human resource and well-being strategies do not apply to these workers, since they are largely seen as being a workforce that exists to complement the *actual* IT workers.

KEEPING THE IT HOMES IN ORDER

Women, as has already been stated, perform a very important role within the IT lifestyle. They provide the male workers with a stable familial life, one which contributes to their social and individual well-being, that complements their working lives as IT workers. Married working women in the IT sector perform multiple tasks in their everyday lives, many of which directly benefit the structures of accumulation put in place. The role of domestic workers amidst the hustle and bustle of an IT worker's life though marginal is an important one. The importance of paid domestic labour in the lives of the IT workers gets manifested in the kind of effect that their absence has on the urban spaces, as is evident from the statements reproduced below from IT workers in Bengaluru, Pune, and Gurgaon:

> I cannot survive without her. Both me and my husbands have shifts in the morning or at night, so we practically do not have much time to do all the household chores. We get really irritated when she misses a day. I know its harsh but if we are not there, what will these people do? (Woman IT Worker, Bengaluru)

> We have had many domestic workers over the course of last few years. Before Covid, there were a plenty of them available. But now they have decreased. Previously, there used to be a lot of them from Nepal, but now they have decreased. I think after Covid, they have stopped coming. (Woman IT Worker, Pune)

> Living as bachelor is difficult in the city. Having a domestic help always makes things easier because they help you with jobs that are usually very difficult to be done yourself, say cooking in the morning, or keeping the house clean during the weekdays, etc. (Male IT Worker, Gurgaon)

Domestic work in India is a work that is reserved for the most destitute individuals in the society. It is a highly feminised workforce with a significant proportion of women coming from marginalised communities and weaker socio-economic backgrounds (Neetha, 2013). The number of domestic workers in India has increased ten-fold since the 1990s (Jain & Mishra, 2019), and has been characterised by an increased migration of workers from non-urban spaces to metropolitan and highly developed urban centres that has had an effect on the very nature of these urban spaces. Domestic workers, and especially migrant domestic workers, in India are largely rendered invisible within the spaces that they inhabit, both quantitatively and qualitatively (Wadhawan, 2013). Jain and Mishra state:

> In India, paid domestic work was a cultural practice and part of the reproduction of class difference within a society marked by inequality. ... Economic growth, modernisation and change in lifestyle have contributed to an increase in the demand for domestic workers, particularly for 'part-time' workers. Ageing and lack of state provisioning of care too have contributed to their growing demand. (Jain & Mishra, 2019, p. 2)

Migrant workers have become an important and necessary part of the urban spaces because of their roles in fulfilling the everyday chores that are critical to the survival and maintenance of the lifestyles of its middle-class inhabitants (Malpani & Ramita, 2023). The indispensability that migrant workers have come to possess in the urban spaces have made them further exploitable commodities—contrary to what is popularly believed in general economic terms. The increased necessity of domestic workers has occurred simultaneously with an increasing availability or supply of migrant domestic workers which in lieu of increasing their demand has enabled a constant depreciation of their social status. The demand for domestic workers in the lives of IT workers is a result of the ways in which their working lives are structured, which have a great impact on their domestic and private lives as well. Most of the IT workers work difficult hours and in shifts—the problems of which have been noted in Chaps. 1 and 2. And with the salaries being constantly decreasing (Times of India, 2023), most of these workers cannot afford the many luxuries that the urban spaces provide such as take-away food, private transportation, high electricity bills, and so forth on a regular basis. While the decrease in salaries obviously has a financial effect on the workers, it also simultaneously has a socio-cultural effect on them making them further alienated in the society. The decrease in salaries for new entrants has coincided with a constant rise in the price of other essentials of the twenty-first-century urban lifestyle (Parmar, 2023), which have affected the workers' capacity to afford certain desired lifestyle services, as two workers—one male and one female—point out from Hyderabad and Pune:

110   S. DEB ROY

> We cannot expect to have a decent life with a fresher's salary. Twenty years ago, a job in the IT sector was supposed to be a way out of poverty, today it is less about that but more about survival in the cities. A single chicken rice used to cost some sixty rupees five-six years ago, now it is about one hundred twenty rupees. I cannot now expect to have lunch outside every day and in the morning, I do not have time to cook. (Male IT Worker, Hyderabad)

> The major reason behind why domestic helps is hired is because people simply do not have enough time on their hands. The IT sector works in such a way that most people work difficult shifts, trying to make ends meet. In that regard, any opportunity that they get to reduce their expenditures comes as a boon for them. (Woman IT Worker, Pune)

These are the factors that typically influence the hiring of domestic workers among these workers. The demand for domestic workers is increasing on an everyday basis in cities such as Bangalore, Gurgaon, and Hyderabad. There are as many as 4 million domestic workers in Bengaluru city alone, as per data collected by an NGO in 2018 (Somashekher & Mangalamma, 2019). While data for other cities is difficult to found, it can be said with a reasonable level of certainty that the numbers would be somewhat similar for other cities as well, as many IT workers interviewed for the book inform. Domestic workers, like many other informal workers, do not work for the state per se. They do so for individuals, or for certain organisations. Put simply, domestic work can be defined as work related to cleaning, cooking, and care, all of which are related to the reproductive labour performed within the domestic space (Wadhawan, 2013). Because of the informal nature of such jobs, an increasing number of migrant women are being recruited as domestic workers (Sharma, 2022; Tandon & Rathi, 2022) that has contributed to their marginalisation. In Chap. 2, the conditions faced by migrant workers had been hinted at, but the chapter mainly engaged with the formal workers, that is the professional workers who earn a high enough salary too. It was also stated that among migrants, there exists a very distinct class differentiation that makes itself evident in these urban spaces. Migrants feel attracted to the city because of the facilities that urban spaces provide, despite these spaces being prone to issues such as bad air quality, poor sanitation, migration, slum culture, and economic instability (Banerjee & Duflo, 2019). But among the migrants, it is the poorer section of the migrant workforce that gets more exposed to these issues as is the norm in the risk society that capitalist development

5 THE INVISIBLE INFORMATION TECHNOLOGY WORKERS   111

produces.[2] The ethnic and racial composition of migrant domestic workers varies with the context in which one situates them. In Gurgaon, domestic workers are usually migrants who come from the neighbouring areas of Haryana, Uttar Pradesh, and Delhi (Das Gupta, 2017; Vishwakarma et al., 2022). Bengaluru, on the other hand, gets a lot of Bengali and Nepali domestic workers because of the large-scale migration of Bengalis towards Bengaluru in recent times. The migration of domestic workers varies according to the 'perceived' population of middle-class migration to a particular IT hub. Migration of unskilled workers takes place through various means and because of various causes. Most of them are employed either through an agency or through members of their communities already working in these IT hubs. One domestic worker who had migrated from West Bengal and Nepal respectively to Bengaluru stated:

> We do not make a particular choice to be at a specific place. It is just how things are. Sometimes we have people already living here from the community, who bring us here. Sometimes, it is because our husbands migrate here. Basically, there is no fixed reason behind us being here. It is diverse, but yes, we do enquire regarding what kind of work we are going to get here because otherwise coming here will put us further into poverty. (Domestic Worker, Migrant from West Bengal, Bengaluru)

> We migrate as families mostly. I migrated with my husband. In our village in Nepal,[3] we have a few agents who regularly recruit people and send them here. For married people, they say that your husband can work as a security guard or something and you can work in the same complex as a domestic worker. (Domestic Worker, Migrant from Nepal, Bengaluru)

Domestic workers within the IT spaces that are usually populated by a significant middle-class migrant populace are employed based on their ethic or community identities. Within the local middle class, there is a preference of employing the local domestic workers primarily those who speak the same language and are trained in the local customs. Language also constitutes a key role in this regard. The employment of domestic workers within their own communities often ends up replicating the same structures of hierarchy that they wanted to escape through migration to cities. The migration of domestic workers is contingent upon the

---

[2] Deb Roy, S. (2024). *Covid-19 and Social Change: Arguments from and for India.* Abingdon: Routledge (Forthcoming).

[3] There is no Visa requirement for Nepali citizens to travel or work in India.

migration patterns of the middle-class IT workers in the IT hubs. However, regardless of their migration status, there are certain commonalities between all domestic workers. Most of them do not even receive the minimum wage and even fewer possess other employment benefits considered essential for a dignified and well-being oriented employment, such as weekly leaves and sick leaves, as research on domestic workers in Hyderabad points out (Reddy, 2023). Even in places such as Kolkata, where trade unions have historically been a much more effective force and have held a considerable political influence over those controlling the political structures, domestic workers' unions and their issues have often been relegated as being marginal. The exploitation that is meted out to these workers not only occurs on the basis of class but also has a significant caste and religious component.

The exploitation of domestic workers is an important part of the class formation among the IT workers. The power to control that they possess with regard to the domestic workers who work at their homes allows these workers to be more efficient and productive sources of human capital to the global capitalist order. The domination exercised by the workers over the domestic workers, or the security guards is analysed by them as being a direct result of the kind of de-humanisation that they undergo at the workplace, both financially and socially. The financial benefits that they receive as part of their job profiles makes them believe in a false sense of control over the variables that determine the trajectory of their lives. Such structures produce a sense of alienation for many of the IT workers because it provides them with an illusion of power.

The interactions that the formal IT sector workers have with other workers, especially those working informal jobs, form the basis of their class consciousness. The peculiar conditions of life that the formal IT sector workers undergo on an everyday basis make them ideal candidates for propagating a de-humanising social psychology that is suitable to the generation of a de-humanised society. For the middle-class women employed in the formal sectors, navigating through such circumstances becomes a bit easier because their class and familial positions place them at a higher pedestal than other women. However, women have always been used as tools by the state and the market to further their own agenda and have tended to be looked down upon as inferior beings (Greer, 1991; Davis, 1983/2003). The struggle of the domestic workers often takes place within a paradigm whereby they do not struggle against the socio-economic structure per se on an everyday basis but rather do so against other women—the women of the household.

> Most of them do not talk to us that much. Sometimes madam does, but Sir almost never speaks to me. I go there, work and come back. They pay the money on time though, but there is no dignity in this work. They use all those expensive things, which we cannot think of possessing. It hurts us when we see that they throw away so much food and all every single day, but that is how life is. (Domestic Worker, Bengaluru)

> Most of the madams do not talk to us. It is true that they do not ask us about our caste, but they do ask about our religion, and where we come from. But once we get employed, the women just try to control us. I have to do all kinds of work, from cleaning the bathrooms to taking care of the child. (Domestic Worker, Pune)

The class distinctions which exist between these women create the conditions within which the gender of the informal workers gets reinforced upon them by other women from the middle class. Class here occupies an important position, and acts alongside other factors such as caste and gender to produce the exploitative social reality that domestic workers experience. The lack of social reproductive and political consciousness aids the generation of such consciousness constitute the most critical part of the internal contradictions for the women workers. Internal contradictions in the lives of these non-standard workers have become highly urbanised in nature because of the way in which contemporary capitalism has used spatiality as a mode of exploitation by creating spaces which exclude the marginalised from occupying them while constantly using them to create the spaces meant to exclude them (Harvey, 2012). The spatial nature of contemporary capitalism constitutes the basis for the large-scale influx of informal workers in these spaces, who can fulfil both economic and social needs of the individuals occupying these spaces.

Urban spaces under contemporary capitalism have become crucibles of structural violence, because they have resulted in the creation of conditions and associated processes which have not only excluded large sections of the populace but also rendered the exploitation of the already marginalised normal in the society. These spaces have become the mediums within which different kinds of exploitative models keep on regenerating themselves using the already existing systems of exploitation and oppression. The way in which caste, class, and gender intersect with each in these spaces has been one of the major features of the postcolonial development of the Indian society. Harriss-White (2003) argues that the trajectory of development in India has created the conditions within which factors such as caste and other socially attributed characteristics, which should have ideally been replaced by economic and new social contracts, became a part and parcel of the corporate capital after the institutionalisation of the neo-liberal reforms after 1991.

Most of the invisible IT workers suffer from states of psychological security, which is an essential part of their ability to experience the space and time. Berman (1983) mentions the experience of time and space with respect to both the self and the others to be a vital criterion of living through modernity itself. Routines enable the proper functioning of solitary activities, which become important elements to construct the consciousness of the individual. Consciousness forged out of a feeling of being secured enables them to navigate their ways through the everyday life created by and creating the urban space and temporalities around themselves. It is this consciousness which enables the individuals to live and work with others while protecting their ideas of their own selves within the urban space.

'Securing' the Techies

Domestic work—a sector where women compose most of the workforce—provides one with a glimpse of how pre-capitalist forms of social relationships continue to dominate the lives of women, regardless of their class position. However, domestic work mostly encompasses the dynamics of the private sphere of the IT workers and, the IT space that has come into existence in these cities does not only rely on the internal dynamics of the household, but also is contingent upon the overall nature of the space. While domestic workers mostly work inside the homes, security workers work outside the homes. Security workers in urban India have come to occupy an important position because of the growing middle-class demand for security that goes hand-in-hand with the growth of affluence in the society (FICCI, 2013). The private security industry in India employs more than seven million people, making it a bigger employer than even the healthcare sector in the country (Grant Thornton, 2015; Kishore, 2018)—particularly employing people from the economically weaker sections, migrant workers, and the like (NSDC, 2013). In recent times, the growth of the private security sector has been an exemplary one with an annual growth rate of 20 per cent (Mahajan, 2019).

The urban space that the IT workers inhabit is a space that is dominated by the politics of signs. Factors such as affluence and lifestyle maintenance become intertwined with the class consciousness that is usually generated among the IT workers in India's IT hubs. Security guards within that milieu do not only make the inhabitants feel safer but also act as a border-land between the IT workers and the wider society—'protecting [them] from the unruly slums that surround the gated communities where most of the IT workers live'. Security work in India, is however, characterised by a growing precarity and long graveyard shifts that contributes to not only the declining health of these workers but also affects their mental health (Vyas, 2016; Noronha et al., 2018; Cannizzaro et al., 2020). The quality of life that draws a significant proportion of the middle-class professional workers to these regions is determined not only by the facilities that these spaces provide but also by the kind of ideological opportunities that they provide to individuals. A very experienced trade unionist, in an interview given to the author, had stated:

> When those in power cannot provide for the workers, they use different kinds of services to lure the workers into doing those lowly paid jobs for them. They lure them with different kinds of services, benefits, easy money, incentives, etc. All with the intention that these workers will do anything that they want them to do. Most of these techniques shroud the fact the IT companies provide no job security to the workers. These are supposed to make the workers feel grateful rather than agitated.

Because of the way in which the entire sector is structured in the country, they fail to effectively realise the importance that factors such as job security and belongingness contribute to the well-being of the workers. A recent report suggests that as much as half of the Indian workforce feels highly insecure in their jobs (Sarkar, 2023). The sense of material insecu-rity that they face as workers makes them to look for a sense of security and control in their non-working lives. The difficult conditions of life that the IT sector workers face in their lives as economic beings makes them sus-ceptible to tendencies of de-humanisation that capitalism renders main-stream in the society. The IT firms tend to substitute the issues of social and employment insecurity by providing these workers with a sense of alienated empowerment within the workplaces. The results of such

116   S. DEB ROY

alienated and powerless empowerment make the workers exert their class privilege over other workers placed below them within the socio-economic hierarchy.

Most security guards, as one report states, are migrant workers to the cities who resort to such jobs as a last option to support themselves in the urban spaces (NSDC, 2013). Working as a security guard in India is a difficult job. The security industry in India is one of the highest recruiting industries in the country (Kishore, 2018). It often employs ex-service personnel and also provides employment option for many unskilled individuals desiring a job that lets them escape conditions of rural poverty that have increased constantly since the early 1990s (Patnaik, 2007). There is an increasing propensity for agencies to pay these security workers in cash instead of direct account-to-account transfer. One of the major reasons for the same is that a significant section of these workers is employed under employment conditions designed through opaque terms of employment where they are denied knowledge of the minute aspects of the job that they are supposed to perform.

Security workers are an important part of the IT workforce. Their job description usually encompasses not only the ensuring of the security of the workers but also ensuring a constant manipulation of the consciousness of the formal IT sector workers. They work simultaneously as hospitality workers along with their security work, performing odd jobs for the workers therein. The security guards mostly perform dual roles. Their first roles are usually focused on them working as hospitality workers. Their job description usually involves bowing or greeting the workers when they come into their offices and when they leave, speak to them in a courteous manner, and fulfilling requests made for errands. The idea of 'security' becomes mostly secondary in their cases because their primary responsibility becomes aiding the generation of a false consciousness of empowerment of the IT workers, making them feel important, as a security worker recounted:

> It is in our job description. We have to greet them and make them feel comfortable and all. The employees like that. Our responsibility is not only about keeping them secure, and anyway we do not protect them, we protect the office. The employees get us as extra benefits. That is what usually is the brief given to us. (Security Guard, Bengaluru)

5 THE INVISIBLE INFORMATION TECHNOLOGY WORKERS   117

Security guards in most major IT hubs can be classified to be performing their duties in three kinds of spaces: residential, commercial, and official spaces. Most security guards prefer to work in commercial sites because of three factors: better pay, better working hours and, most importantly, lesser interactions. They prefer commercial spaces to work in because such spaces usually do not have much additional job responsibilities, and even if there are certain additional responsibilities, it is only marginal in nature:

> In shopping malls or in those other commercial spaces, the customers do not expect us to greet them. In fact, they do not even want to be greeted sometimes. Most of them do not pay much attention that we exist. In these offices, it is difficult. Here they expect us to greet them, they will return our greetings and then there are these additional responsibilities—take care of the sanitation I mean check that everything is done properly, run small errands for the workers, etc. (Male Security Worker, Bengaluru)

> Commercial spaces are better because they provide us with better dignity. Yes, in commercial spaces also, sometimes you get weird customers, but that is once in a while. In the city, nobody has the time to notice security guards. But in offices, they do notice. We have to say 'sir', 'madam' to them. Otherwise, they will complain. The only problem is the CCTVs though, you cannot take rest or talk to people or sneak out for smoking a *biri*. (Male Security Worker, Kolkata)

While commercial spaces are highly preferred by the security personnel, office spaces are the preferred second option for them. The only disadvantage that office spaces have in comparison with commercial spaces is that within office spaces, there is a very specific hierarchy that engulfs their work. In shopping malls or in ATMs, the customers do not expect much from them, while in office spaces, there is an expectation of a certain level of compliance from the security workers. The kind of atmosphere that is usually found in such spaces makes these workers question the social status that they enjoy in comparison with others in those spaces. The formal sector IT workers usually do not pay much attention to these workers, except when they need something very specific from them:

> Most of the management does not pay much attention to us. The only time that people higher up in the workplace hierarchy will talk to us is when they need something done or when there is a security issue or there is a complaint. But usually, when you get called to the HR or somebody in the office, it is usually bad news. (Woman Security Worker, Gurgaon)

The least preferred sites are residential spaces because security work in residential spaces is usually characterised by the longest hours, poorer pay, and more interaction with residents. The preference for official and commercial spaces is also because of the fact that in residential spaces, security workers are frequently given odd jobs such as grocery shopping and petty daily chores by the residents and are subjected to longer hours and harsher job descriptions. Male security guards negotiate with such issues utilising the better access and engagement that they have with the urban space, but it is particularly harsher on the women security guards. Security workers have a highly skewed gender ratio among themselves. Women security guards are few and far between, and when they are usually employed, it is usually in spaces where women outnumber men. Women security guards are often treated differently than their male counterparts with many of them having to perform odd favours to get a 'tolerable' shift or a site that suits their capacities and vulnerabilities as women workers. One female security worker stated:

> We have very bad shifts. Most of us work in the night shifts in the campuses. The problem is that even if we want, it is difficult to get normal shifts. Most of the supervisors ask for favours, some are even of sexual nature. Some of the women are coerced into doing that. Some do not, some who do not end up like me in this wretched night shift for half of the month or get thrown out. (Woman Security Guard, Bengaluru)

The worker's narrative brings out a crucial aspect of security work: the issue of shifts and the fear of being dismissed. Shifts and their humane management are extremely important to these workers because most of them do not only work one job, but rather remain engaged in multiple jobs. So, if they are overworked in one particular shift, it naturally has an effect on the next job that they do. While in residential spaces, the shifts are at times close to 24 hours—which is often justified by the employers saying that they are often given accommodation at the same property. At the same time, the behaviour of the formal sector workers towards the workers also changes once they make the transition from their workplaces to their residential spaces. Two security workers, one man and one woman, who have worked for more than five years as security guards in various residential, commercial, and office spaces in Gurgaon narrate:

In residential spaces, the shifts are just gruelling. Most of it is 24 hours in duration, and we are not only restricted to security work but are often treated as house servants, They will ask us to get them groceries, clean their flats, etc. That is why I do not like to work there, but then I do not have control over that. Some of the people who are good with their supervisors have some control but I do not. (Male Security Guard, Gurgaon)

The major problem is with shifts only regardless of what anybody says. See, in a commercial space, or even in an ATM or an office, there will be five to six guards, so it is sometimes possible to just get some rest, that is not the case in a residential complex. Here you have to be on your feet everytime. (Woman Security Guard, Gurgaon)

One of the major issues that arise in these narratives is the question of shifts. Some of the security guards even at times have a full-day's shift, that is, they come into the office when the office opens and leave only after all the employees have left the office. The nature and duration of their shifts not only makes them part of a highly exploited workforce but also makes them vulnerable to intra-working-class violence. The security guards in the IT offices usually have shifts that range from 8 hours to 12 hours with half an hour of lunch break included in their shifts. The lunch-hours for the workers are usually different from those of the formal IT workers. They are structured in such a way that the interactions between them and other workers can be decreased as much as possible. While to the bare eye, such methods of social control might seem trivial, but in reality they have a drastic effect on the class consciousness of these workers—both the formal and the invisible workforce—which constitutes an important part of what the present book refers to as the 'Metro Middle Class' in India. The security workers in the IT industry are seen to be appendages to the formal sector industry and are usually analysed to be complementing the formal sector workers. The difference between domestic workers and the security workers lies in the ways in which their exploitation contributes to the de-humanisation of the formal sector workers turning the formal sector workers into agents of capitalist exploitation.

CLEANING THE HI-TECH SPACES

Different kinds of informal jobs are created and sustained by the bourgeoning IT sector in India. The work that IT workers do is managed in an environment that is sought to be resembling the west. Business parks and

120   S. DEB ROY

technology firms in India usually harbour a significant number of other services than merely work desks and cubicles and cabins. These services are supposed to be working towards transforming the offices into aspirational spaces that can adequately cater to the growing lifestyle demands of the middle classes that the IT sector employs. Most IT workers' workplaces are structured in such a manner that has to maintain adequate safety, cleanliness, and hygiene to suit global standards. The technology and business parks that house most IT companies in the country have sanitation practices that are different than the usual ones practised in the country. The standards set are more stringent and more rigorous than the accepted social norms in India. They desire these spaces to be highly sanitised, automated, and sophisticated that can conform to their global standards:

> I do not even understand what kind of techniques they use. They could have given us simple broom and a liquid to wash the floor and washrooms, but no, here they have given us a host of different liquids that we are supposed to use. Not using one of those results in the supervisors coming and scolding us. (Sanitation Worker, Bengaluru)

The perception of a particular space depends on the ways in which capitalism structures such spaces. The structuring of a particular space becomes an integral part of the perception that it generates among those that inhabit the same and play an important role in structuring the lives of the people who live and work in those spaces (Lefebvre, 1991). Domestic workers make the IT workers feel empowered and provide them with a certain class belongingness making them *feel different than the traditional working class*. The security guards keep them protected from the broader society that is experienced on an everyday basis by the working class and other marginalised populace. While domestic workers are usually employed through community relationships or through networks of acquaintance within enclosed spaces such as gated communities, security guards are usually employed through an agency or a service provider. Even though domestic and security workers form an important part of the gentrification project of the cities, their work remains incomplete without the cleanliness that sanitation workers provide.

Like the security workers, every major IT office or tech park usually has a contract with an agency or service provider which provides them with outsourced sanitation workers. Many of these workers, like their counterparts in the security jobs, are migrant workers, engaged in jobs considered derogatory by most of the urban middle class. Though an essential job, sanitation work has historically been relegated to the lower castes in the Indian society. The total number of sanitation workers in India is around 1.2 million most of whom come either from the Dalit community or from de-notified tribes (Shruti, 2021). Writing in *The Wire*, Kumbhare writes:

> The caste system continues to 'reserve' sewer and sanitation work for Dalits ... For instance, around 30,000 sanitation workers are employed by the Greater Mumbai Municipal Corporation and all 30,000 are Dalits. Estimates say that 40–60% of the six million households of Dalit sub-castes are engaged in sanitation work. (Kumbhare, 2020, Para 18)

Sanitation jobs in India thus are primarily a caste-based occupation. Even though the Supreme Court had passed a judgement banning manual scavenging in India, there has been no enactment of a law penalising those who violate the terms of the judgement.[4] The system of caste-based employment has been particular harsh towards Dalit women, who have suffered tremendously throughout the pandemic. The occupation of being a sanitation worker in India is a difficult one and is ridden with stigmas and social corruption to the extent that even their deaths often do not get the attention that they deserve even though, their death rates are pretty high in comparison to other sectors (Shruti, 2021). India's issues with serious public health concerns such as sanitation encompasses the methods in which sanitation responsibilities are often portrayed to be the sole domain of one particular caste. However, sanitation workers in most urban spaces in India are not only defined by their caste identity, but also by their gender identity. Both security workers and domestic workers suffer from skewed gender ratios among themselves (NSDC, 2013; Wadhawan, 2013). Structures of skewed gender ratio and low wages are more evident in other sectors of informal work such as sanitation, hospitality, and retail. As a Participatory Research in Asia (PRIA) paper states:

---

[4] According to the *International Dalit Solidarity* Network, the number of dry latrines which are cleaned by human beings in India amounts to a staggering figure of 794,390, along with which around 497,236 toilets remain unattended until a human being, or an animal comes in to clean it (Parvati, August 31, 2020).

The occupation of sanitation work is intrinsically integrated with caste in India. This link earmarks sanitation as the sole concern of just one caste—the Dalits, and among them *Valmikis*.[5] An even wider gap of injustice appears on disaggregating the Valmiki community by gender. Women sanitation workers (specifically lower caste women) in a country in which patriarchy still thrives, live and work under the double burden of labour. (PRIA, 2019, p. 5)

The informal workers remain the most vulnerable sections of the workforce not only due to economic reasons but also due to the social exclusion that they face, which is often of a gendered nature. The International Labour Organisation (ILO) (2018a, 2018b) notes that women are more likely to work in the informal sector because they lack the desired resources to access better jobs, and as only 29 percent of the women are employed in the organised sector (Tandon, 2021). Women workers in the informal sector because of the structural and financial limitations that they face constitute an easier basis for exploitative tendencies to grow in the society and become much more effective agents to provide a sense of alienated control and empowerment to the formal IT workers. Ideas and services such as these evade documentation in mainstream literature and documents that the companies or tech parks. These parks, located geographically in the Global South, present to the workers a sense of being placed ideologically in the Global North evoking feelings of empowerment, modernity, and a general sense of superiority. However, the modernity that the alienated empowerment that these spaces provide becomes the basis around which the class identity of the formal IT workers is constructed. The growing-class confusion among the IT workers increases the tenacity of the false consciousness that they possess. Most of the middle classes globally harbour a sense of class confusion that drives their analysis and perception of the space that they live and work in.

Sanitation workers in the IT offices often perform similar roles as the domestic workers do at home with job descriptions that range from childcare (in case of offices which provide such services to their employees) to maintenance of mini-kitchens, washrooms, and toilets. While, as Chap. 2 has mentioned, the formal Dalit IT workers often come into the IT sector to escape the pre-capitalist forms of exploitation that is meted out to them in their communities, the situation is quite different for the migrant

---

[5] A sub-caste among the Dalits that mainly engages in sanitation work.

sanitation workers. Urban municipal governments have tended to institutionalise the relationship between caste and labour by bringing in significant numbers of Dalit workers to perform sanitation work in urban areas to maintain urban sanitation. For example:

> The large majority of sanitation workers are also migrant worker from another state. In our field sites in Karnataka, most workers were from Andhra Pradesh or Telangana but had settled in Karnataka for two or more generation, in Mumbai many sanitation worker households are from Gujarat, Haryana or Karnataka but have been in Mumbai for more than 70 years. (Shruti, 2021, pp. 167–168)

Migrant sanitation workers live under some of the worst conditions imaginable to the human society with extremely bad conditions of sanitation and public health (Nazeer, 2014). Though an essential sector, sanitation workers find themselves to be further excluded from the society with newer forms of exclusionary measures being enacted (MWSN, 2020). Most of the mainstream approaches have tended to resolve the issues faced by such workers through a reduction of rates for public services that is often linked to better accessibility—like how the Municipal Socialists once advocated for (Gehrke, 2016). Economistic agendas do not attack such structures directly, but rather perceive economic upliftment to be a sufficient precursor to social upliftment creating a segregation between economic liberation and philosophical interventions into exploitative social processes (Dunayevskaya, 1973). The IT workers—most of whom, as has already been stated, come from middle-class backgrounds, and do not experience caste atrocities like the sanitation and hospitality workers who even if come from similar caste backgrounds—come from very different class backgrounds. The class that the sanitation workers come from affects the kind of urban experience that they have, both within their workplaces and in general. The sanitation workers at the technology workplaces are treated akin to sub-human beings and are often exposed to caste-based slurs and gender-based exclusion.

The experiences of the sanitation workers in the IT workplaces reflect the deep-seated nature of caste violence in the country. The treatment meted out to them by the formal IT workers is a testimony to the segregations that capitalism brings forward within the workforce. The kind of relationships that the sanitation workers, mostly Dalits, form with other Dalit formal sector IT workers is one that is dictated by the class structure

124   S. DEB ROY

in the society. The prevailing segregation between Dalit formal IT sector workers and the sanitation workers who work in their offices provides one with a glimpse of how class differences continue to operate within the same caste. The sanitation workers have failed to garner an effective support from their fellow Dalits in the sector. The idea of caste belongingness being a more effective structure of solidarity over class consciousness has not held good in the case of sanitation workers, at least in the IT spaces as can be analysed from the following narratives from sanitation workers in major tech parks in Bengaluru and Pune:

> We get treated like garbage in these spaces. There is one incident that I can remember, I was cleaning up the bathroom in the office and this young person came up and started complaining. Later I came to know that he is a Dalit as well, from my own state. What will you say to these people? If they do not understand our issues, then we cannot expect others to understand as well. (Male Sanitation Worker, Bengaluru)

> The idea of caste being a factor of integration does not work everywhere. The Dalit person who works in the cubicles is very different than me. He or she will not eat with me, will not talk to me, and will never speak good of me. Most of them try to find issues with the work that I do. Of course, I do not know all the backward caste people in the offices, but at least some I know and almost all of them are like that only. (Woman Sanitation Worker, Pune)

Such problems are manifestations of the contradictions that exist between middle-class Dalits and the impoverished Dalits. The exploitation that their own fellow Dalits inflict upon them contributes to an already de-humanised state of existence for the poorer sections of the Dalit populace in the country. This is in stark contrast with the relationship that formal IT workers from certain communities—such as those who come from Bihar or Uttar Pradesh—come to share with other marginalised workers from their native regions, such as those who work as security workers or as gig workers. While sanitation workers remain segregated—and often even exploited by—from their caste brethren, the caste-dimension of their exploitation has rarely been acknowledged by the ruling class in the public domain. On the other hand, the discrimination that is inflicted upon people from Bihar or Uttar Pradesh is widely criticised in the public domain. And since the middle classes today get attracted to issues that garner more socio-cultural attraction (Jha & Pushpendra, 2022), it naturally finds itself in a better position to assert its regional identity in certain specific contexts. The middle class, thus, in urban areas, schooled in accordance with bourgeois and petty-bourgeois values, becomes the perfect manifestation of the uncritical working class that capitalism desires to create in the society (Althusser, 2014). The exploitation that the sanitation workers face proves that '[t]he colonization of [...] sociability by the market has not only generated a new source of profit making but has also helped to drive wedges into the fabric of their social lives, undermining the basis of future solidarities' (Huws, 2014, p. 12).

There has been a constant effort from the governmental structures to relegate the impacts of caste atrocities to promote an idea of India that suits its neoliberal positioning as a capitalist free-market economy free from pre-capitalist structures of exploitation. These workers suffer from structural and material exploitation fuelled by caste violence that the IT workers often inflict upon them on an everyday basis. Because these workers are not part of the mainstream IT workforce, their issues and problems often do not get the attention that they deserve. While the formal workforce has human resource managers to listen to and resolve their problems, these workers do not enjoy any such mechanisms of grievance redressal. Any issues that they face in their working lives are transferred to their supervisors, who mostly do not pay much attention to their problems and the occupational hazards that they face, and because they are also excluded from the

The Foundations of the Metro Middle Class

Any capitalist socio-economic structure is based on the production of commodities through structures and ideologies which convert everything, including emotions, into tradeable goods (Marx, 1867/1976; Illouz, 2007). In the contemporary context of India, it has meant that entities which had been previously categorised as essential entities produced and consumed by communities have begun to be exploited as profitable entities, like all other commodities (Harriss-White, 2008, 2011). The conditions of life faced by the invisible workers of the IT sector are a result of the transformation that has been brought forward within the Indian economy since the late 1980s. The constant gentrification of the IT hubs with highly vulnerable and socially marginalised workers creates the ideal conditions for the emergence of a highly de-humanised social structure. The creation of the invisible workforce that sustains the IT industry in India is not created out of a vacuum but is rather a result of the large-scale migration of the rural populace that has characterised India in the past decade. Primitive accumulation in India has produced the basis for the transition of the agrarian economy to a neoliberal one, and as such has decimated the agrarian relations of production in the country resulting in a growing reserve army of labour for capital in the urban spaces to exploit (Gopalakrishnan, 2009). The formal IT sector workers today merely act as a part of the system of production with other workers from the marginalised sections enabling them to satisfy their lifestyle requirements. The class consciousness of the formal sector workers is not only formed out of their economic positioning in the society but also formed out of the kind of interactions that they have with other workers in the space that they occupy.

The working-class identity today is not only constructed by economic policies and financial structuring, but by the intersections of various social and biological attributes possessed by individual workers and the kind of relationship that these attributes share with pre-existing modes of exploitation (Bahl, 1995; Veeraraghavan, 2013). It is a dynamic one shaped by the socio-economic and cultural conditions that the workers find in their everyday lives (Thompson, 1963; Wright, 1976). Such complicated social positionings characterise the new workforce that is coming into employment in the formal sectors. The formal IT sector workers have come to be an important part of the de-humanisation of the society desired by the capitalist structures in place. The IT workers have become important actors in the processes through which the capitalist structure in place effects changes at a socio-psychological level. The destruction of the social solidarity mechanisms by neoliberal value structures has also infiltrated the various collectives and unions which function within the IT spaces that becomes explicit when one considers these invisible service workers. While many IT unions and collectives have worked among the formal IT sector workers, the invisible workers have more often than not been left out of these organisational forms. The response to such effects of neoliberalism by the trade unions is contingent upon the power that they represent in specific social and political systems in place (Bound & Johnson, 1992). The reaction that the trade unions could generate against neoliberalism in India was thus contingent upon the effects that neoliberal reforms' institutionalisation has had on the workers, especially those who were or would be employed in the private sector.

The power that the formal IT workers have over their domestic workers allows them to generate a sense of empowerment that is akin to a false consciousness that many workers embody within themselves. The management of the society becomes a major factor in the way in which the working individuals articulate their socio-political existence, which in many developing societies depends upon the way in which the state exists for them because they remain dependent on the state for basic commodities and services (Swaminathan, 2003). Socio-economic restructuring of the state affects at a macro-level but also affects the communities and cities that individuals live in, making an impact on prices, affordability, and credit structures in the society (Woldoff et al., 2016; Stebenne, 2020)—factors which are critical to middle-class employees. The changes are highly noticeable in the interaction which occurs between the blue-collar workers and those who can be categorised as being upper middle-class professionals or white-collar workers. The latter often act against the interests of the former without taking into consideration the way in which the broader political scenario in the society is constructed (Reeves, 2017).

Human beings, within such a space, become mere signs to cater to the psychological needs of other human beings placed above them in the socio-economic and cultural hierarchy. Neoliberalism's inherent desire remains the production of a sense of individualisation that is based on the destruction of structures of social solidarity (Navarro, 2007). It renders the state in a substitutive state of existence, one which has little functional power except the power to create newer markets in domains where a market does not exist (Harvey, 2007; Berry, 2022). The absence of an interventionist state that can provide them with opportunities for vertical social mobility produces the social conditions whereby the impoverished populace has no other option but to engage in jobs created by the market to satisfy the methods of profit accumulation in place. The urban space that is developed within these IT hubs is one that is increasingly tilted in favour of generating and fetishising signs that promote a social, ideological, and material consciousness of the marginalised (Lefebvre, 1996). The urban space that IT hubs develop is a space that is dominated by such alienating signs of affluence and consumerism—one of the key characteristics of the *Metro Middle Class.*

REFERENCES

Adnan, S. (2014). Primitive Accumulation and the 'transition to capitalism' in Neoliberal India: Mechanisms, Resistance, and the Persistence of Self-Employed Labour. In B. Harriss-White & J. Heyer (Eds.), *Indian Capitalism in Development*. Routledge.

Ahalya, R., & Pal, S. B. (2017). *Identification and Characterization of Middle Class in India and Its Comparison with Other Economic Classes*. ISID Retrieved April 5, 2023, from https://www.isid.ac.in/~epu/acegd2017/papers/AhalyaRamanathan.pdf

Althusser, L. (2014). *On the Reproduction of Capitalism: Ideology and Ideological State Apparatuses*. Verso.

Bahl, V. (1995). *The Making of the Indian Working Class: A Case of the Tata Iron and Steel Company, 1880–1946*. SAGE.

Banerjee, A. V., & Duflo, E. (2019). *Good Economics for Hard Times*. Juggernaut.

Bell, B., Codreanu, M., & Machin, S. (2020). *What Can Previous Recessions Tell Us About the Covid-19 Downturn? A CEP Covid-19 Analysis*. Centre for Economic Performance, London School of Economics and Political Science.

Berman, M. (1983). *All that Is Solid Melts into Air: The Experience of Modernity*. Verso.

Berry, C. (2022). The Substitutive State? Neoliberal State Interventionism Across Industrial, Housing and Private Pensions Policy in the UK. *Competition and Change, 26*(2), 242–265.

Blundell, J., & Machin, S. (2020). *Self-Employment in the Covid-19 Crisis. A CEP Covid-19 Analysis*. Centre for Economic Performance, London School of Economics and Political Science.

Bound, J., & Johnson, G. (1992). Changes in the Structure of Wages in the 1980s: An Evaluation of Alternative Explanations. *American Economic Review, 82*, 371–392.

Cannizzaro, E., Cirrincione, L., Mazzucco, W., Scorciapino, A., Catalano, C., Ramaci, T., Ledda, C., & Plescia, F. (2020). Night-Time Shift Work and Related Stress Responses: A Study on Security Guards. *International Journal of Environmental Research and Public Health, 17*(2), 562.

Chakraborty, I. (2021). *Invisible Labour: Support Service Workers in India's Information Technology Industry*. Routledge.

Chen, M., & Skinner, C. (2014). The Urban Informal Economy: Enhanced Knowledge, Appropriate Policies and Effective Organization. In S. Parnell & S. Oldfield (Eds.), *The Routledge Handbook on Cities of the Global South*. Routledge.

Das, R. J. (2015). Critical Observations on Neo-liberalism and India's New Economic Policy. *Journal of Contemporary Asia, 45*(4), 715–726.

Das Gupta, M. (2017, February 6). Delhi, Gurgaon, Gautam Buddh Nagar Favourite with Migrants: Economic Survey. *Hindustan Times*. Retrieved December 3, 2023, from https://www.hindustantimes.com/india-news/delhi-gurgaon-gautam-buddh-nagar-favourite-with-migrants-economic-survey/story-d1i4C0zMJfA8HMjDfptyyK.html

Davis, A. (1983/2003). *Women, Race and Class*. Navayana.

Dunayevskaya, R. (1973). *Philosophy and Revolution*. Humanities Press.

FICCI. (2013). *Private Security Services Industry: Securing Future Growth*. Retrieved December 15, 2023, from https://www.capsi.in/files/ficci-report.pdf

Gehrke, J. P. (2016). A Radical Endeavor: Joseph Chamberlain and the Emergence of Municipal Socialism in Birmingham. *American Journal of Economics and Sociology, 75*(1), 23–57.

Godelier, M. (1967). System, Structure and Contradiction in "Capital" (B. Brewsters, Trans.). In R. Miliband & J. Seville (Eds.), *Socialist Register: Volume 4*. Merlin Press.

Gopalakrishnan, S. (2009). *Neoliberalism and Hindutva: Fascism, Free Markets and the Restructuring of Indian Capitalism*. Aakar.

Grant Thornton. (2015). *Private Security Services in India*. Retrieved December 15, 2023, from https://www.grantthornton.in/insights/articles/private-security-services-industry-in-india/

Greer, G. (1991). *The Change*. Bloomsbury.

Harriss-White, B. (2003). *India Working: Essays on Society and Economy*. Cambridge University Press.

Harriss-White, B. (2008). Market Politics and Climate Change. *Development, 51*(3), 350–358.

Harriss-White, B. (2011). Revisiting "technology and underdevelopment": Climate Change, Politics and the "D" of Solar Energy Technology in Contemporary India. In V. Fitzgerald, J. Heyer, & R. Thorp (Eds.), *Overcoming the Persistence of Inequality and Poverty* (pp. 92–126). Palgrave Macmillan.

Harvey, D. (2007). Neoliberalism as Creative Destruction. *The Annals of the American Academy of Political and Social Science, 610*, 22–44.

Harvey, D. (2012). *Rebel Cities: From the Right to the City to the Urban Revolution*. Verso.

Huws, U. (2014). *Labor in the Global Digital Economy: The Cybertariat Comes of Age*. Monthly Review Press.

Illouz, E. (2007). *Cold Intimacies: The Making of Emotional Capitalism*. Polity.

International Labour Organisation. (2018a). *Informality and Non-Standard Forms of Employment*. Retrieved December 3, 2023, from https://www.ilo.org/wcmsp5/groups/public/%2D%2D-dgreports/%2D%2D-inst/documents/publication/wcms_646040.pdf

International Labour Organisation. (2018b). *Women and Men in the Informal Economy*. Retrieved December 3, 2023, from https://www.ilo.org/wcmsp5/groups/public/%2D%2D-dgreports/%2D%2D-dcomm/documents/publication/wcms_626831.pdf

Jain, S., & Mishra, U. S. (2019). Demand for Domestic Workers in India: Its Characteristics and Correlates. *The Indian Journal of Labour Economics*. https://doi.org/10.1007/s41027-019-0150-y

Jha, M. K., & Pushpendra. (2022). Contextualising India's New Middle Class: Intersectionalities and Social Mobility. In M. K. Jha & Pushpendra (Eds.), *Beyond Consumption: India's New Middle Class in the Neo-Liberal State*. Routledge.

Kishore, R. (2018, September 26). Private Security Industry Is a Bigger Employer than Healthcare in India: Study. *Hindustan Times*. Retrieved December 3, 2023, from https://www.hindustantimes.com/india-news/private-security-industry-is-a-bigger-employer-than-healthcare-in-india-study/story-ROQwoKDbzVA3NQevqqdRBK.html

Kumbhare, S. (2020, May 7). Sanitation Workers: At the Bottom of the Frontline Against COVID-19? *The Wire*. Retrieved December 3, 2023, from https://www.thewire.in/article/urban/sanitation-workers-covid-19

Lefebvre, H. (1991). *The Production of Space*. Basil Blackwell.

Lefebvre, H. (1996). *Writings on Cities*. Blackwell.

Mahajan, S. K. (2019). Private Security Guards in India: The Paradox of a Booming Industry and Burden of a Low Status Occupation. *Think India Journal*, *22*(33), 153–157.

Malpani, M., & Ramita, D. M. (2023, August 28). Migrant Workers Forced to Flee Back Home, Gurugram High-rises Feel the Pinch. *The Hindu*. Retrieved December 3, 2023, from https://www.thehindu.com/news/cities/Delhi/migrant-workers-forced-to-flee-back-home-gurugram-high-rises-feel-the-pinch/article67238760.ece

Marx, K. (1867/1976). *Capital: Volume 1*. London: Penguin.

Migrant Workers' Solidarity Network. (2020). *Citizens and the Sovereign: Stories from the Largest Human Exodus in Contemporary Indian History*. MWSN.

National Skill Development Corporation (NSDC). (2013). *Human Resource and Skill Requirements in the Private Security Services Sector (2013-17, 2017-22)*. Retrieved December 15, 2023, from https://skillsip.nsdcindia.org/knowledge-products/human-resource-and-skill-requirements-private-security-services-sector

Navarro, V. (2007). Neoliberalism as a Class Ideology; or the Political Causes of the Growth of Inequalities. *International Journal of Health Services*, *37*(1), 47–62.

Nazeer, M. (2014, February 1). Health and Hygiene in Times of Migration. *The Hindu*. Retrieved December 3, 2023, from https://www.thehindu.com/

news/national/kerala/health-and-hygiene-in-times-of-migration/article5642482.ece

Neetha, N. (2013). Paid Domestic Work: Making Sense of the Jigsaw Puzzle. *Economic and Political Weekly, 48*(43), 35–38.

Negri, A. (1989a). *The Politics of Subversion.* Polity.

Negri, A. (1989b). Archaeology and the Project. In *Revolution Retrieved.* Red Notes.

Noronha, E., Chakraborty, S., & D'Cruz, P. (2018). Doing Dignity Work: Indian Security Guards Interface with Precariousness. *Journal of Business Ethics, 162*, 553–575.

Parmar, B. (2023, November 7). IT Pays? Now Not Much Higher for the New Hire. *Economic Times.* Retrieved December 3, 2023, from https://economictimes.indiatimes.com/tech/information-tech/it-pays-now-not-much-higher-for-the-new-hire/articleshow/105020685.cms?from=mdr#

Participatory Research in Asia. (2019). *Lived Realities of Women Sanitation Workers in India.* PRIA.

Patnaik, U. (2007). Neoliberalism and Rural Poverty in India. *Economic and Political Weekly, 42*(30), 3132–3150.

Patnaik, P. (2008). The Accumulation Process in the Period of Globalisation. *Economic and Political Weekly, 43*(26–27), 108–113.

Reddy, S. (2023, July 18). 81% Domestic Helps in State Do Not Get Minimum Wages. *The Times of India.* Retrieved December 3, 2023, from https://timesofindia.indiatimes.com/city/hyderabad/81-domestic-helps-in-state-do-not-get-minimum-wages/articleshow/101840804.cms

Reeves, R. V. (2017). *Dream Hoarders: How the American Upper Middle Class Is Leaving Everyone Else in the Dust, Why that Is a Problem, and What to Do About It?* Brookings Institution Press.

Sarkar, B. (2023, July 7). Five in 10 Employees in India Worry About Job Security: Survey. *Economic Times.* Retrieved December 3, 2023, from https://economictimes.indiatimes.com/jobs/hr-policies-trends/five-in-10-employees-in-india-worry-about-job-security-survey/articleshow/101563596.cms?from=mdr

Sengupta, A. (2007). *Report on the Conditions of Work and Promotion of Livelihood in the Unorganised Sector.* National Commission for Enterprises in the Unorganised Sector.

Shah, M. (2008). Structures of Power in Indian Society: A Response. *Economic and Political Weekly, 43*(46), 78–83.

Sharma, S. (2022). Contradictions of Neoliberal Urbanism: The Case of Paid Domestic Workers in Indian Cities. *Critical Sociology, 49*(4–5). https://doi.org/10.1177/08969205221112827

Shruti, I. (2021). Of Sewage, Struggle, and the State: Caste and Contractorization in Contemporary Sanitation Work. In *India Exclusion Report 2019-20*. Three Essays Collective and Centre for Equity Studies.

Somashekher, C., & Mangalamma, K. M. (2019). Women Domestic Workers in Bangalore City: A Sociological Study. *International Journal of Innovative Science, Engineering & Technology, 6*(11), 100–107.

Stebenne, D. (2020). *Promised Land: How the Rise of the Middle Class Transformed America, 1929–1968*. Scribner.

Stein, S. (2019). *Capital City*. Verso.

Swaminathan, M. (2003). *Weakening Welfare*. Leftword.

Tandon, A. (2021, September 27). Only 29% of Women Workforce in Organised Job Sector. *The Tribune*. Retrieved March 3, 2023, from https://www.tribuneindia.com/news/nation/only-29-women-workforce-in-organised-job-sector-317042

Tandon, A., & Rathi, A. (2022). Sustaining Urban Labour Markets: Situating Migration and Domestic Work in India's 'Gig' Economy. *Economy and Space*. https://doi.org/10.1177/0308518X22120822

Thompson, E. P. (1963/2013). *The Making of the English Working Class*. Vintage.

Times of India. (2023, November 7). *IT Sector Job Switch Not Paying Off?* Retrieved December 3, 2023, from http://timesofindia.indiatimes.com/articleshow/105030320.cms?from=mdr#&utm_source=contentofinterest&utm_medium=text&utm_campaign=cppst

Tronti, M. (1962). *Factory and Society*. Operaismo in English. Retrieved December 3, 2023, from https://operaismoinenglish.wordpress.com/2013/06/13/factory-and-society/

Veeraraghavan, D. (2013). *The Making of the Madras Working Class*. Leftword.

Vishwakarma, V., Khanam, T., & Manchanda, R. (2022). Analysis of Labor Migration in Gurugram: A Study of Construction Workers. *Journal of Perspectives in Social Science and Humanities Research, 1*(1), 24–44.

Vyas, M. (2016). Sleepless in Mumbai Spotlight on Elderly Security Guards. *Economic and Political Weekly, 51*(26/27).

Wadhawan, N. (2013). Living in Domesti-City: Women and Migration for Domestic Work from Jharkhand. *Economic and Political Weekly, 48*(43), 47–54.

Woldoff, R. A., Morrison, L. M., & Glass, M. R. (2016). *Priced Out: Stuyvesant Town and the Loss of Middle-Class Neighbourhoods*. New York University Press.

Wright, E. O. (1976). Class Boundaries in Advanced Capitalist Societies. *New Left Review, 1*(98).

CHAPTER 6

The Arrival of the 'Metro' Middle Class

INTRODUCTION: IT HUBS AS URBAN MIDDLE-CLASS SPACES

Urban spaces get constructed through the constant, and often sudden, transformation of traditional economic structures in place. The transformation of the traditional space results in the modification of the workforce and their social dynamics therein. Most IT hubs in the country have been formed out of changes within the traditional economic structures in place, which have had an effect on the kind of spaces that these urban IT hubs have presented to their inhabitants. The manifestations of such restructuring can be noticed in all the contemporary IT hubs in India as has been mentioned in the previous chapter. These hubs are formed through the hyper-mobile nature of the contemporary workforce, regardless of their skill levels (Huws, 2014). The middle-class migrants who come to these urban spaces and embody within themselves a significant amount of social capital attempt to re-engineer the spaces in their own light through the consciousness that they gain as workers, as citizens, and as human beings.

Neoliberalism in India has altered the traditional class structure in the Indian society, and the IT workers remain at the core of this massive structural process. Neoliberalism has modified human lives globally by bringing forward newer modes of domination and control. In the process, it has given rise to a distinct middle-class *way of life* that has become one of the

© The Author(s), under exclusive license to Springer Nature Switzerland AG 2024
S. Deb Roy, *The Rise of the Information Technology Society in India*, Dynamics of Virtual Work,
https://doi.org/10.1007/978-3-031-58128-1_6

133

most persistent features of contemporary global capitalism because of its role in generating a sense of consumerism in the society (Nunlee, 2017; Weiss, 2019). The middle class in India has grown from being less than 1 per cent in the 1990s to around 5 per cent in 2004, and further to around 6 per cent of the entire population, that is, around 70 million, in 2010, with it being expected to be around 547 million in 2026 (Lahiri, 2014; Roy, 2018). The growth of the middle class in the past two decades is constructed on the basis of a highly ambiguous perception of growth and development, both economically and socially (RUPE, 2008a, 2008b, 2008c, 2014). Regardless of how they are defined or analysed, they have been an integral part of the plans and policies pertaining to economic and industrial growth since the 1991 economic reforms (Kohli, 2006). Despite the rise in people claiming themselves to be members of the middle class, no clear definition of the same has been available to either scholars or activists (Leigh, 1994). Some of the definitions have focused on their economic characteristics, while some others have focused on the kind of work that they do.

In most societies, the creation of the middle class is a distinctly political process welcomed by both the right and the left wing because the middle class often serves as the basis for generating a discourse favouring the status quo (Le Grand & Winter, 1986). It is the political role of the middle class that makes it an extremely important part of the neoliberal reimagination of the society. The role of the middle class under capitalism varies with regard to the society concerned as societies are subjective entities that act as parts of the global mode of production in conjunction with the local means and relations of production (Dunayevskaya, 1973, 1979, 1983). The subjective nature of the social contradictions creates the conditions under which neoliberalism affects the working individuals therein coming to mean different things for different individuals and groups contingent on their socio-economic and cultural position (Ong, 2006; Birch, 2015).

In plain terms, the middle class is the group of people who fall in between the socio-economic hierarchy that capitalist development produces in the process of constructing the bourgeoisie and the working class (Roy, 2018). They have often been defined as a heterogeneous group, largely composed of 'professionals (architects, clergymen, doctors, civil servants, administrative grade, lawyers, teachers, nurses, accountants, engineers, scientists, etc.), employers and managers plus the immediate members of their families' (Le Grand & Winter, 1986, pp. 402–3). They are 'people who are beyond the poverty line but not in the category of the rich' (Lahiri, 2014, p. 37), and have no issues in purchasing the basic necessities of life (Varma, 2014). Noted economist, Meghnad Desai (2015) argues that 'the middle class is somewhere between the bottom three income deciles and the top two' in India with incomes above the mean income which makes it a minority in an unequal society (pp. xv–xvi). The middle classes have been important parts of the ideological and political construction of the social consensus that neoliberalism attempts to create in the society, especially pertaining to privatisation and austerity policies. The constantly deteriorating public discourse centred on the inability of the public sector to perform effectively in India helped the neoliberal reforms to establish a neoliberal consensus (Jha & Pankaj, 2021). The middle classes have played an important role in that regard. The middle classes do not serve antagonistic purposes like the working class, but rather have become a normalised component of the neoliberal process appreciating the benefits that it draws from neoliberalism (Ehrenreich & Ehrenreich, 1979).

As a class, the PMC is employed in mid-level to lower managerial jobs and has often harboured a hostility towards the waged workers (Ehrenreich & Ehrenreich, 1979). The PMC in the Indian IT sector is similar but also has its own distinct characters. It does possess, similar to the PMC, a common lifestyle, educational backgrounds and training, and kinship networks, but at the same time, it is also characterised by the effects of internal migration that has had a considerable influence on the kind of aspirations and dreams that it has come to internalise. Aided by an urban space that fetishises productivity, and constantly attempts to undermine the human aspects of existence (Harvey, 2006, 2016), along with an inherent desire to create a better upwardly mobile lives for themselves through permanent migration to urban centres (Tumbe, 2018), the PMC in India has evolved into a section of the workforce that evades being restricted to the classical contours of the PMC. The chapter will refer to this particular section of the global PMC as being the Metro Middle Class (MMC)—a class formed out of the PMC in India by widespread migration to the IT hubs.

Because of the global economic slowdown, high inflation, and loss of formal employment opportunities, an increasing number of individuals from the middle class have begun to see themselves as being exploited under capitalism (Curtis et al., 2020). Despite being oppressed as citizens, the formal IT workers possess a certain empowerment because of the social and cultural security that is provided by their jobs. The economic security provided to them by their high-paying jobs coupled with the

136   S. DEB ROY

socio-cultural security that they often possess dictates their attitudes towards the urban reality that they find themselves and the other workers placed below them in the socio-economic and cultural hierarchy that they find therein. At this point, it is important to consider that the creation of the middle class in India, and especially the new middle class after 1991, gradually dismantled of the structural effects of pre-capitalist factors such as caste and gender for individuals in positions of privilege (Sheth, 1999). The old middle class as Pannekoek (1909) explains was a commercial one, one which had some form of capital in its possession. The only similarity which the new middle class has with the old middle class is its median income, while it differs considerably in terms of the two other important dimensions: '(1) access to large-scale industrial bureaucracies ... [and] (2) ownership as opposed to management of capital' (Nelson, 1968, p. 184). The rise of the new middle class was often analysed as being a marker of liberal progress rather than revolutionary change (Dahrendorf, 1959; Kerr et al., 1960). The construction of this new middle class depends on how the power of capital manifests itself in the society constructing the middle class as the class between the 'class of great capitalists ... [and] the class of wageworkers ... [and] constitutes the social group with medium incomes' (Pannekoek, 1909, p. 316).

The Metro Middle Class that the chapter speaks about, or the MMC in short, is different than both the old and new middle classes in the sense that it encompasses both their characteristics within itself in varying proportions. It does possess capital in the sense of its investments because investments and funds in the banks constitute a critical part of capital in the twenty-first century where *no money is idle money* (Lotz, 2016). At the same time, it is not a class with median incomes and is not placed in between the two classes, because it is economically closer to the urban upper class if not the capitalists per se. Class consciousness in the IT hubs is a complex aspect of the lives of the IT workers, one that encompasses both objective and subjective factors. The genesis of the MMC lies in the middle-class migration that occurred to the IT hubs beginning from the late 1980s, which has reached abnormal levels in the twenty-first century. The reduction of public sector jobs, uneven development, and the growing concentration of jobs in the metropolitan areas resulted in these waves of migration and since most of these individuals do not possess land—unlike the old middle classes—the traditional aspects of class segregation and consciousness do not apply to them. The formation of the MMC instead takes place through their sense of alienated belongingness to the urban space and the perceived power that they possess—even if both these aspects contribute to their own marginalisation.

A combination of underdevelopment in their native regions, the formation of a consumption-oriented achievement society, and the constant gentrification of the cities in which the IT hubs are located create the MMC in a manner whereby their consciousness begins to get dictated by the alienated social reality that they become a part of. The IT workers, despite belonging to the working class economically, self-identify themselves with the middle class socially—a factor that affects the ways in which the workers organise themselves. The subjective experience of some women as middle-class individuals makes them distinct from other women workers. The IT workers form their class identity mainly through their financial positioning that if often not determined necessarily through their incomes but rather by their ability to consume. In other words, the act of consumption itself becomes a process through which they internalise the society within themselves (Marcuse, 1964). Taking cognisance from these issues, the chapter is divided into two sections. The first section discusses certain aspects of the traditional middle classes in India, while the second section goes into a detailed discussion surrounding the ramifications of the Metro Middle Class (MMC) formation in the IT hubs.

THE *TRADITIONAL* INDIAN MIDDLE CLASS

The changes in the structural character of the social classes in India has come in the wake of most high-ranking officials such as administrators, officers, and bureaucrats in India coming from the middle-classes (Subramaniam, 1971). The middle class in India has historically been a dominant class in India because of its role in patronising various forms of cultural and economic movements, both economically and politically (Sil, 2004). It has often occupied leadership positions in various social-justice oriented movements and organisations and has been the critical vanguard of mainstreaming capitalist ethos such as consumerism and anti-political behaviour which aid neoliberalism. In doing so, the middle class has played a very important role in the transformation of the nature of the State, the market and the society in India. With neoliberalism becoming a mainstream way of life, neoliberal middle-class values based on the patronisation of pro-capitalist values have come to be celebrated as *the only* authentic social values (Sheth, 1999). The wide scale acceptance of capitalist value structures has constructed a neoliberal consensus that undermines

138   S. DEB ROY

democracy and modes of social administration creating a social compliance towards established rules and institutions often serving the existent status quo and normalising structural and socio-economic violence (Harvey, 2005; Evans & Lennard, 2018; Weiss, 2019).

The security provided to them by their jobs manifests itself in the form of subjective interactions that occur within the very selves of the workers. With the coming of neoliberal capitalism, the ways in which the working class has begun to construct their subjective selves has undergone a significant change (Nunlee, 2017), both within the workspace and outside it. The workers earning fixed wages at regular intervals and enjoying a certain degree of socio-economic freedom have begun to term themselves as being 'salaried employees' rather than as workers and such processes of changing self-identification have had an impact on the trade unions working among such workers. As a result of the middle-class-based restructuring of the society, an increasing number of people now live their working lives as being members of the salariat—a term used by Goldthorpe (2016) to refer to salaried service workers—that places them at an advantageous class position than the wage-earning working classes. The subjective interactions taking place between their oppressed selves and their empowered selves that effect their understanding of the society and the institutions therein (Freeman & Hannan, 1986). Class confusion and apathy towards traditional trade unionism and political engagement affects the negotiations between their identities as workers and customers and exposes the relationship shared by the workers' selves in their workplaces and the consciousness that shapes their social totality under the consumerist ideology propagated by neoliberal capitalism (Fleetwood, 2008). Two IT union activists state:

> These are aware workers, who have come to work in the IT sector. They are aware of what is going on in the country, the kind of poverty that is there and the constant issues that have been arising. But at the same time, they are also confused. They think that they are middle class for whom politics and unionism do not matter much. Whenever there are issues of sexual harassment and we say that we can address that through the union, they move towards the Internal Complains Committee. The management's solution attracts them. Their perspective might be different. But so was ours when we came into the union. The new workers know their rights. They might be a bit reluctant to be politically active but if we can engage with them through their perspective, then only can we progress. They are much more likely to talk to the administration and negotiate rather than do militant collective

bargaining like the trade unions used to. The point, I think is to utilise that for the benefit of the union. It will be reformist, but it will be a step forward. (IT Union Activist, Gurgaon)

In some sectors, we can mobilise the workers based on economic demands. If their daily payments get stopped, we can go there and do that. That helps. But when it comes to salaried employees, it is different. They know that they are going to receive the money. Our condition has not changed. So, this point about salaries and wages do not apply to us, I guess. But there is a difference. Previously people were passionate about their salaries, they did not count themselves as managerial staff, which many of them were. One of my colleagues had lived his entire life as a unionist, never as a manager, but it is different now. I know employees, who have recently begun working, but they are already coming to union meetings and saying that we are not workers, we are middle class people and that certain demands do not affect them. Although, in reality, we know that those demands do affect them. (IT Union Activist, Pune)

Such changes in the ideological and socio-cultural self-reflection of the workers have not occurred in a vacuum. Much of the changes are aided by a bourgeoning urban structure that actively promotes alienation, segmentation, and marketisation of the society (Lefebvre, 1991). The urban spaces that are being constructed in the Global South are characterised in such a way that they marginalise the importance of solidarity structures and networks by fetishising the idea of the atomised individual (Stahl et al., 2021), something that the middle class internalises within itself (Fernandes, 2006). The roots of the middle class in India 'lay not in industry or trade, [which were] increasingly controlled by [others], but in government service or the professions of law, education, journalism or medicine' (Sarkar, 1989, p. 68). Equipped with the social and economic capital that was bestowed upon them, the middle class had penetrated into the core of the Indian public sector, and then subsequently into the formal private sector, because it could use the welfare state, and then subsequently the neoliberal state, to its own benefits, more than the subaltern or the working classes (Ram, 2014; Khanna, 2015; Teltumbde, 2018). The rise of the middle and service classes in India is a manifestation of the hegemonical control of finance capital and neoliberalism in the society, restructuring the economic structure and the class composition of the workforce. The restructuring of the economy is dialectically related to socio-economic and cultural changes in the society, that in turn affect the everyday lives of individuals alter the structure of desires and aspirations that individuals possess that get altered by the change in the kind of jobs available for them (Deb Roy, 2021).

The middle class as it exists today was born out of the various processes brought to life by twentieth-century capitalism with highly complicated models of division of labour, cultural interventions, and through a distinction created between life and lifestyles (Giddens, 1973; Pakulski & Walters, 1996; Inglehart, 1990; Flemmen & Haakestad, 2018). With the development of the middle class, newer modes of segregation have arisen within the society. They have given rise to diverse patterns of consumption and created new aspirational lifestyles aiding the construction of compliant neoliberal subjects (Lahiri, 2014; Inglis, 2019; Deb Roy, 2021; Saraswati, 2021). The compliant *neoliberal subject* is often the middle-class worker because it is the only element in the class structure which has come to uncritically accept that the most effective method of engaging with conditions of crises is not through political resistance but by practicing a form of escapism which allows it to retain its sense of belongingness and happiness in the society despite the hardships (Faux, 2012). The complete subsumption of the unhappy consciousness that is embedded within the citizens constitutes the foundations for a compliant society where the ability to consume and adhere to established norms become the basis of one's lifestyle (Marcuse, 1964; Dekker, 2022). Under such circumstances, certain oppressive social institutions and symbols become methods of empowerment because it allows them to bypass certain institutionalised restrictions. Two women IT workers narrated about their negotiations with the society:

> The issue with most of the women IT workers is that we do realise that the system is against us. But then again, you just have to be a little bit careful, if you are careful then nothing will happen. The financial standing that we have in the society is very important for us, so it is up to us to protect it via whatever means possible. (Woman IT Worker, Pune)

> Things like sexual harassment are quite normal in the IT sector. It is not exactly reported in the media or in official company reports. But the fact that it is still continuing reflects the state of affairs. But at the same time, it is also true that because we have the money from the job, we can at least talk about these things. The poor people cannot even talk about these issues. If we go to a police station, the police at least listen, that is not the case with many women out here. (Woman IT Worker, Gurgaon)

6 THE ARRIVAL OF THE 'METRO' MIDDLE CLASS 141

For people coming from marginalised sections, the 'mainstream' mode of social existence is a cause of concern because most social spaces represent the multiaxial attributes of inequalities and power disproportionality that dominate the everyday social realities under capitalism (Bondi, 1990; McDowell, 1993; Rose, 1993; Massey, 1994; Gilbert, 1997). The existence of exploitative social relations makes the middle class subservient to the restrictive framework of lifestyle that capitalism provides. The growing quantity and quality of choices surrounding lifestyles and professions that a certain section of the working population has come to possess has had an effect on the class identity of the working individuals (Goldthorpe, 2014, 2016). The major challenge for any kind of social transformation at such a juncture, as Žižek insists, remains the reintroduction of 'the Leninist opposition of "formal" and "actual" freedom: in an act of actual freedom, one dares precisely to *break* this seductive power of symbolic efficacy. … the truly free choice is a choice in which I do not merely choose between two or more options *within* a pre-given set of coordinates rather I choose to change this set of coordinates itself' (Žižek, 2017, 'Introduction').

The development of capitalism in any society changes the structural and ideological composition of the non-capitalist classes. The new kind of public policy which emerged in India after 1991 within a rapidly changing social landscape in India aided the complete marginalisation of what many trade unionists refer to as the *actual* working class of the country. The political power enjoyed by the middle class in the *new India* however 'is nothing new … but where the so-called new middle class stake their claim to status more exclusively on economic standing, the outward sign of which is participation in rituals of consumerism evidenced and experienced within the new … India' (Donner, 2012, p. 130). Within a socio-political and cultural milieu put in place by the neoliberal management of the society, the middle class has become in India has been a powerful and instrumental force in shaping politics, especially after the economic reforms of 1991, with the economy taking a turn towards the production of social consumerism (Jaffrelot, 2008; Baru, 2016; Deb Roy, 2021). Most of these issues have become important political issues considering the rightward shift exhibited by the new middle class (Burris, 1986). The creation of the middle class in India was accompanied by the creation of a public sphere conducive to the growth of neoliberal globalisation and capitalist accumulation structures that provided ample opportunities to the growing middle class to consume (Joshi, 2001; Robinson, 2014). The middle-class expression of one's class position in such a socio-economic situation is largely based on the ability of an individual to consume. For the sustenance of the capitalist system, capital attempts to place an absolute control over both production and consumption under which human consumption becomes an act mediated by capital to enable the 'total process of reproduction of capital' (Tronti, 1973).

Under contemporary capitalism, the reproduction of capital becomes the basis of the political restructuring of the society. The middle classes engage in political processes by focusing on various aspects related to their socio-economic temporalities and cultural loyalties and not purely based on the class that it belongs to (Clark & Lipset, 1991; Goldthorpe, 1995). The service workers were supposed to, like their global counterparts, benefit from the liberalisation programmes drawn by the state because 'the less well-to-do [usually] opt for the redistribution of wealth and social welfare of the Left, whereas the better-off [usually] would deem their interests best served by' policies from the Right wing (Flemmen & Haakestad, 2018, p. 403) and advocate in favour of policies of privatisation and austerity. Capital uses the existing social consensus to generate support for reforms which are conducive to the profitability measures that it attempts to implement in a particular socio-economic and cultural context. Heath (1997) argues that because privatisation promotes marketisation and trade, it comes to have different effects on the poor and marginalised in different contexts depending on how privatisation policies are implemented. Privatisation 'is a means towards a better life for everyone, not an end in itself. Privatisation and the more widespread introduction of markets can indeed result in large improvements to efficiency if there is effective competition or regulation, but it can also result in a worsening of income distribution to such a degree that the fabric of society is threatened' (Heath, 1997, p. 31). The latter often characterises large-scale privatisation in countries of the Global South, which in turn results in further segmentation of the workforce (Cleaver, 1979/2014).

The formation of the new middle class in India often transcended caste and religious lines and created a fertile ground for the propagation of neoliberal values in the Indian society (Fazal, 2021). In much of the services sectors, since the majority of the formal workforce is middle class in nature, they have been able to better utilise these processes that have enabled them to mitigate some of the disadvantages that have been historically presented to them. Many of these processes have resulted in the generation of a certain notion of compliance among the middle classes because of the privileges that had been bestowed upon it (Dekker, 2022).

The middle-class disavowal of active politics and its dislike for the workers' movement have caused a consistent rise of apolitical collectives. Two IT workers—a backward caste worker from Gurgaon and a Muslim IT worker from Bengaluru—narrate:

> What will happen with all the politics? We have been doing it for years, but things have not improved. OBCs still get cursed at in almost all the offices. We get called as 'freeloaders' and other casteist slurs. At least with the IT sector and all that we have jobs. The public sector and traditional industries are completely destroyed, and so are the relevance of the trade unions. Being part of an NGO or a collective is far better, at least they do not have a political agenda. (OBC Male IT Worker, Gurgaon)

> The trade unions and some political formations take up our issues but most of them only do that to fulfil their own agendas. What we need now is citizen's politics? The citizens need to come out, the politicians and all these rallies and all will not do anything for us. I am a part of a Muslim collective at the neighbourhood where I live where I do small things to help the poor and others. The trade unions and political parties do not do anything, for them or for us. If it was up to them, they would have shut down the company itself. (Muslim IT Worker, Bengaluru)

Even though such collectives have grown up even in the public sector, they have not affected the trade unions in the public sector quantitatively because in most of the PSEs, trade union memberships are often compulsory, and workers do not have a choice of whether they want to join the union or not. However, they have affected the unions qualitatively such that they have taken over the role that the trade unions used to play among the workers. Trade unions working among the middle-class have begun to face a decrease in their influence among the employees with the rise of de-politicised collectives that have risen focusing on issues such as women's health, lifestyle, and the consumer-identity. Most of these conform to the values propagated by the consumer society—a highly deterministic society mandated by the ideals of mass consumption and increasing manufacture of consumer goods at rates higher than usual (Lefebvre, 2002, p. 10). The underlying aim of this increased production lays upon the desire of capitalism to manufacture, not commodities, but also consumers. The Marxist roots of the theorisation of the consumer society lie in its theorisation regarding money being the sole need generated by the capitalist economic system, with '*Excess* and *intemperance* [coming] to be its true norm'

144   S. DEB ROY

(Marx, 1844, p. 307) resulting in the continuous creation of fetishes, fantasies, and whims and legitimising them through the positing of money as a means through which everything is quantified. As McKendrick argues, in a consumer society:

> What men and women had once hoped to inherit from their parents, they now expected to buy for themselves. What were once bought at the dictate of need, were now bought at the dictate of fashion. What were once bought for life, might now be bought several times over. What were once available only on high days and holidays through the agency of markets, fairs and itinerant pedlars were increasingly made available everyday but Sunday through the additional agency of an ever-advancing network of shops and shopkeepers. (McKendrick, 1982, p. 1)

The act of consumption, in Bowlby's (2001) opinion, 'involves much more than the situations in which actual buying takes place' (p. 6) and is intimately connected to the way in which individuals perceive of the society around them. The birth of a consumer society, as McKendrick (1982) informs, is related to the increasing standards of living, desire to assert status and wealth, and most importantly, to a complete commercialisation of the society itself. The questions of health and lifestyles necessarily intersect with the economic understanding of the society because their social existence is often mediated through the framework of lifestyle as their economic status is analysed to be complementary to their ability to consume. The ability to consume has become a marker of one's social identity—something which is quite natural in the kind of one-dimensional society that capitalism constructs in its advanced stages (Marcuse, 1964). The growth of the middle class in India has intersected with the constant impoverishment of the marginalised populace that denied most of the latter with the means required for achieving positive vertical social mobility (Fernandes, 2006). The processes associated with a safe and secured life becomes more complicated because the alterations that neoliberalism brings with itself changes the general aspirations of the society, especially among the young people (Dolan & Rajak, 2016). It changes the way in which individuals react to the society and the kind of aspirations that they have which, in turn, also alters the ways in which the working individuals come to define concepts such as poverty, unemployment, and precarity. The ideological condition of mainstream India has been dominated by a bourgeoning middle class which has had greater control and access to financial and social resources.

Most of the workers in the IT sector come from the middle classes because the middle classes are more capable to take benefits of the opportunities that neoliberalism provides (Jha & Pankaj, 2021). The middle-class nature of the workers can be either based on one's generic identity within a particular society or focused on the location within which one is based (Reed, 2023). Being middle class is associated with a diverse range of social characteristics that usually result in a change of the structural characteristics that individuals come to possess. The domination of the middle class, within the urban space, and within a liberalising Indian economy, schooled in petty-bourgeois values, becomes a manifestation of the uncritical working class that capitalism desires to create in the society for its continued reproduction (Althusser, 2014). The domination of such values, which often rest upon factors such as a subjective sense being 'English' in India enabled the upwardly mobile class and the individuals therein to imitate the mores and social norms of the British which helped them to explore their own modern selves within a conflicting relationship with the broader social reality and society in general (Chattopadhyay, 2022). In other words, these value structures helped them in articulating their own selves as an exceptional element within the social structure, very different from the waged working class.

The Metro Middle Class Comes Into Being

The growth of the middle class in India has coincided with an increasing inequality in the society. The rise in inequality has not only changed the economic structure of the society but has also had an effect on the society at a deeper psychological level. When privatisation occurs in the society, certain changes take place both within the workers' personal lives and their public lives. This also results in altering the ways in which they analyse class positions and the associated structures of morality and ethics which accompany those class positions (Thompson, 1963). The MMC comes into being through the waves of middle-class migration that occurs in India to the IT hubs, from a diverse range of geographical entities: rural, semi-urban, and urban. Migration and the mobility of labour under contemporary capitalism, as Huws (2014) informs, is one of the basic characteristics of the formation of contemporary forms of labour. The class consciousness of the MMC, like the middle classes, encompasses various aspects of the social relationships that individuals have among each other both as individuals and as communities (Dickey, 2016).

The changes within the class structure in any society also bring forward certain changes within the established norms of morality and ethics in the society as class formation is a gradual process (Thompson, 1963). The implications of the same under neoliberal capitalism—a social ordering that promotes individualisation (Navarro, 2007; Giroux, 2014) and normalises violence—create the social basis for the construction of violent social interactions, both structurally and materially, which is evident in the ways in which the social interactions between the formal IT workers and the invisible IT workers have been explained in the previous chapter. Their social interactions prepare the foundations through which individuals witness the world, and aim to struggle against its internal contradictions, through their everyday concrete entities and processes rather than abstract universal entities and concepts such as the state and globalisation (Soper, 2020). These interactions are also critical to the manifestation of a working-class identity among these workers. Social interactions between individuals and communities create the foundations for exploitation and the development of social subjectivity among the people (Rathod, 2023). These interactions are usually dominated by the individual subjectivity of a worker that is framed in accordance with the dominant ideological conditions in the society (Marx & Engels, 1845). And, the dominant ideological conditioning of the society is one that is formed by a repressive domination and the widespread commercialisation, objectivisation, and alienation that makes individuals and the society they constitute impervious to the evils of the developmental, consumerist, and affluent society. Ideas such as consumerism and affluence in India as a whole, of course, come with their own set of internal contradictions. The existence of '*multiple India's*' is an idea which has never been contested much but under neo-fascist regimes such as the present, it becomes important to take it into account to adequately analyse the problems associated with class, gender, religious, and caste issues in the country.

Concentrated into different kinds of service work, the middle class is the most important component of the consumer citizenship that neoliberalism desires to produce (Kamath & Vijayabaskar, 2009; Roy, 2018). The idea of being consumers determines the dynamics of the employment relations that the middle class get engaged in along with their own unique conception of rights and duties that are often not in complete synchronisation with the ideas of mainstream trade unionism. The proliferation of individuals coming from such class positions within the workplaces has affected the methods in which the trade unions are engaging with the workforce. It has become further complicated for the trade unions because the middle class has found itself benefiting from the neoliberal reforms in India even though it has found itself to be struggling for survival in recent times (Fernandes, 2006; Wenger & Zaber, 2021). Being from the middle class in a poverty-stricken country such as India is a matter of privilege as it designates a relatively better way of life than most of the population. But at the same time, such a social status also makes one protective of the privileges that one has—which again constitutes the basis of compliance in the society (Dekker, 2022).

Means of disciplining and ensuring compliance in the IT sector are usually implemented through two common methods—performance reviews which ensure accountability from the workers and instilling a fear of unemployment within them that makes them highly vulnerable and uncritical towards the exploitation meted out to them. Performance reviews and periodic assessments are used by companies to increase salaries and productivity—which at times also has a positive implication on the individual worker's social positioning as they are the basis upon which promotions are accorded to the workers and inspires them to work harder (Citon, 2015; Indeed Editorial, 2022). Both of these measures are related to the ideological constructions of higher productivity being not only an aspect of their workspaces but rather a way of life. This brings one back to the emphasis on everyday life and the patterns of exploitation that are usually rendered mainstream in the everyday lives of working women that also have a drastic effect on their working selves. Two migrant women IT workers state:

> Among the IT workers, and among the BPO workers in particular, there are numerous issues which we need to consider. The first is that most of these workers are migrant workers, maybe coming from a higher social class than the informal workers, but migrant, nonetheless. Women here face numerous issues while being a migrant working woman in the city, many of which are not being able to be addressed by the union such as sexual harassment at home, extremely deplorable housing conditions, etc. (Woman IT Worker, Bengaluru)

> Coming from a different town or a village to the metropolis comes with its own set of challenges. It is very difficult for single woman, more so for the married ones. For the single women the struggles mostly focus on getting a home, getting good service, etc., while for the working women it is mostly about finding that balance between work and home, or between your free time and your time for the family. (Woman IT Worker, Kolkata)

148   S. DEB ROY

The MMC has become an important part of the neoliberal value structure in the country because it not only self-identifies with neoliberal economic structures, but also contributes to the growing neoliberal de-humanisation of the society. The expression of being a part of the MMC is a core part of the class consciousness that the IT workers come to imbibe within themselves. The MMC consciousness is formed on the basis of not only an opposition towards more publicly funded benefits and service provisioning, but rather an active opposition towards the same. It is denoted by a constant hate towards public provisioning, 'free loading', reservations, and other forms of affirmative action which make them have a very optimistic attitude towards privatisation because to them it denotes the emergence of a highly meritocratic society. Three workers—one Dalit and one woman among them—state:

> The Private Sector's growth has been highly beneficial to middle class people like me. After passing out of my engineering college, I sat for many competitive examinations, and continue to do so till date. It is my fault that I am still working here while I could work in a public sector company if I could just crack that exam. Jobs in the PSEs are very limited. So, private sector is the only option, does not really matter whether I like it or not. (Dalit IT worker, Bengaluru)

> Although PSEs remained the first preference because for women it is safer— proper working hours, no late and night shifts, and good pay, along with respect in the community. But those jobs are hard to get. Privatisation has actually helped people like me in getting a job and earning a job. It might be bad for some people, but it has been a boon for me because it provided me with easy employment after my education was completed. (Woman IT Worker, Pune)

> The public sector helps in the growth of the country. The role there is not only to earn but also to ensure that all our nation's wealth is distributed based on an equitable structure so that the poorest of the poor can be. I know this is all true. I think the growth of private companies has actually been bad for the country, especially for the poor. But these poor people also come to depend on the private sector only, for jobs and all. (Male IT Worker, Gurgaon)

These statements highlight some critical issues faced by workers in the private sector ranging from their appreciatory attitude towards privatisation to their ideas surrounding socio-political change and social justice. The problems that most of the MMC face become a manifestation of their inabilities to either perform or excel in the work that is given to them. More often than not, they analyse themselves as the causes of their own failures. Their idea of a human life remains restricted by a sense of privilege that enables the creation of an alienated humanity divorced from radical change in the order of things. So, while the traditional middle classes were a vanguard class within the radical movement in India, the MMC does not harbour any such desire within itself, as one IT worker from Assam and now settled in Noida since the past seven years stated:

> The problem is politics. I have no issues with whoever comes to power, we should get the services that we are paying taxes. Even with the current BJP government, has anything changed? No, I know that. My home state is Assam and we have a BJP government, there also it is the same. Now I am in Noida, and the politics in Noida is all that matters to me, even if it does matter. I do not think there is any logic in getting affected by politics any-where. Our situation is very different than others. We only get affected if something happens in the United States. (Male IT Worker, Noida)

The MMC becomes an active advocate of the privileges that neoliberal capitalism provides them with and prevents any change in the existing order of things in the urban space. Most of them, as the statements above reveal, remain oblivious of the political occurrences in the society including those of their native places. They remain proud of the benefits that their migration to the IT hubs provides them with because they see that as something that makes them distinct from their—often middle class—parents and other fellow citizens from their native places. It contributes greatly to their meritocratic analysis of the various socio-political changes and the associated cultural processes at play in the society. Neoliberal capitalism believes that meritocracy and personal responsibility need to be established as supreme values in the society (Giroux, 2014) neglecting the underemployment that neoliberalism produces at a mass scale in developing societies because the very nature of everyday life has changed with an increase in insecurity for marginalised populace (Navarro, 1998; Filiz, 2020). Neoliberal policies with their focus on the privileging of aspects such as personal responsibility, reduced welfare measures, and privatisation often create conditions where the effects of privatisation and neoliberalism are most acutely faced by the people from the marginalised communities, and especially the women among them—the implications of which have been noted in Chaps. 2 and 3.

With the coming of neoliberalism and affirmative action, a new middle class has emerged in India which goes beyond the limitations imposed by the traditional contours of caste and class (Sheth, 1999). This middle class was the creation of a more subjective analysis of the existing class contradictions in the society than the objective ones and as such shared a highly ambiguous relationship with welfare states globally (Barbehön et al., 2020). The middle class globally is the result of the kind of discourse, which is promoted by neoliberal modes of governance, which promotes a proliferation of guilt, acceptance of overwork as a normal routinised part of the job profile, and personal responsibility based social structuring where each individual is constructed as a capitalist or a to-be-capitalist (Weiss, 2019). Most of these individuals struggle to keep up with the way in which the dominant discourse around lifestyles and consumption gets altered (Frank, 2007). Aspirations and desires have become central to the construction of the middle class in India (Inglis, 2019). The middle class is often accredited to be the driving force behind the democratisation of the society (Lu, 2005), but the growth of middle-class unionism often occurs at the expense of the blue-collar workers' unionisation (Suh, 2002). This prohibits the formation of a working-class democracy even within the trade unions. Middle-class unionism methods, such as the ones that mostly constitute the unions in the public sector, is often cut off from the stark reality India faces on an everyday basis.

Neoliberal governance ensures that public problems are twitched in such a manner that they become personal issues—issues which can be resolved through better personal management concerning the personal responsibility of the individuals in the society (Giroux, 2014). This results in individuals not seeking systematic change but rather begin to see themselves as being the source of their own problems (Uchitelle, 2006). The growth of this atomic consciousness is one of the critical components of the neoliberal generation and dictates the various kinds of work that individuals do in the society by influencing their interpretation of social mores and norms. The denunciation of social responsibility and its acceptance by the workers makes the workers more prone to becoming foot soldiers than acting as vanguards. These changes are taking place simultaneously with the generation of a new middle class completely entrenched in the service of the class that already possesses some form of capital (Pannekoek, 1909).

In traditional industrial societies, class relations are often straightforward in nature contingent upon property relations and authority (Dahrendorf, 1959). In the specific case of India, it was often through caste that acted along with class, property relations, and positions of authority (Veeraraghavan, 2013). Likewise, the kind of relationships that the formal IT workers share with the invisible IT workers and other kinds of informal workers in the IT hubs constitute the core nature of these spaces which is more often than not dictated by forms of structural and verbal violence inflicted by the formal workers on the informal ones. The Metro Middle Class bases itself upon the distinctions that once existed between the old middle class and the new middle class. The basic foundations of the MMC are not economic but are rather social and cultural in nature—with their roots in the economic structure that neoliberal capitalism creates. It is similar to the traditional middle class in the sense that the MMC is also formed by its adherence to a combination of traditional and modern value structures (Fazal, 2021), but it is different in the sense that while the old and new middle classes did interact with the society, they never attempted to change the existing order of things. Most of them remained subservient to the existing order of things. The MMC, contrastingly, desires to alter the society in its own light. It is most explicitly visible in the ways in which the MMC values their ability to live a life that is highly spontaneous. Herein lies the importance of poorly paid workers such as the platform workers within the IT hubs who provide the formal IT workers with convenience. Convenience becomes one of the major ways in which the MMC expresses their sense of the society, which in turn, shapes their individual consciousness and their attitude towards workers placed below them in the socio-economic hierarchy. The ability to live spontaneously is a major part of the process. While the traditional Indian middle class was much more conservative in nature towards planning and often abhorred spontaneous decisions, the MMC does not do that. In fact, the MMC analyses its ability to live spontaneously as a marker of it being the MMC—a point that will be further analysed in the next chapter.

The MMC's political stagnancy makes it different than the middle classes, who were often perceived to take upon a radical progressive role in politics and social engineering because of their socio-cultural positioning that often puts it within leadership positions in most socio-political movements (Sil, 2004). It was assumed that the middle class would subsequently uplift other sections of the marginalised populace. However, because of it being one of the major beneficiaries of the development of neoliberal capitalism, the middle class has failed to fulfil that role. It has always been widely believed that an educated and socio-politically active middle class ensures democracy and equality according to most popular notions, but the kind of democracy and equality that it aspires to establish has grave implications for the marginalised because these conceptions remain subservient to the status quo that the middle class mostly serves (Suh, 2002; Lahiri, 2014). The middle-class adherence to forms of capitalist democracy and values is largely because of the class interests that it represents, its attitude towards class formation and its ideas surrounding class struggle and social conflicts. The MMC in this regard conforms to the ideological and organisational stagnancy that has characterised the middle class in India.

The relationship that they share with the traditional new middle class is also complicated because most of them do not see themselves as being parts of the middle class—unlike the new middle class which still held close its middle-class affiliations. Their self-identification as being parts of the professional workforce differentiates them from other sections of the populace. While the differences with the working class are formed on the basis of their relative affluence, their differences with the traditional middle class are much more cultural in nature. While the traditional middle class was passively inducted into the consumer society, the MMC actively participates in the same. The consumer society gains social legitimacy by providing a certain freedom to the MMC who do not enjoy much freedom elsewhere. It is this supposed freedom towards realising individual choices that make consumer markets attractive to them even though it is the market itself which exists as a force of social control reproducing capitalism not through the suppression of individual freedom but through its realisation in a form mediated by the market, within the market (Bauman, 1988, p. 61). Consumer markets, in other words, act in ways similar to other emotion regulatory frameworks under capitalism employed to control the emotional display of workers' emotions and the importance of the same in creating a certain mode of interaction in the society (Hochschild, 1983; Gross, 2013). The manner in which the MMC interacts with others becomes a critical part of their class consciousness because it forms the core of their interaction with the social reality. It interferes most fundamentally with what Dunayevskaya (1973, p. 26) refers to be the subjective determination of the selfhood and 'the need to master' oneself remaining entrapped within a paradigm whereby the consumer is supposed to be always happy. Happiness in itself becomes the basis of exploitation, and not being happy is considered to be detrimental to one's human existence under contemporary capitalism (Ehrenreich, 2010).

The idea of a perennial happiness dominates the well-being strategies that the contemporary IT sector believes in. Well-being, as Chap. 4 has shown, becomes a method through which certain sections of the IT workforce are privileged over others. So, while happiness is considered to be very important factor in the lives of the workers, its subjective analysis is rarely attempted while devising well-being strategies for the ensuring the same. The MMC's conceptualisation of well-being is mostly focused on the idea of a managerial solution to their issues that often need political solutions. The creation of the MMC remains contingent upon the MMC's constant lack of interest or a sense of detachment towards the socio-political trajectory of the country and its notion of defining privilege through its capacity of remaining oblivious towards political issues.

De-politicisation is an important part of the drive towards the establishment of a social basis of compliance and disciplinary control in the society (Hardt & Negri, 2000). Compliance and discipline are two of the most important aspects of neoliberal capitalism. Wilful compliance that becomes a norm under contemporary capitalism depends more upon control rather than abject domination (Hardt & Negri, 2000). To achieve this, it devises multiple techniques, one of which is to utilise the common public powers and consciousness because capitalism has come to realise that the most effective method of enforcing its hegemonical logic over the workers (Fraser, 2014; Gramsci, 1977). The conditions of alienation constructed by the neoliberal social order and their active embracement of the same make the workers look for alienated solutions to their problems—solutions which enable a transformation of the oppressed to the oppressor, a trait that is evidently visible within the MMC.

The creation of the MMC has resulted in a change of the strategies that most of the organisations have adopted in organising the IT workers. Most of these organisations have faced grave challenges because trade unions and other forms of collective representations of workplace radicalism and restructuring of employment relations are perceived to be antithetical to the general profitability of private enterprises (Freeman & Kleiner, 1999; Sherk, 2009). While in the public sector, the formation of a trade union is a legal right of the workers (Bhowmick, 2012), no such rights exist in most of the private sector that constitutes one of the major issues for trade unions working in the private sector. The biggest challenge for many of the unions is the propagation of the idea that the private sector service workers are also affected by the state of unionisation in their workplaces by focusing on the role that the unions can play in providing

154   S. DEB ROY

them with an alternative framework of employment relations (Burawoy, 1979) and employee welfare mechanisms. Welfare of the employees has become an important concern for most of the IT firms, be it in India or across the globe. In Chap. 4, it has been exhibited in detail that most of the welfare strategies that the IT firms follow are often designed in such a manner that they are supposed to keep their employees 'happy' based on their objective conditions, without making many interventions into the subjective nature of human lives under contemporary capitalism.

The fetishisation of happiness under contemporary capitalism is a manifestation of the way in which capitalism in its advanced stage complete subsumes, what Marcuse (1964/2002) referred to as the unhappy consciousness within itself. The choices that most IT workers possess are the manifestations of capitalism's ability to make the society function on capitalist terms, while still managing to sustain the superficial existence of the autonomous subject. The freedom to choose itself is used as a tool of oppression because within a neoliberal capitalist social structure '[only] when freedom is exploited are returns maximised' (Han, 2015, p. 10). The processes through which the new middle class engages with the available choices is determined by a lack of class identity and 'class confusion' especially among intellectual and semi-intellectual labour-based professions (Nunlee, 2017). The MMC, on the other hand, engages with the available choices through a paradigm dominated by violence towards workers placed below it in the socio-economic hierarchy in addition to class confusion. The existence of such characteristics has changed the nature of the workforce that the tech firms and the representative bodies interact with. The upsurge of the MMC as a distinct social, cultural, and economic category has grave impacts on the workers' ability to resist their exploitation, which also has a subsequent effect on the workers' movement of the country as well as the social characteristics and definitions that one associates with the workers' definitions of their own class positions.

References

Althusser, L. (2014). *On the Reproduction of Capitalism: Ideology and Ideological State Apparatuses*. Verso.

Barbehön, M., Geugjes, M., & Haus, M. (2020). *Middle Class and Welfare State: Making Sense of an Ambivalent Relationship*. Routledge.

Baru, S. (2016). 1991: How P. V. Narsimha Rao made History. Aleph Book Company.

6 THE ARRIVAL OF THE 'METRO' MIDDLE CLASS   155

Bauman, Z. (1988). *Freedom*. University of Minnesota Press.

Bhowmick, S. K. (2012). *Industry, Labour and Society*. Orient Blackswan.

Birch, K. (2015). Neoliberalism: The Whys and Wherefores ... and Future Directions: Neoliberalism. *Sociology Compass, 9*(7), 571–584.

Bondi, L. (1990). Progress in Geography and Gender: Feminism and Difference. *Progress in Human Geography, 14*, 438–445.

Bowlby, R. (2001). *Carried Away: The Invention of Modern Shopping*. Columbia University Press.

Burawoy, M. (1979). *Manufacturing Consent: Changes in the Labor Process Under Monopoly Capitalism*. University of Chicago Press.

Burris, V. (1986). The Discovery of the New Middle Class. *Theory and Society, 15*(3), 317–349.

Chattopadhyay, S. (2022). *Being English: Indian Middle Class and the Desire for Anglicisation*. Routledge.

Citon, R. M. (2015, September 2). Performance Appraisals: How Do They Affect Employees? *Geneva Business News*. https://www.gbnews.ch/performance-appraisals-how-do-they-affect-employees/

Clark, T. N., & Lipset, S. M. (1991). Are Social Classes Dying? *International Sociology, 6*, 397–410.

Cleaver, H. (1979/2014). *Reading Capital Politically*. Phoneme Books.

Crouch, H. (1979). *The Indian Working Class*. Sachin Publications.

Curtis, B., Maynard, A., & Kanade, N. (2020). Exploring the Squeezed Middle: Aucklanders talk about being 'squeezed'. *Kōtuitui: New Zealand Journal of Social Sciences Online, 15*(1), 8–21.

Dahrendorf, R. (1959). *Class and Class Conflict in Industrial Society*. Routledge and Kegan Paul.

Deb Roy, S. (2021). *Social Media and Capitalism: People, Commodities and Communities*. Daraja Press.

Dekker, S. (2022). *Compliance Capitalism: How Free Markets Have Led to Unfree, Overregulated Workers*. Routledge.

Desai, A. R. (1984). *India's Path of Development: A Marxist Approach*. Sangam Books.

Desai, M. (2015). Foreword. In L. Lobo & J. Shah (Eds.), *The Trajectory of India's Middle Class: Economy, Ethics and Etiquette*. Cambridge Scholars Publishing.

Dickey, S. (2016). *Living Class in Urban India*. Oxford University Press.

Dolan, C., & Rajak, D. (2016). Remaking Africa's Informal Economies: Youth, Entrepreneurship and the Promise of Inclusion at the Bottom of the Pyramid. *The Journal of Development Studies, 52*(4), 514–529.

Donner, H. (2012). Whose City Is It Anyway? Middle Class Imagination and Urban Restructuring in Twenty-First Century Kolkata. *New Perspectives on Turkey, 46*, 129–155.

Dunayevskaya, R. (1973/1982). *Philosophy and Revolution: From Hegel to Sartre, and from Marx to Mao*. Humanities Press.

Dunayevskaya, R. (1979). Marx and Engels' Studies Contrasted: Relationship of Philosophy and Revolution to Women's Liberation. In *The Raya Dunayevskaya Collection—Marxist-Humanism: A Half Century of its World Development*. Wayne State University Archives of Labor and Urban Affairs.

Dunayevskaya, R. (1983/2002). Marxist-Humanism: The Summation That is a New Beginning, Subjectively and Objectively. In P. Hudis & K. B. Anderson (Eds.), *The Power of Negativity: Selected Writings on the Dialectic in Hegel and Marx by Raya Dunayevskaya*. Lexington Books.

Ehrenreich, B. (2010). *Smile or Die: How Positive Thinking Fooled America and the World*. Penguin.

Ehrenreich, B., & Ehrenreich, J. (1979). The Professional-Managerial Class. In P. Walker (Ed.), *Between Labor and Capital*. South End Press.

Evans, B., & Lennard, N. (2018). *Violence: Humans in Dark Times*. City Lights Books.

Faux, J. (2012). *The Servant Economy: Where America's Elite is Sending the Middle Class*. Wiley.

Fazal, T. (2021). The Muslim Middle Class: Structure, Identity and Mobility. In S. Patel (Ed.), *Neoliberalism, Urbanization and Aspirations in Contemporary India*. Oxford University Press.

Fernandes, L. (2006). *India's New Middle Class: Democratic Politics in an Era of Economic Reform*. University of Minnesota Press.

Filiz, A. (2020). Underemployment, Unemployment, Gender and Changing Conditions of (Non) Work Under Neoliberalism. *Journal of Economy Culture and Society, 61*, 341–353.

Fleetwood, S. (2008). Workers and Their Alter Egos as Consumers. *Capital & Class, 32*(1), 31–47.

Flemmen, M., & Haakestad, H. (2018). Class and Politics in Twenty-First Century Norway: A Homology of Positions and Position-Taking. *European Societies, 20*(3), 401–423.

Frank, R. H. (2007). *Falling Behind: How Rising Inequality Harms the Middle Class*. University of California Press.

Fraser, N. (2014). Behind Marx's Hidden Abode. *New Left Review, 1*(86), 55–72.

Freeman, J., & Hannan, M. T. (1986). Niche Width and the Dynamics of Organizational Populations. *American Journal of Sociology, 88*, 1116–1145.

Freeman, R. B., & Kleiner, M. M. (1999). Do Unions Make Enterprises Insolvent? *Industrial and Labor Relations Review, 52*(4), 510–527.

Giddens, A. (1973). *The Class Structure of the Advanced Societies*. Hutchinson.

Gilbert, M. R. (1997). Feminism and Difference in Urban Geography. *Urban Geography, 18*, 166–179.

Giroux, H. (2014/2020). *Neoliberalism's War on Higher Education* (2nd ed.). Haymarket Books.

Goldthorpe, J. H. (1995). The Service Class Revisited. In T. Butler & M. Savage (Eds.), *Social Change and the Middle Classes*. Routledge.

Goldthorpe, J. H. (2014). The Role of Education in Intergenerational Social Mobility: Problems from Empirical Research in Sociology and Some Theoretical Pointers from Economics. *Rationality and Society, 26*(3), 265–289.

Goldthorpe, J. H. (2016). Social Class Mobility in Modern Britain: Changing Structure, Constant Process. *Journal of the British Academy, 4*, 89–111.

Gramsci, A. (1977). *Selections from Prison Notebooks*. Lawrence and Wishart.

Gross, J. (2013). Conceptualizing Emotional Labor: An Emotion Regulation Perspective. In A. A. A. Grandey, J. M. Diefendorff, & D. E. Rupp (Eds.), *Emotional Labour in the 21st Century* (pp. 288–293). Routledge.

Han, B. (2015). *Psychopolitics*. Verso.

Hardt, M., & Negri, A. (2000). *Empire*. Harvard University Press.

Harvey, D. (2005). *A Brief History of Neoliberalism*. Oxford University Press.

Harvey, D. (2006). *Spaces of Global Capitalism*. Verso.

Harvey, D. (2016). *Rebel Cities*. Verso.

Heath, J. (1997). Privatisation in Perspective. In A. Bennett (Ed.), *How Does Privatisation Work?: Essays on Privatisation in Honour of Professor V. V. Ramanadham*. Routledge.

Hochschild, A. R. (1983/2003). *The Managed Heart: Commercialization of Human Feeling*. University of California Press.

Huws, U. (2014). *Labor in the Global Digital Economy: The Cybertariat Comes of Age*. Monthly University Press.

Indeed Editorial. (2022, July 22). 12 Benefits of Performance Appraisals. *Indeed Career Development*. https://www.indeed.com/career-advice/career-develop ment/benefit-of-performance-appraisal

Inglehart, R. (1990). *Culture Shift in Advanced Industrial Society*. Princeton University Press.

Inglis, P. (2019). *Narrow Fairways: Getting by and Falling Behind in the New India*. Oxford University Press.

Jaffrelot, C. (2008). 'Why Should We Vote?': The Indian Middle Class and the Functioning of the World's Largest Democracy. In C. Jaffrelot & P. van der Veer (Eds.), *Patterns of Middle-Class Consumption in India and China*. New Delhi.

Jha, M. K., & Pankaj, A. K. (2021). Neoliberal Governmentality and Social Policymaking in India: Implications for In/Formal Workers and Community Work. *The International Journal of Community and Social Development, 3*(3), 198–214.

Joshi, S. (2001). *Fractured Modernity: Making of a Middle Class in Colonial North India*. Oxford University Press.

Kamath, L., & Vijayabaskar, M. (2009). Limits and Possibilities of Middle-Class Associations as Urban Collective Actors. *Economic and Political Weekly, 44*(26/27), 368–376.

Kerr, C., Dunlop, J. T., Harbison, F., & Myers, C. A. (1960). *Industrialism and Industrial Man: The Problems of Labor and Management in Economic Growth*. Harvard University Press.

Khanna, S. (2015). The Transformation of India's Public Sector: Political Economy of Growth and Change. *Economic and Political Weekly, 50*(5), 47–60.

Kohli, A. (2006). Politics of Economic Growth in India: 1980–2005. *Economic and Political Weekly, 41*(13), 1361–1370.

Lahiri, A. K. (2014). The Middle Class and Economic Reforms. *Economic and Political Weekly, 49*(11), 37–44.

Le Grand, J. (1984). The Future of the Welfare State. *New Society, 68*, 385–386.

Le Grand, J., & Winter, D. (1986). The Middle Classes and the Welfare State Under Conservative and Labour Governments. *Journal of Public Policy, 6*(4), 399–430.

Lefebvre, H. (1991). *The Production of Space*. Basil Blackwell.

Lefebvre, H. (2002). *Critique of Everyday Life: Volume 2*. Verso.

Leigh, N. G. (1994). *Stemming Middle-Class Decline: The Challenges to Economic Development Planning*. The State University of New Jersey.

Lotz, C. (2016). *The Capitalist Schema*. Rowman and Littlefield.

Lu, C. (2005). Middle Class and Democracy: Structural Linkage. *International Review of Modern Sociology, 31*(2), 157–178.

Marcuse, H. (1964/2002). *One Dimensional Man*. Routledge.

Marx, K. (1844/1975). Economic and Philosophical Manuscripts of 1844. In *Marx Engels Collected Works: Volume 3*. Lawrence and Wishart.

Marx, K., & Engels, F. (1845–1846/1976). The German Ideology. In *Marx Engels Collected Works: Volume 5*. Lawrence and Wishart.

Massey, D. (1994). *Space, Place and Gender*. University of Minnesota Press.

McDowell, L. (1993). Space, Place and Gender Relations: Part 2: Identity, Difference, Feminist Geometries and Geographies. *Progress in Human Geography, 17*, 305–318.

McKendrick, N. (1982). *The Birth of a Consumer Society: The Commercialization of Eighteenth Century England*. Indiana University Press.

Navarro, V. (1998). Neoliberalism, "Globalization", Unemployment, Inequalities, and the Welfare State. *International Journal of Health Services, 28*(4), 607–682.

Navarro, V. (2007). Neoliberalism as a Class Ideology; or the Political Causes of the Growth of Inequalities. *International Journal of Health Services, 37*(1), 47–62.

Nelson, J. I. (1968). Anomie: Comparisons Between the Old and New Middle Class. *American Journal of Sociology, 74*(2), 184–192.

Nunlee, M. (2017). *When Did We All Become Middle Class?* Routledge.

Ong, A. (2006). *Neoliberalism as Exception: Mutations in Citizenship and Sovereignty*. Duke University Press.

Pakulski, J., & Walters, M. (1996). *The Death of Class*. SAGE.

Pannekoek, A. (1909). The New Middle Class. Trans. William E. Bohn. *International Socialist Review, 10*(4), 316–326.

Ram, R. (2014). Jawaharlal Nehru, Neo-Liberalism and Social Democracy: Mapping the Shifting Trajectories of Developmental State in India. *Voice of Dalit, 7*(2), 187–210.

Rathod, B. (2023). *Dalit Academic Journeys: Stories of Caste, Exclusion and Assertion in Indian Higher Education*. Routledge.

Reed, E. (2023, February 8). What is the Difference between Working Class and Middle Class?. *The Street*. https://www.thestreet.com/personal-finance/working-class-vs-middle-class-14881073

Research Unit for Political Economy (RUPE). (2008a). *India's Runaway Growth: Distortion, Disarticulation, and Exclusion: Part I*. RUPE.

Research Unit for Political Economy (RUPE). (2008b). *India's Runaway Growth: Distortion, Disarticulation, and Exclusion: Part II*. RUPE.

Research Unit for Political Economy (RUPE). (2008c). *India's Runaway Growth: Distortion, Disarticulation, and Exclusion: Part III*. RUPE.

Research Unit for Political Economy (RUPE). (2014). *A Middle Class India?* RUPE.

Robinson, T. P. (2014). *Café Culture in Pune: Being Young and Middle Class in Urban India*. Oxford University Press.

Rose, G. (1993). *Feminism and Geography: The Limits of Geographical Knowledge*. University of Minnesota Press.

Roy, A. (2018). The Middle Class in India: From 1947 to the Present and Beyond. *Education about Asia, 23*(1), 32–37.

Saraswati, L. A. (2021). *Pain Generation: Social Media, Feminist Activism, and the Neoliberal Selfie*. New York University Press.

Sarkar, S. (1989). *Modern India, 1885–1947*. Palgrave Macmillan.

Sherk, J. (2009, May 21). *What Unions Do: How Labor Unions Affect Jobs and the Economy*. The Heritage Foundation. https://www.heritage.org/jobs-and-labor/report/what-unions-do-how-labor-unions-affect-jobs-and-the-economy

Sheth, D. L. (1999). Secularisation of Caste and Making of New Middle Class. *Economic and Political Weekly, 34*(34/35), 2502–2510.

Sil, K. L. (2004). Beyond the Boundary: Middle-Class Women in Income-Generating Activities in Burdwan, India. *Contemporary South Asia, 13*(3), 255–270.

Soper, K. (2020). *Post-Growth Living*. Verso.

Stahl, G., McDonald, S., & Young, J. (2021). Possible Selves in a Transforming Economy: Upwardly Mobile Working-Class Masculinities, Service Work and

Negotiated Aspirations in Australia. *Work, Employment and Society,* *35*(1), 97–115.

Subramaniam, V. (1971). *Social Background of India's Administrators.* Publications Division, Ministry of Information and Broadcasting, Government of India.

Suh, D. (2002). Middle-Class Formation and Class Alliance. *Social Science History,* *26*(1), 105–137.

Teltumbde, A. (2018). *Republic of Caste: Thinking Equality in the Time of Neoliberal Hindutva.* Navayana.

Thompson, E. P. (1963/2013). *The Making of the English Working Class.* Vintage.

Tronti, M. (1973). Social Capital. *Telos,* No. 17. *Fall, 1973,* 98–121.

Tumbe, C. (2018). *India Moving: A History of Migration.* Vintage.

Uchitelle, L. (2006). *The Disposable American: Layoffs and their Consequences.* Alfred A. Knopf.

Varma, P. K. (2014). *The New Indian Middle Class: The Challenge of 2014 and Beyond.* Harper Collins Publishers India.

Veeraraghavan, D. (2013). *The Making of the Madras Working Class.* Leftword.

Weiss, H. (2019). *We Have Never Been Middle Class.* Verso.

Wenger, J. B., & Zaber, M. A. (2021, May 14). Most Americans Consider Themselves Middle-Class. But Are They?. *The Rand Blog.* https://www.rand.org/blog/2021/05/most-americans-consider-themselves-middle-class-but.html

Žižek, S. (2017). *Lenin 2017: Remembering, Repeating and Working Through.* Verso.

CHAPTER 7

Techie Unionisation in the IT Society

INTRODUCTION: UNIONISING THE TECHIES

Organised sectors under neoliberalism have been constantly pushed towards a condition where they are having to operate with increasingly reduced financial and human resources. The way in which the state has reacted to the questions of powerlessness has been contingent upon the political formation at the centre and the people who control them (Sheth, 1999). The liberalisation of the market in India has meant that many social groups who had been previously exploited because of their socio-biological attributes could now take certain advantages produced by the upward social mobility that the reforms-led economy produced (Sheth, 1999). The scale of liberalisation is a result of the ways in which the neoliberal reforms have affected both the individual Indian citizen and the Indian society at large—and *the relationship between them*. With the coming of neoliberal reforms, the power of the state as a regulating agency in the society in India diminished greatly (Jha & Pankaj, 2021). The global situation was such that competition between the centres of global finance capital in the years which had followed the second world war aided the constant erosion of the very idea of a welfare state and constructed the institutional, economic, and cultural legitimation which global financial structures needed to create the foundations for a broad public consensus in support of neoliberal reform measures (McClure, 2021).

© The Author(s), under exclusive license to Springer Nature 161
Switzerland AG 2024
S. Deb Roy, *The Rise of the Information Technology Society in India*,
Dynamics of Virtual Work,
https://doi.org/10.1007/978-3-031-58128-1_7

162   S. DEB ROY

Being a member of the middle class in India is related to the ability to consume certain cultural and material commodities in a particular way that exhibits the cultural and social capital that an individual possesses such as 'formal educational qualifications and English language [proficiency which] have been defining characteristics of the new middle-class modernity in urban India' (Ganguly, 2022, p. 98). Being middle class has its own distinct share of advantages as the middle classes are traditionally at a better position to let those in positions of power know that they are unsatisfied with a particular policy than other sections of the populace placed below them in the social hierarchy (Le Grand & Winter, 1986). Such privileges that the middle class has continued to enjoy in neoliberal India has made it equipped enough to generate a sense of belongingness within the spaces that it come to inhabit—which is one of the major driving forces behind the formation of the metro middle class (MMC). Under the conditions presented by the neoliberal reforms in India, the middle class has found itself to be a critical component of the workforce for both the capitalists and the trade unions. The middle classes are affected by both the existing managerial relations in their respective workplaces and the segregation existing within the occupational hierarchies (Burawoy, 1979).

They have also been important parts of the trade union movement in India. Trade unionism in India has a long and, often, tumultuous history. Right from the first organised trade union in India which was the Madras Labour Union—established in 1918—trade unions and other forms of workers' organisations have been an important part of not only the economic structure of the nation, but also played critical roles at various points in the political transformation of the nation. Trade Unions have played important roles in the political transformation of some of the most prominent regions of the country. The importance of trade unions in India also gets manifested in the fact that even far-right political parties such as the *Shiv Sena* and the *Bhartiya Janta Party* (BJP) also have their own trade union wings—the Bharathiya Kamgar Sena (BKS) of the *Shiv Sena* and the Bharatiya Mazdoor Sangh (BMS) of the BJP—through which they attempt to make inroads into the working class. However, there are issues surrounding caste and gender which have influenced the trade union debates in India to a great extent. The IT Workers are no different as well.

The IT workers' movement in India took root in Infosys in Pune, where the Forum for IT Employees (FITE) was the first trade union to get registered as a trade union specifically for IT workers (Balaji & Woodcock, 2019). Trade unions in the IT sector face numerous challenges, which range from class confusion to a growing class segregation within the various kinds of workers in the sector (Sarkar, 2008). Trade unions however have come a long way since then increasing their numbers as well as forming a National Co-ordination Committee. This book is not specifically about the functioning of unions in the IT sector and as such the entirety of all the unions operating within India's IT industry have not featured in within the book. The book focuses on four major IT workers' unions in India: the All India IT and IT Enabled Services (ITeS) Union (AIITEU), the Karnataka State IT/IT Enabled Services Employees' Union (KITU), the Forum for IT Employees (FITE), and the Union of IT and ITES Employees (UNITE). While AIITEU is a national organisation with branches across the country, including Kolkata, Bengaluru, Pune, Noida, and Gurgaon, all the others are mostly focused on one particular city or region.[1] The inferences and observations presented in this chapter are mainly through in-depth interviews conducted with activists from these four unions. It is important to say that in terms of memberships, KITU and AIITEU are the largest of the IT Unions, each boasting of memberships that go beyond 7000. Negligible in comparison with the total number of workers in the IT sector, combined together, according to some of the trade unionists, the unionised workforce comprises of merely 5 per cent.[2]

In the chapter, to protect the identities of the activists, the names of the cities where they belong to or work in have been kept confidential. For the unions, organising the IT workers has been an extremely difficult task, because they have been confronted by a multiplicity of questions pertaining to not only the workers' class positions but also their class aspirations. While in the public sector, the unions are mostly confronted with economic questions even among the middle class, in the IT sector they are also confronted by issues surrounding the individual aspirations, and the subjective self-articulation of their class identity by the workers. As two IT union activists from Bengaluru and Chennai stated:

> IT workers are different. These are upscale women and consider their jobs to be more secured than their own jobs, but their idea is that if they are earning money, they should have the space to spend it. Unions here have to

---

[1] The KITU mainly organises in Bengaluru, while the UNITE mainly does in Chennai and Tamil Nadu. FITE operates in Pune and Chennai. Though the AIITEU is an all-India trade union, its main organisational strength lies in Kolkata, and Delhi (NCR).

[2] It is important to mention here that this number is an estimate. No official data is available.

164 S. DEB ROY

focus on issues pertaining to the conditions of life, rather than issues concerning the workplaces or the political state of affairs in the country. Those are important issues for these workers. (Male IT Union Activist, Bengaluru)

The IT workers are different. They have different aspirations. While a public sector worker dreams of owning a house or a car after he or she retires because of the ways in which public sector salaries are structured, a private sector employee wants that immediately. They can take high loans, get loans from the company and are more prone to spending the entirety of their salaries, something that one will rarely see in the case of a public sector worker. Yes, the private sector workers are more aspirational but that is neoliberal aspiration, not a humane or social one. (Woman IT Union Activist, Kolkata)

The workers in the IT sector come from a variety of different classes. They sometimes come from privileged class positions themselves with no involvement in political movements or even social movements. Their non-involvement in the processes which affect them has become a huge burden for the trade unions working among them because the workers think that they have nothing to gain or lose from the struggles that the union takes up. This makes them a confused class in themselves, something that we as union activists need to engage with. (Male IT Worker, Chennai)

The conditions mentioned by the activists in the narratives above are not unique and are found even within the public sector albeit in a different manner. The distinctions between the public and private sector in the era of neoliberalism have increasingly come to shrink with the state enabling the formation of markets in domains where the market was previously absent (Harvey, 2005). The creation of the market and the neoliberal nature of the state in India particularly benefitted the middle class, who saw in neoliberalism, a solution to their problems concerning youth unemployment, underemployment, and so forth (Vanaik, 2001, 2004). The massive involvement of the middle class in various aspects of neoliberalism, especially in the IT sector, has caused a new kind of middle class to emerge, which has ensured that the scale of the problems caused by these factors in unionisation have increased manifold. Most of these changes have been accelerated and normalised due to a financially liberal political framework which dictates the re-engineering of social and ideological processes in a way that favour the relatively well-off and the elites making them equipped to access education and other privileges while constantly impoverishing the others (Losurdo, 2016). The subjective self-definitions possessed by working individuals, constitutes one of the primary bases for their oppression because that is related to how they identify with the structural benefits that they come to enjoy.

Structures of Techie Resistance

Trade unions in any sector work towards ensuring better payments, social benefits and working conditions to the workers, and the IT sector workers are no different (Bisht, 2010). However, the IT sector as a whole, formed on the basis of a notion of hyper-productivity and punctuality, often at the expense of personal well-being (Ramadorai, 2011; Reddy, 2022), continues to believe that trade unions would come in the way of fulfilling these goals. The processes that have been brought to existence by the IT sector are a result of the various economic restructurations that had been institutionalised by the various governments during the 1970s and 1980s (Kalirajan & Shand, 1996). The domination of the IT sector and its associated socio-cultural processes has furthered the already existing public consensus that privatisation results in better performance (Mohan, 2002). The growth of the IT sector and its associated neoliberal consensus has evolved into an all-encompassing process because of the ideological and material domination that the IT workers and the sector as a whole have begun to assert. The large scale of the IT sector has necessitated the involvement of trade unions in the sector organising individuals whom they had previously categorised to be petty-bourgeoisie agents of capitalist hegemony and consumerism. As one union activist put it:

> The problem with most trade unions is that they suddenly woke up to the fact that now we have so many young people coming into the sector that if we do not work among them then we are gone. I and a few others had been speaking of this since our student activist days, but then nobody listened to us. Now suddenly you have to work with IT workers of 25 or 26 years of age with no background in political education. 10 years ago, most activists would have just shrugged them off saying that they are petty bourgeois elements. (IT Union Activist)[3]

In doing so, the unions have not only had to change their organisational structures but also their organisational philosophies. The structure that a trade union possesses is integral to its functioning. In India, most

---

[3] Identifiers have been hidden because of security concerns.

trade unions can be classified as being either one of the two kinds: (1) Unions affiliated with the 'Central Trade Unions' (CTUs) which are in turn affiliated to political formations and possess a distinct political ideology; and (2) Free and Independent Trade Unions which are not affiliated to any political formation per se but may or may not possess distinct political ideologies. Among the four IT unions mentioned above, AIITEU and UNITE have affiliations with the Centre of Indian Trade Unions (CITU), while FITE is an independent one. The case of KITU is, however, a bit unique. While philosophically, the KITU self-identifies with the Communist Party of India (Marxist) (CPI(M)) and the CITU, it has refrained from taking any direct affiliation from the CITU—which has been often critiqued by many of the other unions affiliated to the CITU. The KITU's non-affiliation also has raised some concerns for the AIITEU, which also identifies itself politically with the CPI(M), regarding its functioning in India's largest IT hub, Bengaluru, because the existence of two unions in the same city affiliated to—either formally or informally—the same CTU often creates grounds for inter-union rivalry.

However, in the IT sector, the CTUs have been of limited success, unlike in the public sector where they have been highly successful in organising the workers. One of the major reasons for the failure of the CTUs in the IT sector has been their approach towards politicisation. The fact that most of the CTUs—the ones which wield the most power within the mainstream workers' movement of the country—often have political connections and affiliations has had a crucial impact on the scale and successes of unionisation in the IT sector. Over time, the trade unions—especially the CTUs—have been equated with a particular kind of politics, which has been detrimental to the growth of trade unionism in the IT sector, which harbours a widespread de-politicised workforce. The attitude towards trade unions is often dictated by their attitude towards left-wing politics, which in contemporary India has faced considerable repression resulting in its dismal public image (Deb Roy, 2022). Four IT workers from four different cities have spoken at length about these issues:

> These are a bunch of *naxalis*,[4] that's it. Their own target is talking bad about the PM, about the BJP. For them everybody is bad. They now say that privatisation is bad, but without privatisation, would there be jobs for all of

---

[4] 'Naxali' is a colloquial Hindi derogatory term used to refer to the Naxalites, trade unionists, and Left-wing activists. Source: https://www.britannica.com/topic/Naxalite [Accessed 05.04.2023]

us? The state cannot help everybody. We have to help ourselves. (Male IT Worker, Chennai)

I do not engage in union politics because I feel it is highly political here. When I see in the West, or even from my own experience when I was in London, the situation there is very different. There, unions are associated with economic reforms and all, but that is not the case in India. Here, if you engage in unions, you will be labelled as a communist. (Woman IT Worker, Gurgaon)

They try to organise now and then, but they will not succeed. Narendra Modi has done so many good things for the country, for the economy. We have received so much money. What is the purpose of all this *unionbaazi*[5] in India anymore. Their bosses have destroyed the economy, see what has happened to West Bengal and Tripura. They have no place in the offices like ours. (Muslim IT Worker, Bengaluru)

See, my approach towards the unions functioning in the office has always been very pragmatic. I feel that they are necessary. But not in the way in which they function. The first thing that a union gives here is a CITU pamphlet, and then next day they will come and say that they are only a trade union and not from any political formation. We are not fools. (Dalit IT Worker, Kolkata)

The reflections of the workers presented above point towards the gradual de-politicisation of the society that has become a norm under contemporary capitalism (Hardt & Negri, 2000). The de-politicisation of the society in general stems from a manipulation of the very idea of politicisation itself, which in recent times has become a highly undesirable phenomenon to the urban middle class and has been aided by a concurrent propagation of the idea that the politics of authority is non-ideological in nature and cannot be challenged. These processes are results of the specific kind of neoliberal economic and social policies that have been institutionalised in India which has successfully produced two India's—one India which is affluent, tech-savvy, and articulate, and another India which is impoverished, hungry, and struggling for survival. The bifurcation within the two categories can be most explicitly noticed in the IT sector with the MMC being the former and the invisible workers being the latter.

---

[5] '*Unionbaazi*' is again a colloquial term used for unionism, mostly in a derogatory sense. Source: https://www.urdupoint.com/dictionary/roman-urdu-to-english/union-baazi-roman-urdu-meaning-in-english/93257.html [Accessed 05.04.2023]

The state of one's employment affects one's material interests, everyday aspirations, desires, mental and physical health (Uchitelle, 2006). Because of the aspirational nature of the IT workers, the trade unions have found it difficult to generate an anti-capitalist consciousness among the private sector workers. It has been unable to convey that neoliberal capitalism, despite its seemingly beneficial effects, is incapable of providing any special benefits to the workers therein. But, therein also lies the critical nature of the MMC. Unlike the working class, or even a significant middle class, the MMC does not see neoliberalism as a threat because the MMC in itself is a creation of neoliberalism. The way in which one conducts one life under the conditions presented by neoliberal capitalism has become an important aspect of one's basic social conditioning which determines the choices that one makes (Banjac & Hanusch, 2022). The idea of dreams and aspirations also has a very distinct class character informed by the conditions of one's life and idea of justice (Bourdieu, 1984). Under contemporary capitalism, aspiration becomes an integral aspect of an individual's involvement in processes that promises a better future to them (Inglis, 2019). Aspirations are both spatial and social in nature, which get affected and affect the processes through which individuals seek to establish their spaces of belonging (Jha, 2022). This process in turn is dialectically related to the social status that individuals seek for themselves and their families within the society.

Organising the IT workers needs to take cognisance of aspirations, social desires, and complicated social constructions surrounding one's class, caste, and gender. The MMC's engagement with their social attributes is determined by the higher access to social resources that they possess that makes them more likely to amass social capital and socio-economic security. Their fear of losing their privileges makes them extra protective towards its access to services and transform them into the causal agents of further exploitation mitigating the revolutionary potential of the non-capitalist classes by bringing them within the aegis of capitalist welfare measures. The functioning of the trade unions in the IT sector needs to be in light of the social composition of the workers in the sector as well as the perception of workers regarding politics and social movements. Both these aspects are socially produced by their interactions with the society in general shaping their social, cultural, and political outlook, which in turn become extremely important determining factors in the attitude that they possess towards representative organisations. The kind of relationship that the workers have with their representative organisations determine the possible future pathways and strategies of the union (Deery & Walsh, 1999), which in turn determine the scope of the that the union can employ in negotiating with the immediate management, and other forms of social and political entities such as the state. It is critical to realise that the middle class in India—of which the MMC is also a part—has been a strong component of the Indian developmental trajectory.

The MMC has been one of the major beneficiaries of the neoliberal developmental model in India. This is, however, not true for the mass of precariat workforce at the bottom of the social hierarchy who serve the middle classes. In the IT spaces, the MMC reserves the working-class identity for itself. Germinating in the context of neoliberal globalisation in India, the modern precariat migrant worker is not a part of the mainstream labour community itself and does not only suffer material alienation but also a very inhumane psychological alienation from one's own selfhood (Standing, 2011). Such issues contribute towards a lack of ontological insecurity among the workers. The psychologist R.D. Laing coined the term, 'ontological security' to refer to the processes which allows individuals to experience the self as 'real, alive, whole, and in a temporal sense, a continuous person' (Laing, 1969/1990, p. 39). Ontological security is a measure of the process in which individuals cope with change—an important aspect of the MMC one of whose basic foundations is based on coping with change. Structures of solidarity can play a critical role in that regard, especially for workers coming from marginalised sections because such structures can initiate a democratisation of the immediate society around them ensuring care and to the most vulnerable individuals (Means & Smith, 1994). The MMC often remain entrapped in harsh working conditions because of the ways in which the IT sector has been structured in the country as has been noted in Chap. 1 and throughout the book itself. As three IT workers narrate:

> We have been working night and day in the company. But our salary is very limited. For me, working in a private company is just a compulsion. Given the chance, I will immediately start working for a public sector. It provides us such great security, great payments, and all other benefits. You do not get those in a private sector company. (Woman IT Worker, Bengaluru)

> I like working here. If I had worked in a PSE, then I might have got better payments, but I will not get the kind of lifestyle I get working here. They place me in such a good place. Working in such a company is much more than an economic choice, it is a lifestyle choice, whether you want to work

170 S. DEB ROY

in a dust-filled government office or an aesthetically designed corporate office. (Male IT Worker, Noida)

There are numerous issues existing in the private sector as it stands today. We get way less payment for the kind of work that we do. Our working hours are extremely long and tedious, often more than 12 hours a day. The PSE workers do not have to do any of that. Being a woman is a big problem again. You work hard in the office and must do so again at home. (Woman IT Worker, Pune)

Apart from highlighting the challenging conditions under which individuals work in the IT sector, the statements above reveal the difficulties that workers face in discerning the camouflaged domination that capital plays in determining their social and life choices. These statements from workers reflect the fetishisation of labour productivity as is the norm under neoliberalism (Harvey, 2005). The neoliberal focus on productivity often results in a situation where the marginalised individuals in the workforce become the worst victims among the workforce because in addition to the work that they must do as workers, they also suffer from other social forms of exploitation that determines their attitude towards their own exploitation and their representative organisations. The problems that marginalised workers face in the IT sector are primarily of two kinds, the first one places them as workers where their issues are somewhat similar to the issues that other workers face such as the length of the working day, wage structures, and so forth. The second one places them as citizens, whereby they are exploited as being parts of the space that they inhabit that include issues such concerning job security, retirement benefits, and so forth that are unique to the IT sector.

For instance, one can consider the case of women in the IT sector, whose conditions of life have been discussed in the book in details. In almost all the formal service sectors, women are usually employed in clerical positions in such a way so that their employment does not affect the gender ratio in higher echelons of the company (Bain, 1968). The reason for evoking the condition of women in this context is that regardless of their caste status and religious affiliations, women constitute one of the most highly exploitable subjects within the workforce because of the structural exploitation meted out to them. Even when women get employed in higher positions, the extent to which they can articulate the issues that they face remains contingent upon their intersectional position both within the workplace and in the society in general. Two narratives can be reproduced here to substantiate this point from two prominent union activists from Bengaluru and Kolkata:

> Most of the problems are faced by workers at entry level. When they go ahead with their careers, the problems decrease proportionately. There are two reasons for the same, firstly they themselves reach positions where they can exploit others, or they generate enough of a social capital within the context of their work where it becomes easier for them to navigate through their marginal positions. And secondly, once you go up the feeding order, you also start dictating certain things, like your schedule, and all. This makes it a bit easier, but in no way does that affect the exploitation at home or in the society in general. (IT Union Activist, Bengaluru)

> There are issues among women at higher positions as well. Dalit women, for example, still find it difficult to exercise their power over others even if they have power. At the same time, take the example of Muslim women, even they face many issues when they have to say give an order. There are issues concerning identity and social attributes which work everywhere. But depending on your upbringing and your class you can navigate around them. So, an informed middle-class Muslim or Dalit woman can effectively navigate these issues because she is trained like that, with better education, more social capital, etc. (IT Union Activist, Kolkata)

If one analyses the narratives above, it will become clear that there is a difference between how the two activists frame the issues presented to them. While the first narrative focuses exclusively on the idea of vertical mobility that an employee can achieve while working, the latter focuses on the multidimensional and intersectional nature of women's oppression. While the new workers coming into formal employment arrangements has benefitted the non-capitalist classes by increasing their quantity, it has also posed a serious challenge to the traditional models of trade unionism because of the changes that they have come to embody within themselves that make them distinct from the traditional working class and the middle classes. The ways in which trade unions get organised in any society is a manifestation of the social context within which they function. The subversion of the women workers within the trade unions is thus a matter of grave concern for the trade unions concerned not only because women constitute a significant percentage of the workforce, but also because they play a critical role in the way in the social reproduction of the workforce itself (Fraser et al., 2019). Unfortunately, these issues have failed to be internalised within what mainstream trade unionism refers to as 'trade union consciousness'—an idea that often reflects the masculine and casteist nature of mainstream and dogmatic trade unionism that has been used to propagate the idea that most individuals from the marginalised sections cannot become effective trade union activists as their consciousness is perceived to be highly restrictive and limited in nature. Their perceived inability to be conscious social subjects makes them incapable of realising their actual revolutionary potential to most trade unionists.

Their marginalisation continues even within the trade unions who often fail to analyse the structural and ideological nature of oppression and the role that they have played in the evolution of the society as historical subjects themselves. The absence or presence of unions has different implications for different individuals. For example, in general, for middle-class upper-caste men, the absence of a union often concerns their economic existence only, while for the women and Dalits, the absence of a collective or a union leaves them more vulnerable to exclusionary and exploitative processes. Three IT Workers narrate their experiences with their respective unions regarding such processes:

> For women, I guess, unions are extremely important. That is because when a young woman comes to a city like Pune or Chennai from a place that does not even speak the same language that a worker does. Struggles such as finding a home or getting a support system up and running are some of the areas in which the union is particularly helpful. (Woman IT Worker, Bengaluru)

> For me, being a part of a union is much more than being a part of a representative body. It is a part of who I am. It has helped me get a community here in this city. Coming from a small city, and that also being a Muslim, the union comrades made me feel at home in the city. They gave me a circle, which is very difficult to get directly in this city. (Muslim IT Worker, Gurgaon)

> The Union helped me become more at home at this place. For the men, it is easier. If a union or any such body are not present for them, it does not make much difference. For women, on the other hand, this can be a harsh city, You need to figure out the safe communities, the safe houses and all that. The Union has helped me do that. Although I agree that they have done that to further their own agenda, but it does not matter. (Woman IT Worker, Chennai)

Trade unions in the IT sector have had to tackle issues that are much more social in nature than merely economic, such as belongingness, structural exploitation, and social impoverishment. Such activities have encompassed a variety of different strategies such as renting assistance, providing community support, and so forth. Some of the social strategies that trade unions have been engaging in are attempts to bridge the gaps existing between the economic and socio-cultural exploitation of workers. While some of the activities that the trade unions engage in might not necessarily be trade unionistic in nature, they are still considered to be important facets of trade unionism in the Indian IT sector, most of which are employed to generate favourable attitudes towards unionisation among the workers. Most trade unions working within the IT sector have come to realise that favourable attitudes towards unions are not constituted only through their economic interventions but rather is constructed by the presence of the unions in easing the various difficulties faced by the workers in their everyday lives, especially the marginalised workers.

Such statements highlight that even if some of the workers do not agree with the demands raised by the trade unions or organisations, they can still be parts of the union provided they develop a sense of belongingness towards the organisation. Being a part of a union provides these workers an opportunity to theorise the exploitation that they face at a social level despite being economically privileged. The intervention of the trade unions at this point becomes critical because trade unions despite being flawed still remain the primary schools of class struggle (Marx, 1847). Being a part of a trade union enables the women workers to analyse the exploitation that they face at the workplace. But the inadequacy of mainstream trade union structures gets manifested in the trade unions' inability to theorise the ideological state of contemporary capitalism that relies immensely on the processes through which it can extract relative surplus value through means of disciplining (Tronti, 1962; Hardt & Negri, 2000). Structures of solidarity can enable one to negate the effects of such disciplining to a certain extent because solidarity structures affect the marginalised people in ways that enhance their understanding of their own exploitation (Dunayevskaya, 1970).

On a progressive note, but albeit out of necessity, some IT unions have also begun operating on the basis of communities rather than workplaces because the accessibility required for workplace unionising in the IT sector is extremely rare in the case of India. Unionising in the workplaces is a difficult task to attain because some of the tech parks where the IT offices are usually located are classified as SEZs, where unionisation is not directly encouraged by the state. Two union activists have spoken about these dynamics in details focusing on Kolkata and Bengaluru:

I have worked as a union organised in this company for around 3 years now. The hostility is there, but then it depends on you regarding how well you can tackle it. If you are motivated enough, I do not think there will be much of an issue. I have done open memberships in the office. The managers know that I work for the union. They can call me out and fire me if they want to, but they will not because I have a good rapport with the workers. The hostility, it is important to say this, is based on the way in which the companies see unions, not these managers. (Union Activist, AIITEU, Kolkata, January 2023)

There are two ways in which we usually organise. The first is organising in the workplace, the second organising at the community. At this point, we have taken the second option because that allows us to escape from the hostility shown towards the union at the workplaces. I must admit that it does reduce our capacities at directly affecting the point of production, but that is important to safeguard our activists. (Union Activist, FITE, Chennai, January 2022)

The MMC is not a homogenous class, as can be inferred from these statements. The MMC in Kolkata is actually a more homogenous MMC because most of the workers there speak the same language—Bengali—or other related languages (such as Assamese and Oriya) and dialects and share a relatively more homogenous workforce culturally and socially. On the contrary, in places like Bengaluru, Pune, and Hyderabad, the rate of growth of the IT sector is much higher, and naturally these cities also attract a significantly higher non-local language speaking workforce into them every year.[6] At the same time, Kolkata has had a rich history of trade union struggles and a rich legacy of left-wing social movements, which has continued to have an influence on the IT sector therein as well, which reflects in the organisational methods adopted in these two cities. Trade unions in the IT sector enable newer workers to obtain a community when they relocate to newer places, which are intrinsically connected to the problems that they face in obtaining safe housing, and a decent standard of living. Women and other marginalised individuals suffer from the structural inequalities in place that restricts their ability to form communities and obtain a decent standard of living—something that men often find automatically. It is keeping these different ramifications in mind that the trade union struggles in the IT sector have to be analysed. The changes are

---

[6] Details have been provided in Chap. 1.

related to the general class structure of the society that has been altered with the growth of neoliberal privatisation and the consumerist lifestyle that it produces changing social aspirations, desires, and lifestyles (Burris, 1986).

The effects of such a denunciation of their identity as workers have grave consequences for the workers' movement as well, especially for workers from the marginalised sections. Workers from the marginalised sections of the society are more affected by the socio-economic conditions produced by the normalisation of mass layoffs because they are more likely to suffer from layoffs because of the existent structures of socio-cultural exploitation. The fear of enforced unemployment results in them having a negative attitude towards trade unionism fuelled mostly by the belief that getting engaged in trade unionism would result in them being in the *bad books* of their employers. The fear of being unemployed has caused a tremendous harm to the trade union movement in the private sector—more so among the women workers or Dalit workers because while for the upper caste relatively affluent men, the prospect of employment signifies a vertical social mobility, for the marginalised sections. They were often seen as being a means of asserting their human existence. Such modes of assertion become critical in contexts such as India where both the management and often the unions as well have been dominated by patriarchal, caste-based, and majoritarian ideologies in place (Teltumbde, 2017; Deb Roy, 2022). The prevalence of such notions has resulted in struggles over questions of leadership and organisational methods within the unions.

The benefit of such tussles has sometimes been enjoyed by the right-wing forces. One of the many reasons for the tussle between the forces is the idea of the conceptualisation of the revolutionary subject. One of the many allegations that the left makes against Ambedkarite forces is that they are too particularistic and in doing so often forget about the universal struggle. The Ambedkarite forces, on the other hand, argue that the left is often *vaguely universal* with no respect for the particular social context in which the struggle is being waged. The cumulative result of these processes is that both the employer and the unions have contributed to the growing exploitation of certain sections of workers. Such structures have failed to address concerns such as patriarchal social relations and caste structures that continue to affect human societies as ideological frameworks and as a force of exploitation (Eisenstein, 1979; Teltumbde, 2017). The continuing relevance of such issues under neoliberal capitalism makes it imperative that their issues are approached through a paradigm informed

176   S. DEB ROY

by class analysis. Trade unions in this respect play a critical role because despite the shortcomings, trade unions are important organisations to develop political consciousness, organisational skills, and leadership abilities (Mead, 1998). The question of leadership becomes extremely critical in the context of trade union activities in India, which have otherwise been dominated by the middle class.

'MIDDLE-CLASS' WORKERS AND THE TRANSFORMATION OF THE WORKERS' IDENTITY

The middle classes in India are a highly heterogeneous class that has been formed due to a combination of their objective class positions reinforced and reinforcing their subjective social statuses. Classes do not play out in the real world like they do in theoretical formulations, and instead work in relation to the particular context in which the individuals find themselves. They are formed in relation to the everyday lives of the working individuals that constitute the concrete reality around them (Lefebvre, 2014; Chattopadhyaya, 2013). The middle class has played an important role, both quantitatively and qualitatively, in progressive struggles in India. But the involvement of the middle classes in a progressive movement is a double-edged sword. While on the one hand, it provides any movement with a certain level of social acceptance (Sil, 2004), it also simultaneously also makes the movement tread a difficult path as far as its reflections upon the problems of the working class per se are concerned (Kennedy & Tilly, 1987) because the middle class often work in favour of the status quo. The middle-class adherence towards the ideas and interests of the status quo is often witnessed in the case of the Dalit middle class, who have often sided with the ruling class rejecting any association with socialists and Marxists resulting a paradoxical situation (Teltumbde, 2017).

Such situations are not unique only to Dalits but can be found across other marginalised sections as well. For example, one can again refer to the state of MMC women. Among middle class women, there has been an increase of structural and material violence exhibited towards the invisible IT workers or the IT support workers as Chap. 5 has noted in detail. The perceived power that the middle class enjoys in certain special circumstances does not hold good universally. For example, even within the middle class, the middle-class women suffer more than the men because while the men frame their relationship directly with the work they do, most of the women do so through the lens of men or the family—as has been shown in Chap. 3. Similarly, in Chap. 5, it was stated that individuals from certain regions are able to form certain structures or networks of solidarity with the invisible workers. However, it is usually the case that it is the men who form such connections. The reasons behind why only men do that takes one to the very structure of the society that the IT workers in India inhabit that is characterised by a combination of capitalism, Brahmanism, and patriarchy whereby women regardless of their caste position are often subverted into a private domain of exploitation (Chakravarti, 1993). Similar kind of treatment is reserved for the Dalits and Muslims in the country as well. Such kinds of intersectional and multifaceted modes of exploitation that organisations and trade working among IT workers often have had to work outside the purview of traditional trade unionism. The domination of the middle class alters the discourse of a particular social movement having an effect on not only the class composition of the organisations involved but also the strategies and tactics that they employ.

The changes within the class structure do not only get manifested in ways that are economic in nature but also get reflected in other mundane aspects like the MMC fetish of weekends. For most of the unions, there is no other option but to organise during the weekends because that is the only time that they can actually organise meetings hoping for attendance and a space to do so. Trade unions like the KITU, who have their own office space,[7] find themselves at a relatively advantageous position here. But, regardless of whether a union owns a space, the weekends for the MMC have simply become *off-limits*. Trade unions in the IT sector thus find themselves in a paradoxical scenario. One Union activist notes:

> That is the major reason why I say that the IT workers are a bit different. Most unions have weekend meetings in the service sector. You ask somebody to attend a meeting during the weekends, and you immediately get negative feedback. That is the problem. But the question is if we do not do it during weekends, when do we actually do meeting? And without meetings, how can we run a union? (IT Union Activist, Pune)

The hyper-productive lifestyles that the IT workers are made to live during the weekdays construct the weekends as a fetishised commodity for

---

[7] The KITU has an office which is named as the 'Stalin Centre'. Many trade unionists have critiqued the naming of the office because of the political connotations associated with the same. This has been discussed in the Conclusion.

them—one which they can use to visit shopping malls, get groceries, and spend some quality leisure time, most of which contribute to capitalist profit accumulation in various ways. The previous chapters have engaged in detail about the hyper-productive nature of the IT sector, and the effects that it has on the workers therein. The struggle for profitability has an effect on the kind of work cultures that these firms or companies create. Globally, work cultures have begun to require lower quantities of workers, but it needs them to work harder and faster—most evidently in the IT sector. The hyper-productive nature of the sector and the class confusion among most of the workers in the IT sector necessitate that trade unions cannot remain restricted to merely critiquing the employers or the management, but also work towards generating a larger working-class consciousness among the workers that constitutes the basis on which the IT sector workforce can become a part of the mainstream workers' movement. As one IT union activist stated:

> It is important to make the IT workers realise that they are a part of the larger labour force in the country and globally, since the workers in the IT sector more often than not directly cater a western audience. Without a realisation that they are a part of the workforce, it is impossible to mobilise them. It is important to make them capable enough to understand their own class consciousness. (IT Union Activist, Pune)

The question of class in any social movement is an important one to consider if one is to analyse the causes of failures or successes of the movement. Participatory classes become extremely important in any theory or movement because they play an important role in determining the class character of the theory or the movement itself (Kennedy & Tilly, 1987). Because of its significant numbers within the workforce, the middle class has become an important part of workers' organisations, political formations, and CSOs. However, despite being an important part of the workforce and the workers' movement, the ways in which the middle class frames the issues concerning their working selves has often been put to question, more so in the case of the MMC. The methods of organising the MMC need to counter the various alterations that technological innovations have normalised which include complicated methods of administrative bureaucracy, and instilling a constant fear of unemployment through the reserve army of labour that technological advancement produces under monopolistic capitalism (Braverman, 1974; Fields, 2012).

Most of these methods that the IT sector management employs are aimed at normalising a mode of larger social control and compliance. One of the key aspects of the social control and compliance generation among the IT workers is to generate a sense of superiority among certain sections of the working populace because it does away with tendencies of class identification and greater working-class co-operation that manifests in the forms of greater intra-working-populace violence. The un-unionised and a significant portion of the unionised workers in the IT sector constantly emphasise that they are distinct from other workers. The workers in the IT sector, especially in specialist job profiles frequently desire to be something which is existentially and epistemologically different than the working class. For these workers, there are multiple social and individual attributes such as their class position and their craft interests that come into functioning when they start thinking about forming or joining any form of representative body. Speaking on this, two IT workers, one among whom is a union activist, state:

> I think the problem is mostly located in the ways in which the trade unions frame their policies in the private sector. It is not surprising that most of the IT workers still feel that the unions are a nuisance. It is because they see themselves as being beneficiaries of the system rather than being exploited by it. The private sector has been manufacturing a feeling among the workers that they are not workers *per se* but rather middle-class professionals, a lot of our comrades are also getting affected because most of their peers are working in the private sector. They want their jobs to be flashy like the others, better paying and more dynamics where they can shift jobs and get hikes. They do this without knowing the kind of issues that workers face in the private sector. (IT Union Activist, Bengaluru)

> Today, we cannot go about preaching class struggle. To some that is a problem, while to some, that is just one of the many problems that we must address as a union. We cannot disregard the fact that we are living in times where being political or having a political opinion is almost considered to be a crime in many sections of the society. The workers that we get in the offices are a part of this social transformation. We need to engage with them. Even in the women's rights movements today, we get a lot of people, who proclaim themselves to be the middle class, does that mean that we need to stop engaging with them. But at the same time, we are not workers. That is the issue. While all the unions treat us as workers, the problem lies precisely in that. We are not workers. We are professionals. Workers, working class and all that stuff about revolution does not apply to us. We have no interest in getting rid of the system. We are its beneficiaries. (IT Worker, Bengaluru)

The idea of the middle class has elevated itself from being merely a subjective existential philosophy to a distinct factor within the workers' movement. The differences in class interests are often dictated by the existence of non-class factors within the workers' movement that have been creating major hurdles for many workers' organisations in implementing their traditional methods of organisation. The construction of such a new working class in India has been based on the grounds of a neoliberal hegemony that constitutes the social basis for the furthering of social control by the generation of wilful compliance that overshadows the socio-economic hardships and cultural marginalisation of the already marginalised. The mass usage of authority plays a significant role in this regard. The popular usage of authority by neoliberal capitalism becomes explicit in the way in which authority has been structurally institutionalised in the country as a basic feature of everyday life. This has made it possible for neoliberal capitalism to further aggravate the effect of the model of compliance which it proposes to instil globally creating a social condition where capitalism and the market not only have the ability and freedom to make rules but also the power to ensure that they are followed (Dekker, 2022).

The consequences of such changes become especially grave for workers coming from the marginalised sections for whom lifestyle becomes an important aspect of social existence because it simultaneously represents the very core of their supplementary socio-cultural existence. Identifying themselves with the working class makes them feel less privileged because the social structure around them makes the idea of struggling for one's rights a domain that is reserved for the working class. Self-identifying themselves as being epistemologically different than other workers is a key part of the MMC consciousness. Such a consciousness is mainly generated through the everyday interactions that the MMC have with the urban social reality and the other sections of the working class therein—particularly the precariat workforce employed as invisible workers in the IT sector. Class consciousness is contingent upon the factors of life that the workers confront on an everyday basis (Thompson, 1963). Since compliance forms a critical part of their lives, it is only natural that a large section of the workforce has come to determine their class consciousness through the ideological framework of wilful compliance such that they fulfil the requirements posed by the disciplinary society (Bond, 2004; Harvey, 2005; Giroux, 2014). Such disciplinary domination at a social level cannot be exercised without the active consent of the middle class because of its control over the requisite resources (Tronti, 1962; Negri, 1989; Hardt &

Negri, 2000). Neoliberalism has allowed the middle class to accumulate considerable wealth and higher income opportunities, while a greater section of the populace has been facing greater inequality, insecurity, unemployment, underemployment, casualisation, and informalisation (Das, 2015; Ahalya & Pal, 2017).

The trade unions' response under such circumstances is contingent upon the power that they represent in specific socio-political contexts (Bound & Johnson, 1992), especially under neoliberal regimes that thrive within a framework of anti-unionism and de-politicisation. The perception of unionisation among the IT workers is a pessimistic one, one which is informed by the dual processes of atomic individualisation and de-politicisation critical to the neoliberal model of control (Hardt & Negri, 2000; Porter & Craig, 2004; Stahl et al., 2021). Science and technology under capitalism attempts to replace senses pertaining to class consciousness with technocratic rationality, which distorts the relationship between one's selfhood and social anxieties presenting a sense of ontological insecurity (Kinnvall & Mitzen, 2020). The MMC, though financially stable, suffers from this lack of ontological security, one which has been heightened with the coming of COVID-19 due to the constant degradation of the working life of the IT workers that directly impacted their style of lives.[8] As two IT workers stated:

> Our lives were horrible during the pandemic lockdown. No time for myself, no time for family. The company became so obsessed that we would not work that they started giving us extra work citing that we were anyway on holiday since we are at home. I would really want my organization to understand that being at home during the pandemic is a challenging task. Practically, there is no difference between my home and office now, which has made it very difficult to find work-life balance. But we have to keep on working because the life of a tech worker is very short, you either update yourself or you get thrown out. (Male IT Worker, Bengaluru)

> There was a constant lengthening of hours during the lockdown. At the same time, there is also the constant pressure of skill upgrading, because all of us know that a recession might hit us anytime. I am not comfortable working from my home. Additionally, now I have to work regularly during weekends which is making it very difficult to address concerns which are outside my official domain but deeply affect my productivity. (Woman IT Worker, Kolkata)

---

[8] Detailed discussion surrounding 'Style of life' has been done in Chap. 3.

182 S. DEB ROY

Trade unions within this milieu can play an important role because trade unions have the capacity to directly engage with the workers bringing forward their perspective regarding their own issues, in addition to bargaining for better wages (Punekar et al., 1978; Bryson et al., 2020). Trade union membership in a firm, as Bryson et al. (2020) argue, can be positively correlated with factors such as job satisfaction, mental health, and so forth. However, the liberal framework within which most IT workplaces operate fails to recognise these issues. At the same time, the IT workers' movement in India has depended on liberal activists from the middle classes and has often failed to posture a distinct working-class activism of its own focusing on these workers but only through an ideological framework whereby their identities as consumers have been the major focus. However, because of the apolitical and de-politicised nature of the movement, they failed to evoke an organisational form suited to the workers, who come from the marginalised sections. The failure to generate a distinct mode of activism manifested itself within the IT sector through a rapid weakening of welfare measures and advocacy programmes that were also reinforced by the nature of the IT workforce. The growth of the middle classes in India resulted in an alteration of the demands and strategies that are usually employed by the workers' movement. While working in the IT sector, the trade unions have had to adopt numerous different strategies that can interfere not only within the economic lives of individuals but also within their social lives. The interventions of the unions in the social space that the women workers occupy has important consequences for the attitude that the workers possess towards the unions in their economic lives. It is the dialectical relationship between the workers' attitudes towards the unions and vice versa that shape their engagement with the unions (Kochan, 1979; Sarkar, 2012). The constant interactions between the economic and social aspects of exploitation are critical to the development of a working-class identity among the IT workers. Such processes when combined with the alienating gentrified urbanisation processes that they become a part of make them different from the traditional industrial and service workers and as such traditional models of trade unionism usually practised by the CTUs and their affiliated unions however have failed to generate a sense of solidarity among the IT Workers. Two union activists state:

> The private sector is beaming with who could be very good activists. However, the major problem for many of them are the way in which they

characterise themselves. We have tried getting them onto the traditional unions, but we have failed. They need a new kind of union, a new approach for them is necessary. (CTU Activist, Delhi)

Sometimes, actually, it is a good thing because we have so many different individuals coming into the union, from various backgrounds. They have even helped us develop a website and have also allowed us to keep abreast of what unions across the world are doing, but we have a long way to go. (CTU Activist, Bengaluru)

These narratives exhibit that despite the workers in the IT sector possessing important trade unionistic skills, their individual and social qualities—many of which is ideologically injected into them—deter them from being involved in trade unions. They have increasingly come to define themselves as being parts of the neoliberal order where their interests are different than the working classes. The creation of ambiguous class positions is particularly evident in the post-industrial service sector where class consciousness and radical working-class identity found themselves difficult to be manifested (Touraine, 1969; Bell, 1973). A significant role in this milieu was performed by the middle class and its advocacy in favour of the exclusionist developmental agenda that India put in place (Desai, 1984; Prasad, 1988).

It was expected that the middle class would help in disseminating the developmental gains to the already marginalised. However, as things stood, the middle class has failed to fulfil that role and its growth and unionisation, in Indian and in general, has an inversely proportional relationship with inequality and blue-collar workers' unionisation (Suh, 2002; Fernandes, 2006). Traditionally, the middle class has been a major bone of contention between the organised and the unorganised left in India. Its existence as a major force within the electoral politics of the country has converted the middle class into an important section of the population that all political formations, regardless of their ideological positions, pay attention to (Jaffrelot, 2008). The creation of the middle class is a distinctly political process whereby both the right and the left wing within any political structure aggravate the conditions under which the creation of the middle class gets accelerated and welcomed (Le Grand & Winter, 1986). The differences that an individual worker's subjective positioning of oneself, that is, whether one belongs to the working class or the middle class, entail within themselves affect the way in which the workers organise themselves. There are contradictions surrounding class, caste, and gender which become extremely important for the unions when they attempt to organise the workers.

Most of these issues were present in the Indian workers' movement even before neoliberalism (Chatterji, 1980; Sherman, 2021). But since the growth of neoliberalism coincides with the gradual decline of trade unions (Harvey, 2005), the problems have increased significantly. Neoliberal capitalism reduces workers' rights, increases the domination of the management, and localises the control that global finance capital possesses over the workers (Harvey, 2006). Most of these processes take place with the active consent of the state. In India, the private sector was given a free reign in India as it was believed that privatisation would allow businesses to thrive resulting in a rise of profits causing a rise in the levels of general prosperity in the society (Mohan, 2002). However, claims such as these are yet to be realised in contemporary India, that has seen a constant increase in unemployment and poverty levels since 1991 (Das, 2015; Jha & Pankaj, 2021). The conditions of organising in the private sector are getting further complicated by the contractualisation of the labour force, which has been made possible because the employment protection legislations (EPLs) had been mostly ignored since 1991 (Sarkar, 2023). The rise of corporate culture results in a monopolistic control of certain corporates which enjoy legal immunity even if they violate labour and industrial laws as one senior trade unionist stated. The way in which corporates enjoy a certain level of protection from the government is integral to the very construction of a neoliberal society based on market values (Perelman, 2005) that results in increased poverty levels. The question of poverty is a central one for contemporary analytical frameworks. There can be no denying the fact that the IT workers are one of the most well-paid workers in the country. However, at the same time, most of the IT workers share the social space with countless invisible workers—who are often better suited to become the working class in the classical sense gradually transforming themselves from their current state of being 'a class in making', that is, precariat workers (Standing, 2011). Precariat migrant workers, even though, possess a class character, fail to represent, and articulate themselves as a class, and as such lose their natural, labour, and human rights in the process becoming denizens having a limited range of rights than others (Standing, 2014). Such Precariatisation is significantly different than the classical process of Proleterisation because Proleterisation enables the worker to possess a sense of security, either through wages or through a job or through the guarantee of a distinct way of life, however marginalised that might be. Precariatisation, on the other hand, completely robs the individuals of all forms of social attributes and converts them into a full-fledged perishable commodity which is worse than being the working class in the classical sense.

Mere sharing of a social space is not a guarantee that forms of prejudice would be done away with (Huws, 2014). Rather, more often than not, such prejudices are more likely to increase because of the effects that neoliberalism has on the individual's perceptions towards solidarity networks. The emergence of a new working class aligned with the traditional one was a very popular conception among intellectuals on both ends of the political spectrum in the Global North, who had been working with the assumption that the new working class emerging out of the various kinds of middle or service classes would align with the traditional working class and produce a rejuvenated working class capable of countering technologically-mediated capitalist exploitation (Braverman, 1974; Mallet, 1975; Bruce-Briggs, 1979; Ehrenreich & Ehrenreich, 1979). However, this ideal is yet to be realised. One of the major causes for the same is the existence of non-class factors within the workers' movement that have been creating major hurdles for many workers' organisations and deterring the generation of a working-class identity among the IT workers.

References

Ahalya, R., & Pal, S. B. (2017). *Identification and Characterization of Middle Class in India and Its Comparison with Other Economic Classes.* Retrieved April 5, 2023, from https://www.isid.ac.in/~epu/acegd2017/papers/Ahalya Ramanathan.pdf

Bain, G. S. (1968). *The Growth of White-Collar Unionism.* Clarendon.

Balaji, & Woodcock, J. (2019, January 26). FITE and Organising IT Workers in India. *Notes from Below.* Retrieved April 5, 2023, from https://notesfrombelow.org/article/fite-and-organising-it-workers-india

Banjac, S., & Hanusch, F. (2022). Aspirational Lifestyle Journalism: The Impact of Social Class on Producers' and Audiences' Views in the Context of Socio-Economic Inequality. *Journalism, 23*(8), 1607–1625.

Bell, D. (1973). *The Coming of Post-Industrial Society: A Venture in Social Forecasting.* Basic Books.

Bisht, N. S. (2010). Trade Unions in Indian IT Industry? An Employees' Perspective. *Indian Journal of Industrial Relations, 46*(2), 220–228.

Bond, P. (2004). Neoliberalism in Sub-Saharan Africa: From Structural Adjustment to NEPAD. In A. Saad-Filho & D. Johnston (Eds.), *Neoliberalism: A Critical Reader*. Pluto Press.

Bourdieu, P. (1984). *Distinction: A Social Critique of the Judgement of Taste*. Cambridge University Press.

Bound, J., & Johnson, G. (1992). Changes in the Structure of Wages in the 1980s: An Evaluation of Alternative Explanations. *American Economic Review, 82*, 371–392.

Braverman, H. (1974). *Labor and Monopoly Capital*. Monthly Review Press.

Bruce-Briggs, B. (Ed.). (1979). *The New Class?* Transaction Books.

Bryson, A., Freeman, R., & Blanchflower, D. (2020, November 11). Unions Raise Worker Wellbeing. *VoxEU*. Retrieved April 5, 2023, from https://cepr.org/voxeu/columns/unions-raise-worker-wellbeing

Burawoy, M. (1979). *Manufacturing Consent: Changes in the Labor Process Under Monopoly Capitalism*. University of Chicago Press.

Burris, V. (1986). The Discovery of the New Middle Class. *Theory and Society, 15*(3), 317–349.

Chakravarti, U. (1993). Conceptualising Brahmanical Patriarchy in Early India: Gender, Caste, Class, and State. *Economic and Political Weekly, 28*(14), 579–585.

Chatterji, R. (1980). *Unions, Politics, and the State: A Study of Indian Labour Politics*. South Asian Publishers.

Chattopadhyaya, D. P. (2013). *Science and Philosophy in Ancient India*. Aakar.

Das, R. J. (2015). Critical Observations on Neo-liberalism and India's New Economic Policy. *Journal of Contemporary Asia, 45*(4), 715–726.

Deb Roy, S. (2022). *Mass Struggles and Leninism: Reflections on Contemporary Struggles in India*. Phoneme Books.

Deery, S., & Walsh, J. (1999). The Decline of Collectivism? A Comparative Study of White-Collar Employees in Britain and Australia. *British Journal of Industrial Relations, 37*(2), 245–269.

Dekker, S. (2022). *Compliance Capitalism: How Free Markets Have Led to Unfree, Overregulated Workers*. Routledge.

Desai, A. R. (1984). *India's Path of Development: A Marxist Approach*. Sangam Books.

Dunayevskaya, R. (1970/2015). The WLM as Reason and Revolutionary Force. In *Women's Liberation and the Dialectics of Revolution: Reaching for the Future*. Aakar.

Ehrenreich, B., & Ehrenreich, J. (1979). The Professional-Managerial Class. In P. Walker (Ed.), *Between Labor and Capital* (pp. 5–45). South End Press.

Eisenstein, Z. R. (1979). Developing a Theory of Capitalist Patriarchy and Socialist Feminism. In Z. R. Eisenstein (Ed.), *Capitalist Patriarchy and the Case for Socialist Feminism*. Monthly Review Press.

Fernandes, L. (2006). *India's New Middle Class: Democratic Politics in an Era of Economic Reform*. University of Minnesota Press.

Fields, G. S. (2012). *Working Hard, Working Poor: A Global Journey*. Oxford University Press.

Fraser, N., Bhattacharya, T., & Arruzza, C. (2019). *Feminism for the 99%*. Verso.

Ganguly, S. (2022). In the Pursuit of Middle-Classness: Exploring the Aspirations and Strategies of the Urban Poor in Neoliberal Delhi. In M. K. Jha & Pushpendra (Eds.), *Beyond Consumption: India's New Middle Class in the Neo-Liberal State*. Routledge.

Giroux, H. (2014/2020). *Neoliberalism's War on Higher Education* (2nd ed.). Haymarket Books.

Hardt, M., & Negri, M. (2000). *Empire*. Harvard University Press.

Harvey, D. (2005). *A Brief History of Neoliberalism*. Oxford University Press.

Harvey, D. (2006/2019). *Spaces of Global Capitalism: A Theory of Uneven Geographical Development*. Verso.

Huws, U. (2014). *Labor in the Global Digital Economy: The Cybertariat Comes of Age*. Monthly University Press.

Inglis, P. (2019). *Narrow Fairways: Getting by and Falling Behind in the New India*. Oxford University Press.

Jaffrelot, C. (2008). 'Why Should We Vote?': The Indian Middle Class and the Functioning of the World's Largest Democracy. In C. Jaffrelot & P. van der Veer (Eds.), *Patterns of Middle-Class Consumption in India and China*. New Delhi.

Jha, M. K., & Pankaj, A. K. (2021). Neoliberal Governmentality and Social Policymaking in India: Implications for In/Formal Workers and Community Work. *The International Journal of Community and Social Development, 3*(3), 198–214.

Jha, S. (2022). Dalit Desires, Middle Classness and the City of Surat. In M. K. Jha & Pushpendra (Eds.), *Beyond Consumption: India's New Middle Class in the Neo-Liberal State*. Routledge.

Kalirajan, K. P., & Shand, R. T. (1996). Public Sector Enterprises in India: Is Privatisation the Only Answer? *Economic and Political Weekly, 31*(39), 2683–2686.

Kennedy, M., & Tilly, C. (1987). Feminism and the Stillbirth of Socialist Feminism in Europe, 1890–1920. *Science & Society, 51*(1), 6–42.

Kinnvall, C., & Mitzen, J. (2020). Anxiety, Fear, and Ontological Security in World Politics: Thinking with and Beyond Giddens. *International Theory, 12*, 240–256.

Kochan, T. A. (1979). How American Workers View Labor Unions. *Monthly Labour Review, 102*(4), 23–31.

Laing, R.D. (1969/1990). *The Divided Self: An Existential Study in Sanity and Madness*. Penguin Books.

Le Grand, J., & Winter, D. (1986). The Middle Classes and the Welfare State under Conservative and Labour Governments. *Journal of Public Policy, 6*(4), 399–430.

Lefebvre, H. (2014). *Critique of Everyday Life*. Verso.

Losurdo, D. (2016). *Liberalism: A Counter History* (Trans. G. Elliott). Verso.

Mallet, S. (1975). *The New Working Class*. Spokesman Books.

Marx, K. (1847/1976). The Poverty of Philosophy. In *Marx Engels Collected Works: Volume 6*. Lawrence and Wishart.

McClure, D. R. (2021). *Winter in America: A Cultural History of Neoliberalism, from the Sixties to the Reagan Revolution*. The University of North Carolina Press.

Mead, R. J. (1998). 'Let the Women Get Their Wages as Men Do': Trade Union Women and The Legislated Minimum Wage in California. *Pacific Historical Review, 67*(3), 317–347.

Means, R., & Smith, R. (1994). *Community Care: Policy and Practice*. London: Macmillan.

Mohan, T. T. R. (2002). Privatisation: Theory and Evidence. *Economic and Political Weekly, 36*(52), 4865–4871.

Negri, A. (1989). Archaeology and the Project. In *Revolution Retrieved*. Red Notes.

Perelman, M. (2005). *Manufacturing Discontent: The Trap of Individualism in Corporate Society*. Pluto Press.

Porter, D., & Craig, D. (2004). The Third Way and the Third World: Poverty Reduction and Social Inclusion in the Rise of 'Inclusive' Liberalism. *Review of International Political Economy, 11*(2), 387–423.

Prasad, P. H. (1988). Roots of Uneven Regional Growth in India. *Economic and Political Weekly, 23*(33), 1968–1992.

Punekar, S. D., Deodhar, S. B., & Sankaran, S. (1978). *Labour Welfare, Trade Unionism and Industrial Relations*. Himalaya Publishing House.

Ramadorai, S. (2011). *The TCS Story and Beyond*. Penguin.

Reddy, B. V. R. M. (2022). *Engineered in India: From Dreams to Billion-Dollar CYIENT*. Penguin.

Sarkar, S. (2008). Trade Unionism in Indian BPO-ITeS Industry—Insights from Literature. *Indian Journal of Industrial Relations, 44*(1), 72–88.

Sarkar, S. (2012). Determinants of Employees' Attitudes Toward Union Membership in India. *Journal of World Business, 47*, 240–250.

Sarkar, S. (2023). Towards a Model of Contractualisation of Labour in India: Testing the Effect of Unionisation of Regular Workers and the Wage Gap. *NHRD Network Journal, 16*(1), 20–31.

Sherman, T. C. (2021). Not Part of the Plan? Women, State Feminism, and Indian Socialism in the Nehru Years. *South Asia: Journal of South Asian Studies, 44*(2), 298–312.

Sheth, D. L. (1999). Secularisation of Caste and Making of New Middle Class. *Economic and Political Weekly, 34*(34/35), 2502–2510.

Sil, K. L. (2004). Beyond the Boundary: Middle-Class Women in Income-Generating Activities in Burdwan. *India. Contemporary South Asia,* *13*(3), 255–270.

Stahl, G., McDonald, S., & Young, J. (2021). Possible Selves in a Transforming Economy: Upwardly Mobile Working-Class Masculinities, Service Work and Negotiated Aspirations in Australia. *Work, Employment and Society,* *35*(1), 97–115.

Standing, G. (2011). *The Precariat: The New Dangerous Class.* Bloomsbury Academic.

Standing, G. (2014). *A Precariat Charter.* Bloomsbury Academic.

Suh, D. (2002). Middle-Class Formation and Class Alliance. *Social Science History,* *26*(1), 105–137.

Teltumbde, A. (2017). Bridging the Unholy Rift. In *India and Communism.* Leftword Books.

Thompson, E. P. (1963/2013). *The Making of the English Working Class.* Vintage.

Touraine, A. (1969). *The Post-Industrial Society: Tomorrow's Social History: Classes, Conflicts and Culture in the Programmed Society.* Random House.

Tronti, M. (1962). *Factory and Society.* Operaismo in English. Retrieved April 5, 2023, from https://operaismoinenglish.wordpress.com/2013/06/13/factory-and-society/

Uchitelle, L. (2006). *The Disposable American: Layoffs and their Consequences.* Alfred A. Knopf.

Vanaik, A. (2001). The New Indian Right. *New Left Review, 1*(9). Retrieved April 5, 2023, from https://newleftreview.org/issues/ii9/articles/achin-vanaik-the-new-indian-right

Vanaik, A. (2004). Rendezvous at Mumbai. *New Left Review, 1*(26), 53–65.

CHAPTER 8

Workers, Middle-Class Employees, Professionals? No, just *the Working Poor!*

Poverty today is increasingly becoming extremely nuanced and intersectional in nature evading most traditional macroeconomic and meta-theory-based explanations disproportionately affecting people living in areas with poor infrastructure and more so if their employment does not guarantee certain rights to them. This process under contemporary neoliberal capitalism has been heightened with 'a double transformation of the sphere of work' both qualitatively and quantitatively (Wacquant, 1999, p. 1642). The former in the sense that under contemporary capitalism, most of the working conditions have been becoming extremely degraded with little benefits or social security being provided to the workers, and the latter through the elimination of jobs that require lower skills because of the increasing pressures created by automation and the competition among workers, especially due to the influx of cheap and often immigrant labour into the labour market. When coupled with the various exploitative models based on caste, religion, and gender, this has resulted in widespread displacement and loss of shelter and work (Harriss-White, 2005; Levien, 2018). The urban reality in India produced by these factors thus is a complicated one, one that is difficult to be explained through the traditional theories that have been rendered mainstream in the Global North. While in the Global North, cities and urban spaces have been equated with the bourgeoning rise of rationality and modernity, transgressing the

© The Author(s), under exclusive license to Springer Nature 191
Switzerland AG 2024
S. Deb Roy, *The Rise of the Information Technology Society in India,*
Dynamics of Virtual Work,
https://doi.org/10.1007/978-3-031-58128-1_8

remnants of the feudal and primitive past, the process of urbanisation in South Asia, and especially in India has resulted in a proliferation of these tendencies with a neoliberal touch to them (van Dijk, 2017), which has been one of the greatest drivers of extreme marginality in India.

The Indian IT industry has played a key role in this process, influencing methods and processes of urbanisation so as to create a social structure that aids the growth of businesses and neoliberal models of development—often under the garb of development as is evident in the cases of Bengaluru (Goyal & Prakash, 2023), Gurgaon (Oldenburg, 2018), or Noida (Vasudevan, 2013). The Indian IT industry has some basic underlying philosophies, the most important of which are the notions of productivity and discipline. Both these aspects have become important factors in the projected growth of the IT sector in India. The rise of the IT sector in India has not only been constrained within the IT workplaces, and technology parks. It has rather initiated a social process which has captured the entire country, influencing urbanisation processes and labour reforms in various sectors and modes of employment. Most of these changes have occurred in the era of neoliberal capitalism where the competitive advantage of traditional caste-based and family-based business models have been relatively eradicated in favour of monopoly and transnational capital, although certain advantages pertaining to access to capital and kinship networks continue to exist (Damodaran, 2008). Neoliberalism has caused a consistent rise of commodification of human selves which has converted human subjects into commodities tradeable on the market. Most of these alterations in the Indian society have occurred alongside a constant quantification of the society, whereby human qualities and subjectivities have been converted into data structures (Marcuse, 1964). The IT hubs, the basic premise of the book, are characterised by newer and more complicated patterns of labour and employment relations in the twenty-first-century Indian subcontinent. The modifications have mostly enabled a transformation of the old middle class to a new middle class, which evolved subsequently into the Professional Managerial Class (PMC) and then the Metro Middle Class (MMC)—and as this chapter will show—and then further on into an urban working poor. The MMC shares a close connection with the public sector in the sense that publicly funded institutes provide the Information Technology (IT) sector with the most qualified engineers and software professionals (Parthasarathi & Joseph, 2004).

The perceived positive impacts of neoliberal reforms often remain ignorant of the relationship that the neoliberal reforms share with the ideas of coloniality, where the poor and the defenceless are made to completely succumb themselves to the idea of market discipline unregulated by the state (Chomsky, 1996), and transforming the state to a substitutive one (Berry, 2022). The transformation of the state has coincided with the constant rise in the number of individuals who can be classified as being working poor in the Global South with higher long-term unemployment rates and poverty (Majid, 2001). The development of neoliberal capitalism has caused an increasing proportion of working individuals to move towards conditions of working poverty where they are subjected to wide-scale insecurities and financial exclusion (Fields, 2012). There has been a constant exploitation of emotions concerning individual security and social status for the benefit of the expansion of profits under capitalism (Jones, 2007; Illouz, 2007). Such processes have hastened the processes of homogenisation at a global scale creating a global capitalist unconscious that exploits the emotional state of human existence creating a lack of ontological security among the non-capitalist classes (Giddens, 1990). This can be most explicitly witnessed in the case of how different IT workers coped with the COVID-19 induced lockdowns. While the precariat service workers, or the invisible IT workers, had to *walk back to their homes* in the absence of any governmental support suffering through tremendous hardships without much governmental or social support (Kapri, 2021), the formal IT and IT Enabled Services (ITeS) workers were provided with the option of *working from home.*

Different sections of the formal IT workers, as well, have been differently affected by the work from home 'regime' that was brought in with the COVID-19 induced lockdowns. During the lockdowns, the social reality of the IT workers has changed drastically. The rapid shifts that these workers had to make from their adopted cities to their hometowns and villages, created a certain vacuum in their lives, which has been negotiated by differently by different individuals. Working from home has also exposed the exploitative nature of the kind of work that they do as has been referred to in the previous chapters, especially for the women IT workers as Chap. 3 has shown. The increase in anxiety among the marginalised sections of the workforce during the pandemic had significant effects on their ideas of selfhood and their ontological security within the IT space. The anxieties had largely been caused, as Chaps. 3 and 4 had shown, been caused by a fear of getting redundant or losing their jobs because of the economic recession that the sector faced, albeit for a brief period in India (Gopalakrishnan et al., 2022). Issues such as unemployment and layoffs within a neoliberal economy often get relegated as mere incidental events (Uchitelle, 2006). The working poor are more vulnerable to layoffs and retrenchments 'because [apparently] their value to their employers [is] less than their cost in wages and benefits. So, they must raise their value [and] must acquire the necessary education and training to qualify for the work that is in demand in the new economy' (Uchitelle, 2006, p. x). The fears of the workers, especially of the women, were reflections of the fact that the world today is a space where the control over production is largely being exercised through a domination over knowledge whereby productive time and the capacity to block the application or possession of knowledge have become the basic contours of capitalist control (Negri, 2016).

A significant part of such a control has been exercised by the constant validation provided to a certain way of life—a consumerist one—as being the only normalised style of life which has produced the social basis for the creation of an uncritical acceptance of socially constructed aspirations, constraints, and limitations in the society (Aday Jr., 1990). Processes aiding such a transformation on a mass scale act in accordance with the homogenising tendencies that lie at the core of the capitalist transition of the world (Anderson, 2020). For neoliberalism to prosper, the construction of a globally homogenous yet unequal society is preferable because it allows the market relations to expand more effectively (Harvey, 2007). Processes of homogenisation become critical for neoliberalism because it helps neoliberalism to simultaneously emphasise the importance of entities such as individual freedom, liberty, and responsibility along with the constant valourisation of market dynamics (Harvey, 2006). The domination of the global trade rules and norms under which these corporations function creates the grounds for the creation of completely de-politicised, uncritical, and a consensual rationality among individuals which is of paramount importance to the global neoliberal order that is simultaneously both neo-conservative and liberal (Porter & Craig, 2004). In doing so, the neoliberal global order attacks the fundamental principles and operating mechanisms in various social contexts attempting to implement its own homogenous value structure aimed at the creation of the perfect consumer citizen who represents and practices market values more than traditional social or communitarian social values.

The conditions of life that exists in most IT hubs in the country—be it in Chennai or in Noida or the nascently developing Business Process Outsourcing (BPO) industry in Guwahati—evoke a sense of homogeneity creating patterns of consumption which are favourable to the creation of a global market. The PMC's role in the reproduction of capital has played a critical role in the reproduction of capitalism's most innate desire: the desire to accumulate (Marx, 1976). Accumulation on an accelerated scale and the maintenance of a continuous cycle of profit accumulation has been achieved through the transformation of contemporary capitalism from being an agency of formal subsumption to an agency of real subsumption (Negri, 2003). This process where the productivity of labour becomes redundant because the production process itself becomes a commodity through a complete reorganisation of work through the application of communication technology, constitutes what Negri (1989), based on Marx's (1976) theory, calls real subsumption, the unequivocal and complete realisation of the law of value (Negri, 1989, 2003). The basic advantage that capitalism possesses today, in addition to the real subsumption of labour, is the relative obliteration of the working-class identity in India, which has made it rather impossible for a united or an effective organisational resistance towards the capitalist onslaught to emerge from the IT sector (Sarkar, 2008). This will be evident if one considers the following statement made by an IT worker in Bengaluru, when asked about the relevance of trade unions in the IT sector:

> We are all middle class here. None of us are quote unquote working class if you go by the classical definitions. We are not even Industrial workers per se. Because of the kind of lifestyle that they have or aspire to have, people have now begun to think that they are not workers at all—that is the problem. The word worker itself has become like a slang.

The denunciation of the working-class identity has played a critical role in enabling the real subsumption of the IT workers within the processes of capitalist accumulation. The contours of middle-class activism have been plagued with a certain ambiguity which has often made it difficult for the middle classes to realise their subjectivity in terms of the broader socio-political and cultural objectives, and they have often restricted seeing themselves as atomised beings. The MMC's adherence to petty-bourgeois values has continued to dominate its perception of politics that abhors a radical change in the order of things (Roy, 2014). The pessimistic perception of politics makes the MMC attracted to various forms of non-radical or overtly non-political forms of organisational set-ups, as is the norm under neoliberalism's modifications of the space that it comes to dominate (Harvey, 2006), that has had a negative effect on the unionisation drives

196   S. DEB ROY

in the IT sector. The complete de-politicisation of the IT workers has resulted in them being completely oblivious, and often antagonistic, to any representative organisation having any kind of direct or indirect political affiliations, even during times of crisis (Roy, 2024).

The space that IT workers occupy in the IT hubs is composed of a variety of individual subjectivities, which are developed through the kind of work that one engages in and the benefits and securities that the work provides, in addition to the wages or salary that one earns (Hardt & Negri, 2000). For example, the nature of work that domestic workers do is different from women performing household labour. At the same time, the very existence of domestic labour in spaces such as IT hubs points towards a basic contradiction that exists between people being technologically savvy enough to use advanced technological devices for housework and their usage of poorly paid human labour to perform the same work as that of a technological device. The usage of technological devices, it must be considered, has often been a domain that has been reserved specifically for the men (Huws, 2003). In the context of India, one can extend the argument that these have often been reserved for upper caste men, because of the influence that Brahmanical patriarchy has held over the class structure of the Indian society (Chakravarty, 2002). The role of domestic workers in the lives of the IT workers is not one that is determined only by measures that enhance productivity materially but also the role that various factors can play in ensuring a psychological alienation of the worker from one's own state of existence.

The reproductive labour performed by the domestic workers adds to the emotional stability enjoyed by the MMC that not only contributes towards a heightened productivity but also creates a sense of psychological empowerment. Such factors contribute towards the creation of an alienated subjectivity whereby the individual oneself submits one's innate human capabilities and sensibilities to capitalism to exploit (Fromm, 1961). The processes at play in the IT hubs produce a scenario where even a critique of exploitation becomes another mode of exploitation. Much of these processes signal towards the genesis of a renewed phase of capitalist expansion and domination, whereby capitalism internalises the modes of resistance available to the non-capitalist sections of the population. The appropriation of the modes of resistance becomes possible because of the de-politicised nature of the contemporary workforce, especially in sectors such as IT which employs workers who desire a vertical social mobility— either out of necessity or out of a socially developed false consciousness.

Typical of contemporary capitalism, the IT workers, as the book has exhibited, suffer from de-politicisation that makes them look for managerial solutions to issues that concern political and legal aspects. For instance, one can look at the questions concerning workers' welfare, which can get positively affected by the growth of unionisation because of the role that unions play in putting forward the views of the workers (Punekar et al., 1978; Bryson et al., 2020). When marginalised people are pushed towards becoming the working poor, their exploitation increases manifold because 'the way in which the urban poor live [is] one marked by a particular kind of temporality and agency, with a set of relations to law and property that are very different from those that characterise the formal domain' leading to a highly diverse, yet unequal social structure (RoyChowdhury, 2021, p. 2). Trade unions can become increasingly important at such junctures because they can provide the workers with a sense of being workers.

In the public sector, trade unions have played a critical role in ensuring employment benefits to the workers such as job security, retirement benefits, compassionate forms of appointment in case of death, and the like. In the absence of any such representative bodies, the IT sector has aided the construction of the urban working poor in India who are almost always at the constant risk of losing their jobs and once they lose the job, find it unlikely to be reabsorbed into the same job thus having no other option but to suffer from—often extremely long—periods of unemployment (Gibbons & Katz, 1991; Keys & Danzinger, 2008). The basic analytical framework that guides one's analysis of the working poor in countries such as India has to be relative. So, while it is true that the MMC remains one of the most highly paid workers of the formal sector, it is also important to consider the kind of urban space that they come to inhabit and the effects of the same on their conceptions of their own poverty.

The conversion of a significant portion of the erstwhile PMC into the working poor has been aided by not only the growing unemployment but also by the constantly rising inflation that these individuals must live through in their everyday lives. Forms of contemporary social development depend upon the exclusion of marginalised individuals and subsuming them under various forms of domination, that makes them more prone to become the working poor. The definition of the working poor as is referred to in this context is of a working individual who suffers from relatively low payments, absence of social security, and a growing uncertainty regarding their jobs and lives (Herzenberg et al., 1998). The uncertainty that these workers face in their everyday lives gets reflected in the kind of socio-political and cultural organisations that they choose to represent them. To most of them, trade unions reflect a political form of organisation that is incapable of addressing their concerns because trade unions often remain constricted around questions of economic demands which possess a direct relationship with the political fabric of the country. The creation of the working poor in India is a distinct political process. The reluctance of the same being accepted by the working poor themselves remains a manifestation of the kind of material and ideological stagnancy that they face. The restrictions put in place by capitalist structures ensure that individuals remain within the structural and ideological contours of expectations which are beneficial to capitalism.

The marginalised sections of the society today have been in fact converted into appendages of the broader capitalist process, through the utilisation of a dual model of exploitation—one which has resulted in the creation of a distinctly neo-feudal mode of exploitation that feeds on the traditional forms of exclusion. Various models of neo-feudal oppression have resulted in diverse kinds of exploitation and appropriation, affecting the structure of property holdings (Ravenscroft, 1999), which have caused widespread phenomenon such as rural-to-urban migration to take place that has become the basis of the construction of a significant portion of the marginalised populace (Tandon & Rathi, 2022). Most of these people suffer from a mode of exploitation constructed by a combination of traditionalism and modernity to bring in newer methods of marginalisation in varying proportions contingent upon the particular contradictions in that social context.

The Indian trade union movement has often remained restricted as far as its engagement with unorganised forms of labour concerned (Mulvey, 1978). This is not to say that trade unions have not engaged with such forms of labour, but rather it means that trade unions' framework of engagement has always been one that has been dominated by their experiences formed among the public sector workers, who are often the middle class or the PMC in the classical sense of the term. The MMC or the working poor are often completely sidelined in the wider socio-political discourse. Both academia and politics give considerable attention to the middle class and the extremely impoverished within academia and politics, the ones who occupy the positions in between these two segments of the population often get neglected. Between the middle class and the extremely poor, there is a wide cohort of individuals at a consistent risk becoming the extremely impoverished, especially those coming from the marginalised sections of the society (Klein & Rones, 1989; Desai & Kharas, 2017).

The individuals belonging to the working poor find it difficult to establish a sense of belongingness to both the middle class and the working class because of their contradictory subjective selves constituted out of their social, cultural, and economic practices (Davies & Harre, 1990). The qualities that most of the workers in the IT sector associate themselves with are qualities that can be more effectively associated with as the working poor rather the middle classes or the PMC such as the fear of unemployment, issues with living conditions and insufficient wages. The working poor remain in poverty because their low wages and their pre-existing familial conditions make them more vulnerable to poverty (Klein & Rones, 1989). The implications of these conditions get accelerated for individuals coming from certain specific social groups because they remain deprived of the necessary educational, nutritional, and other such issues that enables them to escape conditions of poverty (Gilbert, 1998). In India, such social groups are mostly formed by Dalits, Muslims—and especially the women among them—and women in general. The major advantage of using the concept of the working poor is its highly qualitative and subjective category because it is more related to the way in which one lives, rather than how much one earns. The subjective aspects of the category make it an ideal framework for the analysis of human subjectivities within the social factory.

Most of the MMC that the book talks about earn enough to sustain its desired urban lifestyle. However, at the same time, one also has to consider the fact that the growth of salaries in the IT sector currently is much lower than the rate of increase of inflation. The increasing inflation in the metropolitan areas has caused a considerable stress on the lives of the workers. However, it is not the inflation or its rate per se that makes the difference but rather the effects of the same that becomes important. For the IT workers, especially those in senior positions having a significant amount of experience, the salary hikes are more likely to be sufficient to mitigate the effects of the inflation. This however is not true for the freshers and the precariat workers. Even among the senior IT workers, it is possible that women, Dalits, and Muslims will continue to suffer from social exploitation that will constantly risk their economic prowess and stability. The major differences between the MMC and the precariat IT workers is the contradictions surrounding how they analyse the politics of life and lifestyles, the former being related to the needs of basic sustenance that most of the invisible workers face, and the latter being the prime concern of the MMC.

The conditions for the existence of a sustained marginalised populace in the urban areas have been encouraged by a constantly altering capitalist mode of production in the society. This becomes the basic fulcrum around which the relations of production in the society are sustained under capitalism (Lefebvre, 1982). The conditions of urban marginality in contemporary India aptly get manifested in the situation faced by the women, Dalits, sexual and religious minorities. The marginality that they face is intrinsically related to the importance that is ascribed to them in the social hierarchy because '[t]he decision of who is going to be more important in an organisational setup depends upon who is entrusted with the responsibility of performing the most important work in the organisation' (Chattopadhyaya, 1957, pp. 44–45). During ancient times, the most important work was the provisioning of food and since it was the men who did that, they naturally came to occupy a dominant position in the society. Similarly, the social gradation of labouring activities that work in the society produces the notions about dominance under contemporary capitalism such that certain professions are unfairly treated and designated a lower status in the society that gets reinforced by and reinforces their existing ascriptive social attributes such as caste, race, and gender (Harriss-White, 2020). They come to be entrapped within a state of utter hopelessness, losing their abilities to articulate and identify with their problems of everyday lives. These problems have been accentuated in the IT sector where labour laws have been kept relatively redundant through the utilisation of SEZs and outsourced labour (Sarkar, 2008; Paul, 2014; Bisht, 2010).

The constant erosion of the workers' rights along with the rise of neoliberal capitalism has resulted in a condition where globally significant portions of the workforce are now identifying themselves as being working poor because their conditions of life vary significantly from those traditionally attributed to the working class, or the middle class, or even the PMC. And the marginalised sections of the workforce—the Dalits, the Muslims, and the women, for example—are the most vulnerable ones entrapped within this global transition. Being a member of the working poor does not depend directly on whether a person is employed or not, but rather is based on the idea that '[employment] should be a vector to lift people out of poverty, but this is only true if job quality is sufficient, including adequate earnings, job security and safe working environments.

The relationship between employment and poverty depends greatly on the extent to which decent work is ensured in the labour market' (International Labour Organisation (ILO), 2019, Para. 2). The role of a PSE job becomes critical in this respect not because of the financial benefits that it provides but because of the socio-economic benefits that come with it. A public sector job is less likely to push the marginalised workers towards conditions of working poverty because once they are employed, then the likelihood of them losing the job is almost non-existent. In the IT sector however, such securities and guarantees are not present. However, while due to such insecurities, trade unions have an inherent necessity in the private sector, the rates of unionisation within the private sector have remained extremely low, mainly fuelled by the anti-union perception of the IT Sector. While for the upper caste male IT workers, the absence of a union often does not mean many hindrances to their professional development, as has already been stated. The marginalised sections of the MMC get more affected by the absence of the unions because for them, the avenues for grievance redressal are significantly more constrained. For example, women in the IT sector often cannot speak up about their issues within their respective companies because of the absence of women human resource personnel, as Chap. 2 shows. For the men, in such instances, the domestic space becomes a space of recuperation and replenishment using the unpaid reproductive labour of women (Vogel, 1983/2013; Fraser et al., 2019). For women on the other hand, who are often forced to sacrifice their personal subjectivities for maintaining familial or communal ties, such structures of recuperation do not exist and their entire framework of analysing the world remains constrained within a lens dominated by the men in their lives (Baxter, 1993; Ramamurthy, 2004).

Most of the marginalised populace remains trapped within a social consciousness dominated by a certain stagnancy that they come to confront in their lives. The ability to articulate is one of the major obstacles that many individuals face in their everyday struggles in countries such as India characterised by low levels of social and individual consciousness. Despite being affected by the growing inequalities of the society, they continue to appreciate the existent state of affairs constituting a one-dimensional society where they are left without much individual or communitarian agency and hope for a better life (Fromm, 1942; Marcuse, 1964). And the hope for a better life through employment is a key concern for both the MMC and the precariat workers who migrate to these cities.

The working poor are more likely to be affected by structures which restrict their employment opportunities, and once employed restrict the probabilities of upward mobility. Such structures, most notably include the educational and training systems in place which restrict the socio-economic capacity of the working poor to aspire beyond their immediate local contexts increasing the chances of them remaining entrapped within exploitative social relations of production (Tsao et al., 2018; Chen, 2020). The working poor suffer from immense social and economic exploitation through a combination of social and financial exploitation. The working poor are left vulnerable to the problems that an individual faces in not only performing one's job, but also while searching for the same. The working poor constructed through unemployment, unavailability of full-time work, low family incomes, fear of unemployment, subpar living conditions, and so forth constitute a distinct category of the work force (Klein & Rones, 1989; Desmond & Gershenson, 2016). Within the IT workers, the Dalits, Muslims, and women, as the book has shown, are more prone to such processes.

Such a state of powerlessness is also evident in the ways in which the urban spaces are designed in contemporary India. The contradictions that exist between these different elements of the urban space constitute the core of the processes through which marginality within the various components of the urban spaces work. The creation of the urban space is critical to the creation of marginalities under contemporary capitalism because the urban space reinvigorates the multifaceted nature of marginality that lies at the core of capitalism, constituted because of one's class, gender, caste, and race. The kind of urban marginality that exists under contemporary capitalism is constituted by a range of different factors that includes the precarious nature of urban survival to the regimes of dispossession that allows one to analyse urban dwellers in terms of practices of segregation, stigmatisation, exclusionary policies, and socio-economic positions dictated by marginality and exclusion (Aceska et al., 2019). Cities such as Bengaluru, Noida, and Gurgaon, based on the personification of global business hubs such as Singapore, are sustained by a growing migrant labour force that is constantly thrown into the jaws of marginalisation (Searle, 2016; Oldenburg, 2018; Goyal & Prakash, 2023). Such cities, usually posed as solutions to cities such as Jamshedpur, do not change any of the issues that persist in them because both these kinds of cities are built by the forces of private capital creating different kinds of marginality (Kumar, 2015; Sood & Rath, 2017).This is the urban paradox that characterises the contemporary urban spaces leaving such contradictions unchallenged because it continues to thrive within the nexus created by the existent relationship between the global and native forces of capital. One of the basic characteristics of domination in the Global South, as Marx himself had theorised was the complete appropriation of the modes of resistance such that the marginalised populace gets completely subsumed within the various mode of production and exploitation (Marx, 1853/2006).

One of the key methods as applied by the IT unions is the usage of various kinds of organisational methods. Some of the trade unions in the IT sector have been able to inculcate a trade union consciousness among the workers. Unions such as the KITU which have a greater amount of political involvement amidst their ranks have been successful in generating a certain amount of militancy within a specific section of IT workers. The success of the KITU in Bengaluru, however, owes to a large extent to the fact that the Karnataka State IT/IT Enabled Services Employees Union (KITU) has been able to organise the workers on the basis of a strategy that follows community-based organising. Such a strategy involved door-to-door campaigns, constant communications, and so forth. Other unions such as the All India IT and IT Enabled Services Union (AIITEU) have instead followed a more workplace-based approach, which has severely restricted the vibrancy of their activities because of the kind of restrictions that most IT offices have in place as far as trade union activities are concerned. At the same time, the kind of workers that the IT unions seek to unionise are entrapped within a struggle for positionality wherein they remain bound by the statist or the dominant social notions of exploitation—the exploitation of sanitation workers on the basis of caste gets overlooked, while the exploitation of gig workers, or security guards comes to garner increasing attention. Similarly, these workers also possess a multiplicity of different opinions regarding how one characterises typical qualities of a modern IT job. For example, one can take the example of graveyard shifts in this context. While a section of women workers might see shift work as being exploitative as a working woman, a section again might analyse it as being an opportunity to express oneself fully as a worker and as a citizen. The struggle that ensues between capitalism and social transformation in societies such as India is both objective and subjective in nature. While objectively, the struggle occurs in the domain of economic struggles, the subjective struggle is often the more complicated one because that encompasses dimensions of ideology, individuality, and

204   S. DEB ROY

culture. Modes of social transformation in India have been affected greatly by the peculiar conditions of development in India that have ensured that both these aspects of social transformation have come to occupy an important, yet often disjointed, position in the struggle for social transformation.

While the KITU has enjoyed success because of the kind of homogeneous social composition[1] with regard to the linguistic and cultural composition of its members that it possesses, the AIITEU has often struggled in that regard. Regardless of the method of organisational tactics that the unions have followed, they have still found themselves struggling to organise a large section of the IT workforce. The reason for this is manifold which include de-politicisation, class differences between IT and ITeS workers, and so on. Contrary to the IT workers per se, the invisible IT workers have been better organised, although their unions are often not recognised by the industry. That is because for the precariat workers, their identity as workers is often the only one that they possess, and as such a trade union often becomes a natural organisation for them. However, to build a stronger resistance to capitalist exploitation, it is necessary to unite both these sectors together, and therein lies the struggle to find a commonality.

With the changes in the internal composition of the labour force and the organisation of the labour force, it has become necessary to speak in terms of social security rather than salaries or wages (Huws, 2017). Social security can be the thread that binds the footloose and salariat together because both these kinds of workers, and especially the extremely marginalised among them, remain tormented by the lack of social security. The issue of social security becomes particularly important in IT hubs because the IT hubs represent spaces of privilege where experiments on repression, as Negri (2008) mentions, can be carried on inflicting structural and material violence on the most marginalised sections of the non-capitalist classes. Within the IT society, a section of the people enjoys being a part of MMC because their conditions of life allow them to be so, while a significant majority is relegated to living the life of the working poor. The contradictions that one finds in the Indian IT sector are far more nuanced in nature than in other parts of the world, because in India, economic conditions intersect with non-economic conditions to produce an IT sector that goes ahead to produce an IT society—a society where productivity reigns

---

[1] The KITU largely has a Malayali and Telugu membership base, who comprise more than 50 per cent of their total membership.

supreme, often even at the expense of one's health and well-being. And with a rising cost of living, and decreasing contours of social security, both the MMC and the precariat will soon be enroute towards a state of critical urban poverty, that is, being the working poor—socially, economically, and culturally.

REFERENCES

Aceska, A., Heer, B., & Kaiser-Grolimund, A. (2019). Doing the City from the Margins: Critical Perspectives on Urban Marginality. *Anthropological Forum, 29*(1), 1–11.

Aday, D. P., Jr. (1990). *Social Control at the Margins: Toward a General Understanding of Deviance*. Wadsworth.

Anderson, K. B. (2020). *Dialectics of Revolution: Hegel, Marxism, and its Critics through a Lens of Race, Class, Gender, and Colonialism*. Daraja Press.

Baxter, J. (1993). *Work at Home: The Domestic Division of Labour*. Melbourne University Press.

Berry, C. (2022). The Substitutive State? Neoliberal State Interventionism Across Industrial, Housing and Private Pensions Policy in the UK. *Competition and Change, 26*(2), 242–265.

Bisht, N. S. (2010). Trade Unions in Indian IT Industry? An Employees' Perspective. *Indian Journal of Industrial Relations, 46*(2), 220–228.

Bryson, A., Freeman, R., & Blanchflower, D. (2020, November 11). Unions Raise Worker Wellbeing. *VoxEU*. Retrieved April 5, 2023, from https://cepr.org/voxeu/columns/unions-raise-worker-wellbeing

Chakravarty, U. (2002). *Gendering Caste*. SAGE.

Chattopadhyaya, D. P. (1957/2007). *She Juge Mayera Boro* (Trans. Author, pp. 44–45). Anushtup.

Chen, M. (2020). COVID-19, Cities and Urban Informal Workers: India in Comparative Perspective. *The Indian Journal of Labour Economics, 63*(1), 541–546.

Chomsky, N. (1996). Old Wine in New Bottles: A Bitter Taste. *Electronic Journal of Radical Organisation Theory*. Retrieved April 5, 2023, from https://chomsky.info/199606__/

Damodaran, H. (2008). *India's New Capitalists: Caste, Business, and Industry in a Modern Nation*. Permanent Black.

Davies, B., & Harre, R. (1990). Positioning: The Discursive Production of Selves. *Journal for Theory of Social Behaviour, 20*(1), 44–63.

Desai, R. M., & Kharas, H. (2017, July 13). Is a Growing Middle Class Good for the Poor? Social Policy in a Time of Globalization. *Brookings Global Working Papers*. Retrieved April 5, 2023, from https://www.brookings.edu/research/

is-a-growing-middle-class-good-for-the-poor-social-policy-in-a-time-of-globalization/

Desmond, M., & Gershenson, C. (2016). Housing and Employment Insecurity Among the Working Poor. *Social Problems, 63,* 46–67.

Fields, G. S. (2012). *Working Hard, Working Poor: A Global Journey.* Oxford University Press.

Fraser, N., Bhattacharya, T., & Arruzza, C. (2019). *Feminism for the 99%.* Verso.

Fromm, E. (1942/2001). *The Fear of Freedom.* Routledge.

Fromm, E. (1961). *Marx's Concept of Man.* Continuum.

Gibbons, R., & Katz, L. (1991). Layoffs and Lemons. *Journal of Labor Economics, 9,* 351–380.

Giddens, A. (1990). *The Consequences of Modernity.* Polity.

Gilbert, M. R. (1998). "Race", Space, and Power: The Survival Strategies of Working Poor Women. *Annals of the Association of American Geographers, 88*(4), 595–621.

Gopalakrishnan, K., Dayasindhu, N., & Narayanan, K. (2022). *Against All Odds: The IT Story of India.* Noida: Penguin.

Goyal, M., & Prakash, P. (2023). *Unboxing Bengaluru: The City of New Beginnings.* Penguin.

Hardt, M., & Negri, M. (2000). *Empire.* Harvard University Press.

Harriss-White, B. (2005). Commercialisation, Commodification and Gender Relations in Post-Harvest Systems for Rice in South Asia. *Economic and Political Weekly, 40*(25), 2530–2542.

Harriss-White, B. (2020). Waste, Social Order, and Physical Disorder in Small-Town India. *The Journal of Development Studies, 56*(2), 239–258.

Harvey, D. (2006). *Spaces of Global Capitalism: A Theory of Uneven Geographical Development.* London: Verso.

Harvey, D. (2007). Neoliberalism as Creative Destruction. *The Annals of the American Academy of Political and Social Science, 610,* 22–44.

Herzenberg, S., Alic, J., & Wial, H. (1998). *New Rules for a New Economy: Employment and Opportunity in Post-industrial America.* Cornell University Press.

Huws, U. (2003). *The Making of a Cybertariat.* Monthly Review Press.

Huws, U. (2017). A New Bill of Workers' Rights for the 21st Century. *Think Piece,* December, 92. Retrieved April 5, 2023, from https://www.compasson-line.org.uk/wp-content/uploads/2017/11/A-new-bill-of-Workers-Rights.pdf

Illouz, E. (2007). *Cold Intimacies: The Making of Emotional Capitalism.* Polity.

International Labour Organisation. (2019). *The Working Poor or How a Job Is No Guarantee of Decent Living Conditions: A Study Based on ILO's Global Estimates of Employment by Economic Class.* ILO Stats: Spotlights on Work Statistics, 6. Retrieved April 5, 2023, from https://www.ilo.org/wcmsp5/groups/public/%2D%2D-dgreports/%2D%2D-stat/documents/publication/wcms_696387.pdf

8 WORKERS, MIDDLE-CLASS EMPLOYEES, PROFESSIONALS? NO, JUST...   207

Jones, S. (2007). Working-Poor Mothers and Middle-Class Others: Psychological Considerations in Home-School Relations and Research. *Anthropology and Education Quarterly, 38*(2), 159–177.

Kapri, V. (2021). *1232 KM: The Long Journey Back Home*. Harper Collins Publishers India.

Keys, B., & Danzinger, S. (2008). Hurt the Worst: The Rise of Unemployment Among Disadvantaged and Advantaged Male Workers. In K. Newman (Ed.), *Laid Off, Laid Low: Political and Economic Consequences of Employment Insecurity* (pp. 1996–2003). Columbia University Press.

Klein, B. W., & Rones, P. L. (1989). A Profile of the Working Poor. *Monthly Labour Review, 112*(10), 3–13.

Kumar, V. (2015). Trade Unionism and Contract Workers in Selected Industries in Jamshedpur. *Indian Journal of Industrial Relations, 51*(2), 212–222.

Lefebvre, H. (1982). *The Sociology of Marx*. Columbia University Press.

Levien, M. (2018). *Dispossession Without Development: Land Grabs in Neoliberal India*. Oxford University Press.

Majid, N. (2001). The Working Poor in Developing Countries. *International Labour Review, 140*(3), 271–291.

Marcuse, H. (1964). *One-Dimensional Society*. Routledge and Kegan Paul.

Marx, K. (1853/2006). The East India Question. In I. Hussain (Ed.), *Karl Marx on India*. Tulika.

Marx, K. (1867/1976). *Capital, Volume 1: A Critique of Political Economy*. Penguin.

Mulvey, C. (1978). *The Economic Analysis of Trade Unions*. Martin Robertson.

Negri, A. (1989). *The Politics of Subversion*. Polity.

Negri, A. (2003). *Time for Revolution*. Bloomsbury Academic.

Negri, A. (2008). *Empire and Beyond*. Polity.

Negri, A. (2016). *Reflections on Empire*. Polity.

Oldenburg, V. T. (2018). *Gurgaon: From Mythic Village to Millennium City*. Harper Collins Publishers India.

Parthasarathi, A., & Joseph, K. J. (2004). Innovation Under Export Orientation. In A. P. D'Costa & E. Sridharan (Eds.), *India in the Global Software Industry*. Routledge.

Paul, S. (2014). Special Economic Zones and the Exploitation Underneath. *SSRN Journal*. https://papers.ssrn.com/sol3/papers.cfm?abstract_id=2359449

Porter, D., & Craig, D. (2004). The Third Way and the Third World: Poverty Reduction and Social Inclusion in the Rise of 'Inclusive' Liberalism. *Review of International Political Economy, 11*(2), 387–423.

Punekar, S. D., Deodhar, S. B., & Sankaran, S. (1978). *Labour Welfare, Trade Unionism and Industrial Relations*. Himalaya Publishing House.

Ramamurthy, P. (2004). Marriage, Labour Circulation and Smallholder Capitalism in Andhra Prasdesh. In R. Kaur & R. Palriwala (Eds.), *Marrying in South Asia: Shifting Concepts, Changing Practices in a Globalising World*. Hyderabad.

Ravenscroft, N. (1999). "Post-Feudalism" and the Changing Structure of Agricultural Leasing. *Land Use Policy, 16*, 247–258.

Roy, A. (2014). *Capitalism: A Ghost Story.* Haymarket.

Roy, R. (2024). Politics Through Precarity: Tech Workers' Unions in India During the Covid-19 Pandemic. *Journal of Contemporary Asia, 54*(1).

RoyChowdhury, S. (2021). *City of Shadows: Slums and Informal Work in Bangalore.* Cambridge University Press.

Sarkar, S. (2008). Trade Unionism in Indian BPO-ITeS Industry—Insights from Literature. *Indian Journal of Industrial Relations, 44*(1), 72–88.

Searle, L. G. (2016). *Landscapes of Accumulation: Real Estate and the Neoliberal Imagination in Contemporary India.* The University of Chicago Press.

Sood, A., & Rath, S. (2017). The Planned and the Unplanned: Company Towns in India. *IIC Quarterly, 43*(3–4), 91.

Tandon, A., & Rathi, A. (2022). Sustaining Urban Labour Markets: Situating Migration and Domestic Work in India's 'Gig' Economy. *Economy and Space.* https://doi.org/10.1177/0308518X221120

Tsao, J., Hardy, I., & Lingard, B. (2018). Aspirational Ambivalence of Middle-Class Secondary Students in Hong Kong. *British Journal of Sociology of Education, 39*(8), 1094–1110.

Uchitelle, L. (2006). *The Disposable American: Layoffs and Their Consequences.* Alfred A. Knopf.

van Dijk, T. (2017). The Impossibility of World-Class Slum-Free Indian Cities and the Fantasy of Two Indias. In T. Kuldova & M. A. Varghese (Eds.), *Urban Utopias: Excess and Expulsion in Neoliberal South Asia.* Routledge.

Vasudevan, V. (2013). *Urban Villager: Life in an Indian Satellite Town.* SAGE.

Vogel, L. (1983/2013). Marxism and Oppression of Women: Toward a Unitary Theory. Brill.

Wacquant, L. (1999). Urban Marginality in the Coming Millennium. *Urban Studies, 36*(10).

Index[1]

A
Abstract labour, 53
Abstract space, 53
Abstract time, 53, 54
Affirmative policies, 22
Alienation, 9, 11, 14, 50, 57, 61, 83, 94, 112, 139, 146, 153, 169, 196
Anxiety, 13, 39, 94, 181, 193
Asiatic mode of production, 26
Atomised subjects, 90
Authority, 33, 72, 91, 93, 150, 151, 167, 180
Autonomy, 14, 50, 68, 70, 72

B
Bengaluru, 5, 5n3, 5n4, 6, 8, 15, 23–25, 28, 33, 40, 41, 54, 56, 58, 62, 64, 65, 68, 80, 82, 84, 85, 88, 93, 108, 110, 111, 113, 116–118, 120, 124, 143, 147, 148, 163, 163n1, 164, 166, 167, 169, 171–174, 179, 181, 183, 192, 195, 202, 203
Biopolitical control, 77, 85
Bourgeoisie, 2, 134
Bureaucracy, 26, 136, 178
Business, 1, 3, 5, 60, 119, 120, 184, 192, 202

C
Capitalism, 4, 6, 7, 9, 11, 14, 26, 29, 30, 35, 38, 43, 49–51, 53–55, 59–66, 69–72, 77, 78, 81–86, 90, 93, 94, 96–99, 105, 107, 113, 115, 120, 123, 125, 134, 135, 138, 140–146, 149, 151–154, 167, 168, 173, 175, 177, 178, 180, 181, 184, 191–193, 195–198, 200, 202, 203

[1] Note: Page numbers followed by 'n' refer to notes.

© The Author(s), under exclusive license to Springer Nature Switzerland AG 2024
S. Deb Roy, *The Rise of the Information Technology Society in India*, Dynamics of Virtual Work, https://doi.org/10.1007/978-3-031-58128-1_8

209

210 INDEX

Caste, 21, 22, 26, 26n2, 28, 30–33,
35, 39, 42, 43, 50–52, 61, 66,
67, 87, 105, 106, 112–114,
121–125, 136, 142, 143, 146,
150, 151, 162, 168, 170, 175,
177, 184, 191, 196, 200–203
Caste consciousness, 22
Caste system, 26n2, 121
Class consciousness, 15, 112, 115,
119, 124, 126, 136, 145, 148,
152, 178, 180, 181, 183
Class struggle, 152, 173, 179
Commodification, 7, 53, 81,
83, 90, 192
Community, 11, 22, 23, 25–28, 31,
34–36, 41–43, 50–52, 55, 65–71,
85, 88, 89, 108, 111, 120–122,
124, 125, 127, 145, 146, 148,
149, 169, 172–174
Compliance, 11, 72, 91, 117, 138,
142, 147, 153, 179, 180
Compulsion, 57, 169
Concrete labour, 53
Concrete time, 54
Consciousness, 8, 14–16, 21, 22, 26,
30, 33, 51, 72, 83, 90, 113, 114,
116, 122, 127, 133, 136–138,
140, 148, 150, 151, 153, 154,
168, 172, 176, 178, 180, 196,
201, 203
Consumerism, 40, 127, 134, 137,
141, 146, 165
Contractual, 16, 69
Cost management, 90
Covid-19, 42, 63, 83, 91, 92, 94, 97,
181, 193

D
Dalits, 8, 15, 21–23, 30–37, 41–43,
71, 80, 82, 87, 95, 106,
121–124, 122n5, 148, 171, 172,
175–177, 199, 200, 202

Decision-making autonomy, 64
De-humanised Subjects, 90
Desires, 6, 9–11, 55, 61, 66, 85, 95,
120, 127, 135, 140, 143–146,
149–151, 168, 175, 179,
195, 196
Dialectical struggle, 60
Digital small-scale commercial
ecosystems, 72
Digital spaces, 64
Diversity, 21–23, 32
Domestic work, 34, 36, 65, 105n1,
106–114, 119–122, 127, 196
Domination, 5, 6, 10, 11, 13, 26, 38,
50, 54, 55, 61, 72, 77, 107, 112,
133, 145, 146, 153, 165, 170,
177, 180, 184, 194, 196,
197, 203

E
Economic empowerment, 63
Economic well-being, 24
Emotional well-being, 88, 98
Employee welfare, 154
Employment relations, 42, 91, 146,
153, 154, 192
Empowerment, 11, 40, 43, 62, 63,
72, 83, 115, 116, 122, 127, 135,
140, 196
Engagement, 12, 31, 37, 51, 57, 60,
77, 118, 138, 168, 182, 198
Ethics, 60, 111, 145, 146
Eudaimonic well-being, 96
Everyday production, 69
Exploitation, 6–8, 14–16, 23–25, 28,
30–37, 39, 41, 43, 49, 50, 52,
55, 59, 62, 63, 67, 69, 70, 81,
83, 84, 86, 87, 89, 90, 112, 113,
119, 122, 124–126, 146, 147,
152, 154, 168, 170–173, 175,
177, 182, 185, 193,
196–199, 202–204

INDEX   211

F

Familial responsibilities, 60
Female IT workers, 16, 108, 110,
    140, 147, 148, 167, 169, 170,
    172, 181, 193
Financial empowerment, 62
Formal IT workers, 8, 16, 57, 67, 69,
    119, 122, 123, 127, 135, 146,
    151, 193

G

Gated communities, 67, 71,
    115, 120
Gender consciousness, 21
Gender discrimination, 35
Gendered division of labour, 55
Gendered exploitation, 37, 39, 41, 43,
    50, 70, 170, 173, 177
Gendered violence, 176
Gender representation, 38, 39
Gender roles, 52
Global capitalist structures, 60
Gurugram, 6, 8, 15, 23, 24

H

Harassment, 33, 36, 37, 62, 138,
    140, 147
Health, 38, 77, 85, 94, 97, 115,
    121, 123, 143, 144, 168,
    182, 205
Hedonic well-being, 82, 84, 87, 91
Heightened productivity, 59, 196
Heterodox communities, 69
Honour, 62, 63
Household work, 56–58
Human capital, 22, 90, 112
Human nature, 99
Human resource management
    (HRM), 33, 78–81, 87, 89, 91,
    94, 95, 97, 98

I

Identity, 1, 9, 14, 21, 25, 28, 31, 32,
    49, 52, 59, 63, 64, 66, 67, 86,
    97, 111, 121, 122, 125, 126,
    137, 138, 141, 144–146, 154,
    163, 169, 171, 175–185,
    195, 204
Ideology, 12, 40, 41, 68, 125, 138,
    166, 175, 203
Industrial capitalism, 55, 63, 64
Industrial growth, 26, 134
Information technology (IT), 1–17,
    21–43, 49–72, 79, 80, 105–127,
    133, 161–185, 192
Intellectual, 154, 185
Islamophobia, 23–30
IT lives, 53
IT parks, 120, 122, 124, 173, 192
IT sector, 1–17, 21–25, 24n1, 28,
    31–34, 37–39, 43, 51, 54,
    58n1, 59, 60, 62, 65–67, 71,
    72, 79, 81, 82, 94, 97, 99,
    105–108, 110, 112, 115,
    116, 119, 120, 122,
    124–126, 135, 138, 140,
    143, 145, 147, 153,
    162–170, 172–174, 177–180,
    182, 183, 192, 195–197,
    199–201, 203, 204
IT space, 21–43, 63, 71, 111, 124,
    126, 169, 193
IT workforce in India, 16, 21

J

Job satisfaction, 93, 96, 182

L

Labour conditions, 25, 31, 80, 83, 90,
    113, 115, 125, 147, 165,
    200, 201

212 INDEX

Labour exploitation, 7, 15, 16, 23, 30, 34, 43, 63, 86, 112, 119, 125, 154, 170, 173, 175, 203
Labour hierarchy, 29, 136, 151, 154
Labour management, 81
Labour market, 191, 201
Labour mobility, 25
Labour policies, 7
Labour process, 27, 29, 43
Labour rights, 138, 153, 184, 200
Labour unions, 162
Landlordism, 26
Liberation, 10n7, 70–72, 123
Liberation of women workers, 53
Life-sustaining entities, 69
Low-waged work, 69

M
Mainstream management, 80, 90, 99
Majoritarian violence, 25, 30
Management, 4, 9, 13, 22, 28, 33, 34, 41–43, 72, 78–81, 87–91, 94, 95, 97, 98, 117, 118, 127, 136, 138, 141, 150, 169, 175, 178, 179, 184
Marginalised communities, 22, 23, 34–36, 41, 42, 71, 85, 89, 108, 149
Marginalised workers, 34, 39, 125, 170, 173, 201
Marginality in Indian cities, 23
Market mediation of human reproduction, 53
Marx, Karl, 26, 53, 54, 69, 93, 94, 125, 143, 146, 173, 195, 203
Material exploitation, 30, 125
Material reality, 71
Material violence, 24, 176, 204
Mechanization, 70
Mental health, 77, 85, 97, 115, 182
Meritocracy, 22, 97, 149

Metro Middle Class (MMC), 13, 16, 119, 125–127, 133–154, 162, 167–169, 174, 176–178, 180, 181, 192, 195–201, 204, 205
Metropolitan, 7, 136, 199
Middle class, 2–6, 9–11, 13, 22, 24–29, 31, 35, 40, 71, 72, 86, 87, 107, 109, 111–115, 120–125, 127, 133–154, 162–164, 167–169, 171, 172, 176–185, 191–205
Middle-class Muslims, 24, 25, 28, 171
Middle-class values, 71, 137
Migrant workers, 8, 24, 109, 110, 116, 121, 123, 147, 169, 184
Minority communities, 25
Monetised 'productive' work, 56
Multinational companies, 27
Muslim IT workers, 24, 25, 28, 30, 80, 82, 143, 167, 172
Muslims, 8, 15, 21–25, 26n2, 27–31, 34–37, 41–43, 71, 80, 82, 85–87, 95, 106, 143, 171, 172, 177, 199, 200, 202

N
Needs, 15, 35, 40, 41, 61, 65, 68, 70, 72, 81, 83, 86, 91, 95, 98, 113, 117, 127, 143, 144, 147, 149, 152, 153, 164, 168, 172, 178, 179, 183, 199
Neoliberal capitalism, 35, 51, 55, 61, 63, 66, 71, 138, 146, 149, 151, 153, 168, 175, 180, 184, 191–193, 200
Neoliberal control, 61, 69–72
Neoliberal reforms, 2, 7, 26, 79, 107, 114, 126, 135, 147, 161, 162, 192

O

Oriental traditions and western modernity, 26
Outsourced work, 16, 69, 106, 121, 200
Overtime, 59

P

Patriarchal values, 72
Patriarchy, 36–43, 50, 55, 60, 71, 122, 177, 196
Personality, 88, 95
Personnel Management, 90
Political arguments, 59
Post-colonial Indian society, 26
Post-industrial society, 42, 56, 61
Potential, 2, 12, 34, 50, 52, 66, 68, 71, 72, 82, 88, 94, 168, 172
Pre-capitalist exploitation, 25, 32, 37, 62, 122, 125
Precariat, 6, 8, 169, 180, 184, 193, 199, 201, 204, 205
Pre-modern societies, 56
Pressure, 30, 34, 40, 58, 59, 64, 65, 68, 82, 181, 191
Private sector, 3, 10, 12, 14–15, 26, 27, 39, 40, 82, 126, 139, 148, 153, 164, 168–170, 175, 179, 182, 184, 201
Private shame, 63
Production mechanisms, 29
Productivity, 12, 29, 34, 43, 52, 54, 59, 65, 72, 77–80, 83–85, 90, 92–94, 96, 135, 147, 170, 181, 192, 195, 196, 204
Professional Managerial Class (PMC), 13, 14, 16, 135, 192, 195, 197–200
Profits, 4, 8, 12, 30, 52, 70, 72, 78, 91, 93, 127, 178, 184, 193, 195
Promotion, 14, 41, 62, 147

Psychological, 16, 25, 38, 61, 64, 70, 81, 87, 88, 90, 94, 96, 98, 99, 114, 127, 145, 169, 196
Public-private dichotomy, 62
Public sector, 4, 9, 12, 14, 27, 31, 84, 135, 136, 139, 143, 148, 150, 153, 163, 164, 166, 169, 192, 197, 198, 201
Public sphere, 57, 60, 64, 141

R

Representation, 32, 36, 38, 39, 153
Reproductive labour, 16, 39, 41, 43, 50–53, 55, 58–70, 110, 196, 201
Reserve army of labour, 72, 107, 126, 178
Retention, 92
Revolutionary subjectivity, 85
Routinisation, 38, 41, 53, 70, 71

S

Salary negotiations, 92
Sanitation workers, 105, 120–125, 203
Security guards, 107, 111, 112, 116–120, 203
Sexual division of labour, 50, 55–57, 59, 60, 64, 65, 68, 87
Sexual exploitation, 36
Sexual harassment, 36, 37, 138, 140, 147
Social activities, 69
Social belongingness, 63
Social category, 36, 52, 70
Social cleavages, 87
Social complexity, 60
Social conditions, 23, 127, 180
Social consciousness, 22, 26, 201
Social control, 13, 63, 119, 152, 179, 180

214 INDEX

Social dynamics, 63, 70, 94, 133
Social identity, 21, 32, 67, 144
Social inequality, 87
Social interactions, 70, 146
Social interpretations, 95
Social justice, 9, 32, 89, 137, 148
Social mobility, 25, 28, 35, 71, 72,
    127, 144, 161, 175, 196
Social norms, 26, 120, 145
Social ontology, 24, 64
Social perception, 29–30
Social positioning, 40, 81, 86,
    126, 147
Social practices, 35, 38, 43, 53, 60–70
Social reality, 6, 11, 22, 23, 30, 50,
    55, 71, 85, 87, 98, 105, 113,
    137, 141, 145, 152, 180, 193
Social reproduction, 43, 49–72, 171
Social solidarity, 9, 49–54, 65, 68, 70,
    126, 127
Social status, 39, 41, 61, 66, 70, 81,
    88, 96, 97, 106, 109, 117, 147,
    168, 176, 193
Social structure, 29, 55, 60, 62, 68,
    70, 79, 90, 107, 125, 145, 154,
    180, 192, 197
Social structuring, 90, 150
Social subjugation, 52
Social support, 71, 193
Software, 1–3, 6, 15, 16,
    21, 33, 192
South Asia, 63, 192
Space, 3, 5, 6, 14–16, 21–43, 49–61,
    63–71, 83, 87, 89, 92, 99, 105,
    108–111, 113–115, 117–127,
    133–137, 141, 151, 162, 163,
    168–170, 177, 182, 184, 185,
    193–196, 201, 204
Spontaneity, 69, 70, 82
Spontaneous lifestyle, 69
State Monopoly Capitalism, 26
Stress, 8, 39, 88, 92, 94, 199

Structural inequalities, 22, 174
Structural violence, 24, 32, 113
Style of life, 58, 59, 181n8, 194
Subaltern classes, 26
Subjectivity, 5, 9, 16, 52, 54, 94, 98,
    99, 146, 192, 195, 196, 199, 201
Surplus capacities, 55, 56
Surplus labour, 26, 59, 63
Surplus value, 59, 63, 70, 173
Surveillance, 92, 93
Surveillance capitalism, 93

T
Tactics, 60, 79, 92, 177, 204
Task identity, 64
Technocratic rationality, 90, 181
Technological development, 29, 35
Technology, 29, 35, 69, 82, 83, 90,
    92, 105–127, 181, 195
Temporal, 60, 70, 169
Tension, 39, 91
Trade Unions, 9–14, 17, 86, 86n2,
    98, 112, 126, 138, 139, 143,
    146, 147, 150, 153, 162–168,
    163n1, 171–179, 181–184, 195,
    197, 198, 201, 203, 204

U
Underdevelopment, 29, 137
Unionisation, 10, 150, 153, 161–185,
    195, 197, 201
Un-monetised domestic labour, 56
Urban life, 61, 63
Urban social spaces, 50, 69
Urban spaces, 6, 8, 14, 16, 30, 31,
    36–38, 43, 50–52, 57, 95, 105,
    107–110, 113–116, 118, 121,
    126, 127, 133, 135, 137, 139,
    145, 149, 191, 197, 202, 203
Use value, 53

W

Wages, 2, 6, 12, 29, 50, 91, 96, 105, 106, 112, 121, 138, 139, 170, 182, 184, 194, 196, 199, 204

Well-being, 8, 14, 16, 24, 24n1, 34, 51, 54, 57, 63, 64, 69, 70, 77–99, 108, 112, 115, 153, 165, 205

Well-being industry, 90

Western modernity, 26

White collar workers, 29, 52, 127

Women workers, 37–41, 53, 61, 62, 65, 67–71, 67n3, 80, 113, 118, 122, 137, 171, 173, 175, 182, 203

Workers' collectives, 143

Workers' rights, 138, 153, 180, 184, 200

Work from home, 25, 64, 84, 91, 92, 193

Working class, 9, 11, 14, 15, 22, 29, 54, 66, 96, 98, 106, 119, 120, 125, 126, 134, 135, 137–139, 141, 145, 146, 150, 152, 162, 168, 169, 171, 176, 178–180, 182–185, 195, 199

Working poor, 10, 11, 192–194, 197–200, 202, 204, 205

Work-life balance, 34, 88, 181